Safety, Health and Environmental Hazards at the Workplace

Also available from Cassell

Evans, *Supervisory Management*
Farnham and Pimlott, *Understanding Industrial Relations*
Gatiss, *Total Quality Management*
Goddard, *Informative Writing*
Maitland, *Recruiting: How to Do It*
Morris, *Health and Safety: A Guide for the Newly Appointed*
Pettinger, *Managing the Flexible Workforce*
Robson, *Essential Accounting for Managers*
Simons and Naylor-Stables, *Effective Communication for Managers*

Safety, Health and Environmental Hazards at the Workplace

★

A. J. P. Dalton

CASSELL

London and New York

Cassell

Wellington House 370 Lexington Avenue
125 Strand New York
London WC2R 0BB NY 10017-6550

First published 1998

British Library Cataloguing-in-Publication Data
A catalogue record for this book is available from the British Library

ISBN   0-304-33289-5 (hardback)
        0-304-33291-7 (paperback)

Typeset by BookEns Limited, Royston, Herts
Printed and bound in Great Britain by Redwood Books, Trowbridge, Wilts

Front cover photograph: a demonstration outside the London headquarters of the
Health and Safety Executive by members of the Construction Safety Campaign
(photo by the author).

For Nicola, Liza and Claudia and the next generation, starting with James, Jack and Lois

CONTENTS

★

FOREWORD

I have known Alan Dalton for over ten years now. We first met in the mid-1980s when I was the shadow minister for employment, with responsibilities for health and safety. He was then working at the independent trade-union sponsored Labour Research Department (LRD), and was also very active in the Hazards Campaign.

At that time there were a series of major disasters – such as Zeebrugge, Piper Alpha and King's Cross – plus a steady rise in 'common' deaths at work. For example, more than three workers were being killed on building sites each week. With information supplied by the Hazards Campaign and people like Alan, we were able to highlight the failure of the government to prevent these disasters and workplace deaths.

Whilst health and safety at the workplace remains a vital issue – just the mention of asbestos or stress confirms that – in the 1990s it is the environment that is big on the agenda; for example, global warming threatens the very world we live in. As the recently published government's chief scientist's advice to the Prime Minister has clearly shown, we have to act sooner rather than later on this issue and we all have a role to play.

And here Alan has been very active too – I feel it is no exaggeration to say that he has personally forced the environmental issue on the trade union agenda, despite some considerable opposition.

I fully recommend this book for its unique approach in combining safety, health and environmental (SHE) issues at the workplace.

Michael Meacher MP,
Minister for the Environment

PREFACE

'You are never too small to win, and certainly never too big too lose' (June Hancock, who was awarded £65,000 compensation for the asbestos-cancer, mesothelioma, that she developed 'just playing around the firm' of J. W. Roberts in Leeds).

The preface to this book has been written six months after the new Labour Party of Tony Blair won a massive landslide victory on the 1 May 1997. Some cracks are beginning to appear, and the honeymoon period seems over. On the issues we are going to look at in this book – safety, health and environmental (SHE) hazards at the workplace – the progress, if you can call it that, has been uneven. To be fair to the new Labour government, perhaps it's really too early to make any real judgement. Nevertheless, an interim report is possible.

A World Health Organisation (WHO) press release, issued in December 1997, gives some idea of the worldwide scale of workplace safety and health hazards, much of which is preventable:

○ 120 million occupational accidents, with more than 220,000 deaths in a global workforce of around 2.6 billion people

○ 160 million new cases of work-related diseases may be caused by various types of exposure at the workplace

○ 40–50 per cent of the world's entire population are at risk through exposure to physical, chemical, biological, psychosocial or ergonomic hazards

○ Globally, about 100,000 chemicals are important health hazards

○ Some 50 physical factors, 200 biological agents and 20 adverse ergonomic conditions, plus innumerable psychosocial factors, have been identified as creating hazardous working conditions

○ The risk of cancer from work and workplace exposure is of special concern. About 300–350 different chemical, physical and biological factors have been identified as occupational carcinogens

○ About 3,000 allergens have been identified which can cause dermatoses and respiratory diseases (e.g. asthma)

○ About 30–50 per cent of workers in industrialized countries complain of psychological stress and overload

○ Only 5–10 per cent of workers in developing countries and 20–50 per cent of workers in industrialized countries (with a few exceptions) have access to adequate occupational health services

○ The total economic loss due to occupational illness is tremendous and amounts to 10–15 per cent of the world's GNP

○ According to a World Bank estimate, two-thirds of work lost due to accidents and ill-health could be saved through the implementation of occupational health programmes.

Because of global warming, worldwide environmental issues are far better known. The turbulent world weather conditions of forest fires, drought and floods, exacerbated by El Nino, serve to emphasize the global nature of environmental hazards.

On workplace safety, the new Labour government appears to have changed little. The 1996–7 Annual Report of the Health and Safety Commission/Health and Safety Executive (HSE) – the government's top health and safety body – showed rises in the crude death rate in several key industries, notably agriculture and construction. These were explained as a possible 'blip' (tell that to the family and friends of those who died) by the Director General of the HSE, Jenny Bacon, and the HSE promised some 'blitzes' in these areas. These have been shown to be ineffective before (e.g. in the construction industry during the 1980s). It will fall again to the trade union movement and the families and friends of the workplace victims to demonstrate outside coroners' courts for justice.

On workplace health, it is not much better. Take, as an example, asbestos hazards. Asbestos kills more than 3,500 people each year, more than are killed on the roads, but road deaths are falling while asbestos deaths are set to rise to 5,000–10,000 a year by 2025. Asbestos was first described as an 'evil' dust 100 years ago in the 1898 Annual Report of HM Factory Inspectorate to Parliament. Several European countries (e.g. Germany, Italy, The Netherlands, Norway, Sweden and Switzerland) have banned the use of all asbestos. On 3 July 1996, the French government announced a ban on the use of asbestos products on its territory, effective from 1 January 1997. Whilst the new Labour government has announced its intention to ban asbestos, there has been no action as yet.

As a result, 1997 ended with a familiar activity of mine: demonstrating with other trade unionists and asbestos victims on 19 December, outside Birmingham Magistrates' Court. A few months before some cowboy asbestos disposers had spread asbestos all over Birmingham, and the HSE inside the court were taking a prosecution. At a magistrates' court the maximum possible fine is £20,000, so we wanted the case dealt with at a crown court; where the fine can be unlimited and can be coupled with a prison sentence of up to two years – the only real deterrent to such asbestos criminals.

On the environment, there is, thankfully, more to report. The new Labour government do really seem to be doing much more and are determined to make this government the first genuinely green government. The year ended with the vitally important Kyoto conference on global warming in Japan. No one could fault the efforts of Deputy Prime Minister, John Prescott, who for two weeks before the conference flew around the world trying to get an agreement. In the end an agreement of sorts was reached, with an international protocol committing the developed nations to a six per cent reduction in greenhouse gases below 1990 levels between 2008 and 2012. Opinions varied on whether this will be sufficient ('not good enough', according to Ritt Bjerregaard, EU Environment Commissioner) and, crucially, on whether the agreement will be enforced – but it is a start. As Prime Minister Tony Blair told the Number 10 Downing Street Green Summit for Business in December 1997: 'British business should see the Kyoto Climate Change Summit as a challenge and not a threat'.

'Here's a buck for your pollution quota, buddy!' (Reproduced with kind permission of Patrick Blower and the London *Evening Standard*)

In November 1997 the Commission of the European Communities published an important communication (COM(97) 592 final) on the environment and employment ('Building a sustainable Europe'), which concludes: 'Environmental policy, if well designed, should be seen as a strong driving force for investment and the building of a sustainable Europe, creating both growth and employment.'

Re-reading my 1982 Cassell book, *Health and Safety at Work for Managers and Supervisors*, I feel that, despite the odds, many improvements in health and safety, and increasingly the environment, at the workplace have occurred. Most of these improvements are due to our membership of the European Union. Workplace health issues such as stress, RSI, backache, bullying, violence, long working hours and shift work are now at least recognized, if not controlled. However, I do not think we have advanced very much on accident prevention, asbestos removal control, noise and vibration control and on the *real* control and substitution of hazardous chemicals and biological hazards at the workplace.

Major advances in the prevention of workplace SHE hazards will take place if the government extends and funds, the TGWU (EU-funded) pilot scheme on 'roving safety representatives' in agriculture, and if the government also extends the current health and safety rights (paid time off for workplace inspection duties and training, etc.) that trade union safety representatives have to environmental issues as well.

On chemicals (and biological hazards), I feel that the new-wave environmental movement will help a lot with its emphasis on 'Life Cycle Assessment' – also called 'cradle to the grave' analysis – and 'Cleaner Technology', the basic principles of which I outline in this book. In fact, I feel that it is the environmental movement, and its practice, that will inject some new life, thinking and action into workplace safety and health issues. That is why this new book deals with safety, health *and* environmental workplace issues as one.

It is impossible to acknowledge, let alone thank, all the people who have helped me in the practice, research and preparation of this book. Like all authors I stand on the shoulders of many other authors – who are acknowledged in both the notes and recommended further reading.

Firstly, the many victims of work-related safety, health and environmental illnesses. I have worked with some victims to prepare parliamentary and local ombudsman reports, to contact the media and to generally campaign for improvements. Many have suffered great pain and anguish while doing this and I know it has been very difficult to fight for prevention while suffering at the same time. Some have even died, such as brave June Hancock – whose quotation starts this chapter – as I finished this book in July 1997. This book is for them most of all.

Secondly, in the past twenty-five years I have been very much supported by the people on the *Hazards* magazine (formerly *Hazards Bulletin*) editorial collective and in the Hazards Campaign network, both within the UK and, in more recent years, in the EU.

Lastly, but not least, there are the many trade union safety representatives whom I have taught – and whom I still teach – who in turn teach me most of what I know. Thanks also to the scientists, doctors, lawyers, safety officers, environmental activists, students, managers, supervisors and other SHE professionals who have helped me over the years.

Some of the above people appear in the following pages, most do not. If this book has any value it is due to them. I also hope that it stimulates some readers to take up the issues of workplace safety, health and the environment. Despite the sometimes depressing facts, there is a lot of satisfaction to be gained in identifying and controlling SHE hazards at the workplace. Finally, being the eternal optimist, I strongly hope that this book will make a small contribution towards the improvement of the safety, health and environment of current, and future, working people, thereby making the world a better place to live in.

Kentish Town, London
1 January 1998

INTRODUCTION

> We should always devote care to maintaining our health, that we may freely perform
> our bodily functions, than to making profits.
>
> Georgius Agricola, 1556

Sixteen years ago, in 1982, I wrote what might be considered as the 'first edition' of this book for Cassell, entitled *Health and Safety at Work for Managers and Supervisors*. It is a sign of the changing times that I made no mention of environmental issues in that book. Therefore this is not a second edition, but a completely new book. However, there is one important connection with the 1982 book. This book is *not* about the fine detail of workplace safety, health and environmental (or SHE) issues. It would be ten times longer, and unreadable, if that were the case. It is an introduction and, more importantly, an *approach* to dealing with SHE issues that comes from more than twenty-five years of practical experience in dealing with these important issues. Whilst the details of the hazard, risk and law are important in any particular SHE issue, the social, economic and political issues surrounding that SHE issue are equally important. Without the latter, you will not see the wood for the trees. I have tried, wherever possible, to integrate both approaches.

There are three key messages throughout the book:

1. A truly effective SHE hazard prevention programme will be achieved only by involving the workforce and community fully.
2. Prevention is better than cure with regard to all SHE issues at work.
3. The current UK SHE law is pretty good – all it needs are some relatively minor additions. What it urgently needs is fair, firm and effective enforcement. This will protect people and the environment, act as a catalyst to produce an innovative and competitive industry and provide a true 'level playing field' for both employees, employers and communities. It *must* be a crime, punishable by imprisonment, for the senior managements of companies and organizations to ignore SHE laws – as they have been doing for the past 150 years or so.

Ironically, when I first became involved in the social responsibility of being a scientist, for the British Society for Social Responsibility in Science (BSSRS) and whilst still a research and development chemist in the pharmaceutical industry, it was environmental issues that I was concerned about. One infamous case in which I was involved on behalf of BSSRS, in the early 1970s, was advising tenants and residents who suffered from the famous 'Battersea smell' in London. Almost certainly it came from the now closed-down Garton's glucose factory, but there may have been a contribution from the nearby gin factory too. Fermenting biological matter often smells, as we all know from our visits to the countryside, and it was – and still is – a difficult smell to remove or mask. Decomposing biological, and other, materials are still causing great problems in all the waste landfill dumps in the UK and elsewhere. They are, effectively, fermenting and giving off explosive methane, and other gases, which can cause damage to anything built on top of them. These gases are having a major impact on global warming. Despite the growing public concern in the early 1970s, and many influential publications of that time (e.g. the 'Club of Rome' report entitled 'The Limits to Growth', Rachel Carson's powerful book, *Silent Spring*, and Fritz Schumacher's *Small is Beautiful*), the 1973 oil crisis effectively killed off the early environmental movement in the UK and elsewhere. But, as we now know, in the late 1980s and 1990s it was to return with a vengeance.

At the same time, and perhaps because of the 1960s 'flower power' and environmental concern, there was worldwide government action about work-place health and safety. Many countries, such as the USA and Sweden, introduced new laws. The UK was no exception, introducing the 1974 Health and Safety at Work Act – still the basis of health and safety law in the UK today. So, trying to earn a living, many budding environmentalists, like myself, became 'health and safety' specialists and taught the subject to managers, supervisors and, after the revolutionary Safety Representative and Safety Committee Regulations of 1977, we taught health and safety to those many thousands of new creatures created by these regulations – 'trade union safety representatives'. At long last the *employees* were to have some say over their health and safety conditions and, as we shall see, increasingly environmental conditions, at work.

Workplace safety has, in fact, been the concern of a few astute observers, mainly medical doctors and alchemists, since the sixteenth century. Mining has always been an especially hazardous occupation and remains so until this day. In 1556 Agricola wrote his classic 12-volume work on every aspect of mining.[1] The fifth book deals with accidents and ill-health in mining. He noted that in the mines of the Carpathian mountains women were known to have married seven times, because of the deaths – from accidents and diseases – of previous husbands. He even suggested some preventative measures, such as face masks and ventilation systems for the dust (Figure 1.1). By 1713 the first ever, and still very readable, textbook of occupational medicine had been written, Bernardino Ramazzini's classic *Diseases of Workers*.[2] He, too, starts off his descriptions of the hazards of many jobs, with that of miners. Despite his fellow clinicians, who he said 'laughed me to scorn', Ramazzini insisted on visiting the mines, and many other workplaces, first-hand to see the reality of the work. That is what makes his work so alive and readable today. And, of course, it remains just as important today for those concerned about workplace SHE hazards to visit reality, at the workplace, as it was some 300 years ago.

It was the advent of the UK's 'industrial revolution' around 1760–1830, with those 'dark satanic mills', that really saw the rise of public and political – and the first ever Factory Acts – concern about workplace safety hazards. Although an up-to-date review of workplace safety (and health) remains to be written, earlier editions of Donald Hunter's brilliant *The Diseases of Occupations* contain a good historical account.[3] The first Factory Act in the world was in Britain, the Health and Morals of Apprentices Act 1802. By 1833 the first four 'factory inspectors' had been appointed to ensure that the Factory Acts were enforced. Then, as now, employers did not like laws that restricted their freedom to kill and maim their workers in the name of profit and many opposed the Factory Acts forcefully. Both Karl Marx, in *Das Capital*, and Frederick Engels, in *The Making of the English Working Class*, wrote in detail of the terrible factory conditions of the time. Marx actually praised the British Factory Inspectorate. Charles Dickens also wrote about the employers' opposition to the Factory Acts and called them the, 'Association for the Mangling of Factory Operatives'.

Up until the 1974 Health and Safety at Work Act , and even up to the present day, safety, and not health (let alone the environment), remained the main concern of the Factory Inspectorate – or Health and Safety Executive (HSE), as they are now known. However, at long last, health is forcefully pushing itself onto the safety agenda, simply because the amount of deaths and suffering it causes far outweighs the safety hazards of work (which are not insignificant). The Factory Acts remained, until recently, the key safety law. The last substantial, 'consolidated' Factory Act was that of 1961, which actually goes back to 1937 and then to 1901 in a recognizable format. A 1997 HSE compendium of current health and safety law quotes Acts of Parliament going back to the early nineteenth century – The Highways (Railway Crossings) Act of 1839.

Throughout the book I have emphasized the need for SHE laws to be enforced effectively and fairly. Thus there would be a true 'level playing field' for all employers and employees. Hopefully, this will be true throughout Europe in the not too distant future, and throughout the world, in the foreseeable future, if the very successful model of the Montreal Protocol, designed to reduce the greenhouse effect, is extended to other SHE issues.

FIGURE I.1   As early as 1556, Georgius Agricola was illustrating devices for the mechanical removal of dangerous fumes and vapours from mines in his classic text, *De Re Metallica*

CASE STUDY 1: ENFORCING EU HEALTH AND SAFETY LAW

In October 1994 Len Stacey, an English bricklayer, was killed on a German building site in Liepzig in the old East Germany. Len fell from an unprotected two-storey block of flats when some bricks hit him in the back. There was no scaffolding or safety netting as required by German, and EU, building laws. The old East Germany is virtually one whole building site, and the laws of the jungle rule. Len was the father of two young children, Laura three and Lenny two, and he was married to Denise Stacey. Denise was devastated. The shock of going over to Germany and collecting Len in a coffin, and the shabby treatment she received both in Germany and from the health service for her bereavement, caused her to be sectioned into the local hospital and her children to be taken into care; to top it all, her house was flooded. As she told me: 'This was my lowest point. I had lost my husband, my children, my sanity and my home. Everything I had loved had been taken from me.'

I first met Denise in October 1996, at the time of the two-year anniversary of Len's death, when she was asking for help in pushing the German coffin, that Len came home in through the German embassy's doors in London – she was a very angry woman. She wanted compensation – she had not received a penny – and justice for Len's death. Her lone actions shamed us all. She phoned and wrote to everyone she could, including trade unions, MEPs, the EU and both the UK and the German governments. She raised the money to go to Germany to lobby the German prosecutor and the German building unions – who were very helpful – and she used television and the media to expose the complacency on health and safety laws. Eventually, after much hard work and emotional effort (she pawned her wedding ring to deliver the coffin to the German Embassy), she was successful in that the German government agreed to prosecute for man-slaughter the British subcontractor who was building the flats, and who should have put up the scaffolding, and two managing directors of the German developers who, the contract documents show, were also responsible for inspecting the non-existent scaffolding.

The trial took place in June 1997, in Germany, and both the British contractor, David Carter, director of Carter Construction, and one of the German developers, Richard Unterhuber of ABN Whon-und Indutreibau, were found guilty of 'negligent manslaughter and endangering life'. The sentences – a five-month suspended prison sentence and a fine of £2800 for Mr Carter (he was also ordered to pay Denise £4500 compensation) and a fine of £4800 for Mr Unterhuber – were derisory. In the words of TGWU national construction officer George Henderson, who accompanied Denise to the trial, 'These fines are a licence to kill all EU workers. There is no EU "level playing field" on health and safety, just a bottomless pit into which EU workers are falling, and dying, daily.'

FIGURE I.2   Denise Stacey delivers the coffin of her husband, Len, to the German Embassy in London, on the two-year anniversary of his death

It is hoped that 'adequate' compensation will automatically follow suit. It has been a long, hard struggle for Denise, leaving her heavily in debt. She told me, 'Of course, I am doing this for Len and my children. But I do not want his death to be in vain. I want conditions on all sites, for all building workers, made safe.'[4]

Some observers feel that strict SHE laws in the industrialized world may cause industry to move to other parts of the world where the SHE laws are less strict. It has certainly been true that in the past many trade unions were not concerned about environmental issues, because they thought that a concern for the environment would lead to job losses. In the past few years there have been many studies that have shown this view to be false. The reasons why companies invest where they do and – even more – why they are successful and profitable, are very complex. One of the foremost researchers in this area, and a former economic adviser to US President Ronald Reagan, is Professor Michael E. Porter of Harvard Business School. In his massive and influential study, entitled *The Competitive Advantage of Nations*, and in subsequent research, he has concluded that:

> I find consistent with the traditional liberal position, for example, that strict antitrust laws, tough health and safety regulations, and heavy investment in training human resources are beneficial ...[5]

> How an industry responds to environmental problems may, in fact, be an indicator of its overall competitiveness ... Successful environmentalists, regulatory agencies, and companies will reject old trade-offs and build on underlying economic logic that links the environment, resource production, innovation and competitiveness.[6]

As might be imagined, Professor Porter's views have not gone down well with everyone, especially the American business and economic community.[7] However, his radical view has recently received significant support from a detailed study[8] by the Organization for Economic Co-operation and Development (OECD) – a key organization of the major world capitalist countries – which found that environmental laws did *not* lead to job losses and countries who embraced 'cleaner technologies' were more competitive; although it was less sure on the impact of 'green taxation'. As we move towards the twenty-first century, there is still an illogical and old-fashioned division between 'safety and health' and 'the environment'. This is a bit reminiscent of the old-fashioned division between 'safety' and 'health' and the 'workplace', between 'safety officers' and 'occupational nurses/doctors'.

This is true, not just in the UK, but worldwide. In general, 'safety and health' issues are seen as 'employment' or 'industrial relations' issues and the government department responsible is the 'Employment Department' or something similar. This is true even in that relatively modern agency, the EU. The safety and health department has just been established in Bilbao, northern Spain, and the environment department is located in Copenhagen, Denmark, each under a different director general (DG) of the EU.

However, at the company and organization level there are signs of change and the more progressive transnational companies have now set up SHE departments and are running SHE programmes – hence the title of this book. Ironically, a few years ago the Conservative government moved the main UK health and safety agency – the Health and Safety Commission and Executive – from the now abolished Department of Employment to the Department of the Environment (now the Department of the Environment, Transport and the Regions). So, uniquely, in the UK we are in a very good position to further the SHE approach at governmental as well as company and organizational (e.g. local government) levels.

Because of this historic, political and legal background, the vast majority of books in this field deal either with 'safety and health' or 'environmental' issues; sometimes an individual chapter deals with the other area. This book will deal with both together and try to integrate them wherever possible, although, to make the subjects manageable, the environment will be dealt with only from a workplace perspective. This is *not* an introduction to general environmental issues, for which there are many excellent books that can be found filling up the shelves in any good bookshop.

Looking at the subjects I have covered, it is clear that there are many important ones that are omitted: fire, transport pollution, ionizing and non-ionizing radiation hazards, working alone, women and health and safety, environmental and occupational exposure limits, toxicology, sampling methods, fork-lift trucks and homeworking, plus many 'hazardous' occupations such as construction, nursing, farming, as well as compensation for occupational and environmental damage and ill-health. (The environmental section is thinner than the health and safety section because, at this time, there is really less of practical value to say. However, I have no doubt that the balance will change in favour of workplace environmental issues in the future.)

Nonetheless, I am consoled somewhat by the words of the first, and greatest, occupational medicine textbook, *Diseases of Workers*, by Bernardino Ramazzini, who wrote in his preface in 1713:

> I admit then that the work which I am about to publish is imperfect, or rather merely intended to incite others to lend a helping hand until we obtain a really complete and thorough treatise worthy of a place in the department of medicine ... Wherefore do you, kind reader, give a friendly reception to my treatise which, though no great work of art, was written for the good of the community, or at all events for the benefit and comfort of the working classes, and, if you please: Make allowance for a work written not from ambition but from a sense of duty and to be of use.

NOTES

1. Georgius Agricola (1556) *De Re Metallica*, translated by Hoover and Hoover, New York: Dover Publications, 1950.
2. Bernadino Ramazzini (1713) *Diseases of Workers*, translated by W. C. Wright, London: Hafner Publishing Co., 1964.
3. Donald Hunter (1955) *The Diseases of Occupations*, London: The English Universities Press Ltd.
4. The sources for this case study are my case notes; (1977) Death in Leipzig, *Hazards* **47**, 4; and (1997) British builder's widow overcomes German disinterest to win manslaughter conviction, *Health and Safety Bulletin*, 268, August.
5. M. H. Porter (1990) *The Competitive Advantage of Nations*, London: Macmillan, p. xvi.
6. M. E. Porter and Class van der Linde (September–October 1995) Green and competitive: ending the stalemate, *Harvard Business Review*, 134.
7. Frances Cairncross (1995) *Green Inc. – a Guide to Business and the Environment*, London: Earthscan.
8. OECD (1997) *Environmental Policies and Employment*, London: The Stationery Office. For a detailed summary, see OECD (1997) Jobs and the environment: an overview from the OECD, *ENDS Report 267*, 16–19 April.

1

WHY BE CONCERNED ABOUT SAFETY, HEALTH AND ENVIRONMENTAL (SHE) ISSUES AT THE WORKPLACE?

WORKPLACE DEATHS BY 'ACCIDENT'

It is the Heath and Safety Executive (HSE) which collects the figures on workplace deaths and injuries due to accidents and ill-health. This section will look only at workplace deaths and accidents; ill-health is considered elsewhere (see page 6). Each year the workplace deaths, injuries and 'dangerous occurrences' are published in the HSE Annual Report to Parliament. Year after year, although funding for the HSE has been cut and extra burdens are placed upon it, the HSE reports a steady improvement in the fall in workplace deaths and injuries. This is demonstrated in Figure 1.1, which come from a recent review of health and safety law since the 1974 Health and Safety at Work Act by John Rimington, the former director general of the HSE from 1983 to 1994.[1] It is worth pointing out that Professor Theo Nichols, in his recent thought-provoking book, *The Sociology of Industrial Injury* (Nichols, 1997), has interpreted the crude accident and serious injury rates for 1975–85 somewhat differently from the HSE.

As can be seen from Figure 1.1, crude workplace deaths of employees have fallen substantially, from almost 2000 a year in 1950, to around 250 in 1993–94. The trend continues – but with a 'blip' for last year – with the crude workplace death rate for employees and the self-employed killed at work in 1996–97, the latest available being 302. This was up from 258 the year before. To this, for 1996–97 we can add 394 'members of the public', not at work, who were killed by work activities (e.g. mothers killed pushing their children in prams on the pavement past building sites, where buckets of tar and slates fall onto them off roofs and scaffolding, children killed in lakes of farm slurry, railway trespassers and suicides). Announcing these results in July 1997, Jenny Bacon, director of the Health and Safety Executive (HSE) said, 'We do not know whether this is a rather tragic "blip" in this country's previously improving safety record, or the start of an upward drift.'

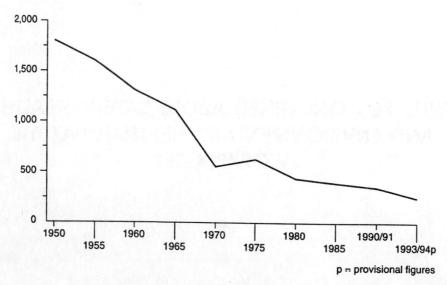

p = provisional figures

FIGURE 1.1   Fatal accidents at work 1950–1993/94
Source: Lecture by John Rimington, 26 April 1995

For the relatives and friends of the individuals concerned, it is a different matter. Their distress is exacerbated by the fact that most workplace deaths are preventable. That is, they are not true accidents in the generally accepted sense of the word 'accident' as an unforeseen event. All the in-depth HSE studies in workplace deaths that have been done have shown that the vast majority of workplace accidents are preventable and that, in most cases, it was management that should have done the preventing (see also page 34).

CASE STUDY 2: A MOTHER FIGHTS FOR JUSTICE

In November 1988 things looked good for 24-year-old window fitter Paul Elvin. His girlfriend Lorna, was to have his baby in a few months, they were to move into a new flat in a few weeks, and he had just started a new job fitting out John Menzies' newsagents at London's Euston Station. He had everything to live for. But on his first day at work, having received no safety training, he touched a live 25,000-volt overhead power cable with an aluminium pole. He caught fire, his hands and feet were burnt off and he died in hospital a day later.

In the normal course of events, his employer would have found a replacement, and there would have been a brief inquest and an HSE investigation. The HSE *might* have prosecuted Paul's employer. The courts may have fined the employer the typical few hundred pounds for such an offence. Paul's death appeared as two lines in the Annual Report of the Railway Inspectorate, part of the HSE. It eventually made up one of the 558 workplace-related death statistics for 1988 in the HSE Annual Report.

FIGURE 1.2   Lorna, baby Kylie and Ann Elvin

But this workplace death was not to result in the 'normal course of events'. It was to be the start of a campaign, yet to fully be realized (see page 35), for workplace deaths to be taken, and investigated, as seriously as non-workplace deaths. After coping, somehow, with her massive grief, his mother, Ann Elvin, and Paul's family – and especially his girlfriend Lorna (who gave birth to Paul's daughter, Kylie, three months after his death) – started a campaign for justice for Paul's death. It involved demonstrations, media and television appearances hundreds of letters (including to the Queen), a petition signed by hundreds of local people, marches and – with support from her local MP, Simon Hughes, and the Construction Safety Campaign (a trade union-based, rank and file, construction safety campaign group) – a lobby of Parliament.

Two years to the day almost, in November 1990, the HSE eventually prosecuted the subcontractor, Cawberry's, to British Rail, that Paul's company worked for. It was fined £5000 with £5000 costs. Needless to say, Ann, her family and Paul's friends and supporters were disgusted at the fine. As Ann says in her moving and excellent book on the campaign, 'Paul was murdered legally. Why didn't they prosecute Paul's employer, GBR Windows and British Rail? It happened to my son. It could happen to yours. We owe it to the future to make the workplace safe. We owe it to our children, and our children's children.'[2]

WORKPLACE INJURIES

It is generally accepted that the figures on workplace deaths are accurate: it is hard to cover up the death of a worker (although the deaths of hundreds of people whose work involves driving for a living – e.g. commercial drivers and sales representatives – and who are killed 'at work' are not recorded as workplace deaths).

The situation with regard to the reporting of other serious and minor accidents is far from satisfactory. In some industries, such as construction, agriculture and small and medium-sized companies (with less than 50 employees), the HSE acknowledges in its annual reports that there may be up to 50 per cent under-reporting even of serious accidents. The reasons are not hard to find. The current system of reporting accidents. The Reporting of Injuries, Diseases and Dangerous Occurrences Regulations, known as RIDDOR (see page 123), depends on the employer filling-in a fairly detailed form and sending it off to the appropriate enforcing authority. There would not seem to be an incentive for an employer to tell the authorities that it is injuring its workers. In 1996/97, there were 45 successful HSE prosecutions under RIDDOR (Health and Safety Executive Statistics, 1996/97), with an average fine of £671 per offence. The fines for not reporting are so low that only larger workplaces take RIDDOR seriously.

Bearing this in mind, the latest figures on accidents at work during 1995-6 are 30,968 major injuries; 132,976 injuries necessitating more than three days off work. (Health and Safety Commission and Executive, 1997).

At the November 1997 publication of the HSC/HSE Annual Report, containing these figures, the Institute of Employment Rights pointed out that in 1997 there were 50,000 major injuries reported to the HSE, but only 2158 (4 per cent) were investigated. (This compares with the 12-15 per cent of cases investigated in the years 1995-6). These include: 6 of 100 blindings (6 per cent); 297 of 1158 amputations; and 53 of 359 poisonings, gassings and asphyxiations (15 per cent). These figures led Bill Morris, General Secretary of the Transport and General Workers' Union, to say that 'the HSE is simply failing to get to grips with the rising tide of reckless disregard by employers for workers' safety' (*Guardian*, 12 November 1997).

THE 1990 LABOUR FORCE SURVEY (LFS)

In my experience over many years, and according to several Parliamentary Ombudsman reports, government officers concerned with SHE issues have been generally obstructive and unhelpful. This attitude presumably comes from their long-term, previous political bosses in the Conservative Party, who did not really care about SHE issues. However, I would like to make one exception to this general rule: the civil servants who thought up the idea of adding health and safety questions to the 1990 Labour Force Survey (LFS).

The LFS is an annual survey that asks people, by means of a detailed and structured interview in their own home, about various aspects of their working conditions (e.g. hours of work, holidays, sick pay and so on). Of course, the key difference with RIDDOR is that working people are being asked, not their employers. There is the added benefit that it is less intimidating to be asked these questions at home, rather than at work. These are both good reasons for the answers to be more honest than those given to RIDDOR by employers.

The 1990 LFS survey covered some 40,000 households and nearly 80,000 respondents in England and Wales, of whom 45,000 were in employment. The results of the special 'add on' health and safety survey have been verified by a variety of means, and the government's HSC has concluded that: 'It is possible to have a considerable degree of confidence that the LFS generally provides an accurate basis for estimating the real level of work-related injuries' (HSEC, 1991).

The 1990 health and safety supplement to the LFS survey (HSE, 1993) found that:

○ 1.5 million people reported work-related injuries in the previous year
○ 2 million people suffered from an illness that they believed to have been caused or made worse by work
○ work-related injuries and ill health give rise to around 29 million working days lost each year – more than one day off per year for every worker (and ten times as many days as lost through strike action that year)

Subsequent (HSE, 1997), but more limited, LFS health and safety surveys by the HSE in 1993/94, 1994/95 and 1995/96 indicate that about 1.06 million people each year suffer a workplace injury:

○ 940,000 were injuries to employees
○ 120,000 were injuries to the self-employed
○ 403,000 were injuries that led to more than three days off work and were therefore reportable under RIDDOR, compared with the 164,288 or so three-day or more injuries actually reported

The more recent LFS surveys do allow some comparison, and it appears that the level of reporting has risen overall from 34 per cent in 1989/90 to 42 per cent in 1995/96. However, the HSE analysis (HSE, 1997, p. 78) of this data notes that, 'it appears that one third of this increase in reporting can be explained by a shift in absence patterns, with workers now less likely to take more than three days off work'. This shows the social nature of 'accidents' and ill health. The better your sick-pay scheme, the more likely you are to take time off work when you are injured and/or ill. The HSE (1997: 78) concludes that the potential reasons for this shift in absence patterns include:

○ workers may now be suffering less serious injuries than in earlier years;
○ they may be taking a shorter time to recover from their injuries than before;
   or
○ workers may feel more pressure to return to work earlier than in previous
   years.

Given the changing nature of British society in the 1990s, it is this last reason that I
suspect is the *real* reason for the apparently falling sickness absence.

WORKPLACE ILL-HEALTH

Whilst, amazingly, there are no truly accurate estimates of the extent of workplace
ill-health in the UK, all authorities admit that it dwarfs the problems of workplace
deaths and injury. Around 20,000 workers a year die from a work-related disease,
for example. The 1990 LFS survey showed that an estimated 750,000 retired and
unemployed people reported being affected by the longer-term consequences of
work-related illness.

   What are the main work-related diseases that we do have some official figures
for? The following figures are taken from the 1995/96 HSE Annual Report (HSE,
1995/96).

○ Asbestos is one of the main killers and the deaths are almost totally work-
   related (but see page 180). Currently around 3500 people die from an
   asbestos-related disease each year (mainly lung cancer; the asbestos cancer,
   mesothelioma, and asbestosis or lung scarring). This is set to rise by 2025 to
   5000–10,000 per year.
○ In general the HSE estimates that around 2–8 per cent of all cancers are
   caused by work (mainly cancer of the lung, skin and bladder) and this would
   lead to around 3000–12,000 deaths in Britain per annum.
○ Around 400 coal and foundry workers were compensated for coalworkers'
   pneumoconiosis and silicosis in 1995.
○ Two hundred and sixty-eight coal miners were compensated for chronic
   bronchitis and emphysema in 1995 (a newly prescribed disease in 1993; there
   were 4000 cases up to the end of 1994 from the backlog).
○ There are around 90 cases of 'farmer's lung' (extrinsic allergies alveolitis) each
   year.
○ There were 589 cases of inflammation or ulceration of the upper respiratory
   tract or mouth ('occupational rhinitis') in 1994–95.
○ There are around 200 other 'biological infections' (e.g. anthrax, leptospirosis,
   hepatitis B, brucellosis, Q fever, legionnaire's disease) reported each year,
   although this may be a considerable underestimate.
○ Five hundred people work with lead, and most have raised blood lead levels,
   although only 205 were suspended from work for high levels during 1994–95.

○ Three hundred and fifty-three workers inhaled significant amounts of chemical fumes during 1995, a proportion of which will go on to suffer long-term illness from such inhalation.

○ At least 14,200 people a year receive compensation for exposure to noise at work.

○ Twenty thousand people suffered from vibration white finger.

○ During 1995 there were 851 new cases of occupation asthma.

○ The 1990 LFS survey indicated that there were 54,000 cases of occupational dermatitis or skin disease said to have been caused by work, and a further 30,000 cases made worse by work.

○ The 1990 LFS survey indicated that there were 593,000 musculoskeletal disorders, such as repetitive strain injury or RSI (a work-related upper limb disorder) and backache: 299,000 were backache and 110,000 were RSI-type diseases. A 1993 Department of Health survey found that one in three people (37 per cent) had suffered from backache lasting more than one day in the previous year. One in three people questioned (35 per cent) thought that the initial cause of their back pain was work-related.

○ The 1990 LFS survey revealed that 183,000 people in England and Wales believed that they had stress, depression or anxiety caused or made worse by work. Of these, 105,000 thought that their illness was actually caused, as opposed to made worse, by work.

○ According to the 1990 LFS survey, at least 2500 people thought that they suffered from 'sick building syndrome' (see page 113), with symptoms of nose and eye irritation, sore throat, dry skin and tiredness.

As we shall see, in the relevant sections of this book, all these 'official' figures are vast underestimates of the real extent of workplace ill-health, and the HSE acknowledges this to be the case.

In America, various studies[3] have identified the top ten workplace diseases as, not in order of priority, incidence or severity:

○ lung diseases
○ backache and RSI
○ cancer
○ major accidents to the spine, head or bad fractures
○ heart disease and strokes
○ reproductive disorders, such as miscarriage, sterility and low sperm count and/or sperm damage
○ nervous system damage, such as from solvents and pesticides
○ noise-induced hearing loss
○ dermatitis or skin problems
○ stress, depression and anxiety

In many ways this list is very similar to that which the government is slowly stumbling towards in the UK, and presumably similar to those in other EU nations

FIGURE 1.3   There are around 90 cases of 'farmer's lung' every year due to inhaling farm dust and biological materials (photo: HSE)

and the rest of the developed world, although they are very different[4] to those in the so-called 'developing world'.

In summary, the indicators of workplace ill-health – as inadequate as they are – discussed above show the signs of a very real and growing epidemic, that the government, employers, trade unions and community have clearly failed to control.

THE COSTS OF WORKPLACE HEALTH AND SAFETY HAZARDS

For many years there has been no national, and even few company or organizational, attempts to calculate the true costs of workplace accidents and ill-health. The last major government enquiry in this area, the 1970–72 Robens Report (see page 42) – which led to the 1974 Health and Safety at Work Act – estimated that the costs to the nation in 1970 were £200–900 million per annum. In February 1994, the HSE[5] released the first ever detailed estimate of the costs to society of work-related accidents and ill-health: £11–16 billion pounds annually! This is equivalent to between 2 per cent and 3 per cent total gross domestic product (GDP), or a typical year's economic growth. The HSE study noted the following:

○ The cost to employers is between £4 billion and £9 billion annually. This equates to between 5 per cent and 10 per cent of all UK industrial companies' gross trading profits in 1990, or between £170 and £360 for each person employed.

○ The cost to employees and their families is estimated to be almost £5 billion. This makes allowances for social security payments, civil compensation, reduced income and allowance for the pain and suffering.

○ Added to these two costs is the cost to society of: unemployment, property damage and treatment, loss of potential output, the costs of medical treatment, Department of Social Security (DSS) costs and so on.

At the press launch of this important study, the HSE restated its long-held view that around 70 per cent of the costs of work-related accidents and ill-health could be eliminated. A year before, in 1993, the HSE had released[6] the results of five detailed case studies on the costs of workplace accidents in the following organizations: a construction company, an oil platform, a transport company, a creamery and a hospital. First, it is important to note that the companies studied were all large, with well-established management systems for health and safety issues and an 'average or better than average' health and safety performance. Further, during the 13–18 week period of study – by the highly respected Accident Prevention and Advisory Unit (APAU) of the HSE – there were no accidents involving death, major injury or explosions, no civil claims and no criminal prosecutions to swell the basic figures. In short, the five organizations studied were the UK's best, at their best time. Therefore, the true costs for many other UK companies and organizations, especially small and medium-sized enterprises, will, undoubtedly, be much higher.

The results are given in Table 1.1.

TABLE 1.1 Financial costs to five organizations[a]

	Total loss (£000s)	Annualized loss (£000s)	Representing
1. Construction site	245	700[b]	8.5% of tender price
2. Creamery	244	975	1.4% of operating costs
3. Transport company	49	196	1.8% of operating costs 37% of profits
4. Oil platform	941	3764	14.2% of potential output
5. Hospital	98	397	5% of annual running costs

[a] Figures quoted are actual at time of study: no adjustment has been made for inflation. Study 1 lasted 18 weeks; studies 2–5, 13 weeks each.

[b] Represents total length of contract (54 weeks).

Source: *The Costs of Accidents at Work*, HSE, HS(G)96, HMSO, 1993

THE CHANGING ROLE OF INSURANCE COMPANIES

Another significant finding of the HSE research was that for every £1 of insured costs there were between £8 and £36 of uninsured costs, depending on the organization (see Figure 1.4 and Table 1.2).

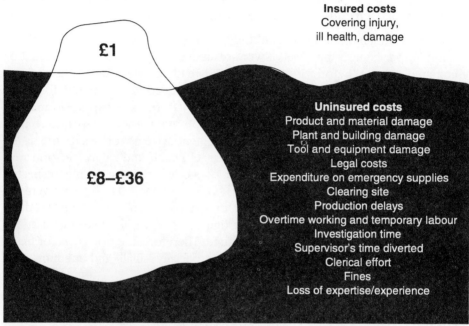

FIGURE 1.4   The accident iceberg
Source: The Costs of Accidents at Work, HSE HS(96), HMSO, 1993

TABLE 1.2   Insured versus non-insured accident costs in four organizations

Organization	Uninsured costs for every £1 of insured costs
Construction site	£11
Creamery	£36
Transport company	£8
North sea oil rig	£11
Hospital	?[a]

[a]   Could not be calculated, as NHS hospitals are self-insured
Source: The Costs of Accidents at Work, HSE, HS(G)96, HMSO, 1993

In addition, during 1993–94 trade unions won £335 million in legal damages for their members injured at work; up by 8 per cent on the total of £310 million for 1993–94. In January 1995, the Association of British Insurers revealed that between 1989 and 1993, insurers had paid out £2.8 billion in claims following accidents and ill-health as a result of employers' failing to ensure a safe and healthy working environment. Speaking at the December 1994 Institute of Occupational Safety and Health (IOSH) annual conference, Ian Helmore, liability manager for the Iron Trades Insurance Group (a major employers' liability insurers), said that, 'Between 1988 and 1992 for every £1 employers liability of premium received insurers paid out £1.24 in claims'. He added: 'If you fail to manage health and safety, initially organizations will face significant premium increases, and, ultimately you may not be able to insure at all (and this is compulsory to trade).'

In a more recent lecture to insurers, a leading insurance company adviser has repeated this progressive view and even gone as far as suggesting that the future may see the development of some form of no-fault government/private scheme that will benefit the employee who is injured, the employer and the insurer. The only losers will be the many solicitors who make a good living off the dead, injured and diseased. Clearly, then, concern and action over workplace ill-health and accidents pays where it counts: on the bottom line!

It is significant that the insurance industry is now a big player in the debate about global warming and other global environmental disasters, for it stands to pick up the tab. The number of major catastrophes is now three times the level of the 1960s. Dr Gerhard Berz, head of Munich Re – the biggest re-insurance group in the world – said the insurance industry had been lucky in recent years as potentially huge losses had turned into near misses. But he predicted a really catastrophic event in the near future (Luck 'must run out' for insurers, *Guardian*, 31 December 1997).

CASE STUDY 3: THE POSITIVE ROLE OF INSURANCE

Insurance companies, well aware of the above information, are now playing much more positive roles in workplace accident and ill-health prevention. A recent experience of my own will illustrate this point. On a teaching course for T&G safety representatives, one, who was employed in a large multinational, mentioned how bad health and safety was at his depot. They were being given a one-day course in 'risk assessment' by a senior member of the companies' insurance carrier. During the morning, the lecturer praised the managing director for his concern about health and safety, but seemed quite out of touch with the real world of the workplace. In the lunchbreak the T&G safety representative took polaroid pictures of five or so different dangerous situations at the plant.

The insurance lecturer was very shocked when he saw them and checked the locations and accuracy of the photographs. Satisfied that they were real, he went into senior management that week, with the photos, and instantly raised the premiums by £50,000! The management soon got its act together, trained all its managers in risk assessment and allowed independent evaluation by the insurance company, to which the trade union safety representatives and the employees had a very important input. Safety and health improved dramatically at the plant.

THE ENVIRONMENT

FIGURE 1.5   Police in London are now wearing face masks when the traffic pollution is high

The environment was hardly out of the news in Britain during the first few months of 1997: global warming, the thinning of the ozone layer and skin cancer hazards, the water shortage, 'Swampy' and his fellow tunnellers protesting against motorway and runway construction and so on. The manifestos of all three major UK political parties – the Conservative Party, the Labour Party and the Liberal Democrats – had all been 'greened' for the 1997 May general election as never before. The manifesto promises varied, with the Liberal Democrats coming out the greenest. In summary, the three political parties promised, on the environment, in their manifestos:

Conservative:
- ○ 'Tough but affordable targets' to improve air quality.
- ○ Sustained improvements in water quality, at an affordable pace.
- ○ Encouragement of low pollution vehicles.
- ○ Continuous exploration of the 'polluter pays' principle.
- ○ Product labelling to show the environmental impact of how goods are made.

Labour:
- ○ All departments to promote environmental policies, with parliamentary audit.
- ○ Integrated transport policy.
- ○ Review of vehicle excise duty to promote low-emission vehicles.
- ○ Tough regulation of water industry.
- ○ Tax penalties for pollution.
- ○ Moratorium on 'large-scale sales' of Forestry Commission land.

The Liberal Democratic Party:
- ○ Cut car tax to £10 up to 1600 cc, while gradually increasing fuel duty by 4p a litre.
- ○ Urban road pricing to finance public transport.
- ○ Carbon tax to finance VAT and employers' national insurance contribution (NIC) cuts.
- ○ Countryside management contracts to help farmers to protect vital habitats.

'Make the polluter pay' is a fine-sounding slogan, but one that has never been put into practice in the UK. It is now well recognized[7] that the traditional measure of a country's wealth, the gross domestic product (GDP), is a poor measure of the 'quality of life' of a country. For example, a hurricane that destroys houses will boost the GDP because of the reconstruction work that follows it; there is no measure in the GDP for the suffering and inconvenience of the occupants of the houses, even without loss of life. That is why it is possible for the economy to be booming – as the Tories claimed during the 1997 election – yet there to be little 'feel good factor' around in people, when there is rising pollution, inequality, crime and social tension.

Linked to this broader criticism of the failure of economics to take into account the environment, is the failure[8] of all the political party policies to grasp the value of 'green taxes' in reducing pollution. A recent report by the Institute of Public Policy estimated that introducing a package of green taxes now could raise £10 billion a year in 2000 and create 252,000 extra jobs; two-thirds of them full-time, if the extra revenue was used to cut national insurance contributions (NICs). In fact, we already have a few green taxes, such as an increased tax on leaded petrol (a great success in reducing lead from car exhausts), an 8 per cent VAT on domestic fuel (but 17.5 per cent was wanted) and a £7 per tonne landfill tax that has boosted household recycling schemes. Green taxes are more common in Europe: Finland introduced a carbon tax in 1990, Sweden and Norway energy taxes in

1991, Denmark in 1993 and The Netherlands in 1996. A number of EU countries levy taxes on acid rain. Six EU countries – France, Italy, Austria, Spain, Greece, Portugal – use road tolls. In France they bring in £2.92 billion. These countries are seeking between a 0.8 and 3 per cent shift in the tax base from constructive activities, such as work and investment, to destructive ones such as pollution. Overall, 'green taxes' are growing worldwide because, 'In effect, [environmental] taxes seek the path of least economic resistance to protecting the environment.'[9]

THE MAJOR POLLUTION PROBLEMS

There are a very wide range of urgent pollution problems, the key ones of which are: global warming, the depletion of the ozone layer, acid rain, vehicle pollution, energy use, water pollution and scarcity, contaminated land, resource depletion, food scarcity, population growth and the loss of rare species. There are many books available that discuss all of these important issues in great detail.

Some of the key UK 'environmental indicators' are published annually.[10] Some of the latest are as follows:

O   *Carbon dioxide* emissions were 148 million tonnes, 11 million tonnes lower than in 1990. Power stations (30 per cent) and road transport (20 per cent) were the major sources of emissions in 1995.

O   *Methane emissions* were 3.8 million tonnes, almost 15 per cent lower than in 1990. The main sources of emissions in 1995 were landfill (46 per cent) and cattle (21 per cent).

O   *Emissions of synthetic nitrous oxide* were 95,000 tonnes in 1995, 21 per cent lower than in 1990. Non-combustion processes amounted for two-thirds (67 per cent) of total emissions.

O   There was a *decrease in the ozone layer* of 5–6 per cent, per decade, in the UK.

O   *Consumption of CFCs* in the EU was 87 per cent lower than in 1994.

O   The UK *supply of CFCs* was 82 per cent lower than in 1994.

O   *sulphur dioxide emissions* fell from 2.7 million tonnes in 1994 to 2.4 million tonnes in 1995, a decrease of 13 per cent. Power stations account for two-thirds (67 per cent).

O   'Poor' air quality, in respect of *sulphur dioxide*, was recorded at 14 of 28 monitoring sites in the UK, on at least one occasion, during 1995.

O   *Total black smoke emissions* fell to 356,000 tonnes in 1995 from 404,000 tonnes in 1994, a decrease of 12 per cent. Emissions from road transport were 50 per cent higher than in 1980, but had fallen by 18 per cent from the 1992 peak. They now constitute around 50 per cent of such emissions.

O   Emissions of smaller particles, known as *PM10*, fell by 14 per cent between 1990 and 1995.

O   The UK standard for *PM10* (50 micrograms per cubic metre of air) was exceeded at all automated monitoring sites during 1995.

○ Emissions of *nitrogen oxides* fell to 2.3 million tonnes from 2.4 million tonnes in 1994, a decrease of 4 per cent. Rod traffic emission account for almost half (49 per cent), but have fallen steadily since 1989 and the introduction of the catalytic converter.

○ 'Poor' air quality for *nitrogen dioxide* was recorded on at least one occasion at 15 of the 29 national monitoring sites in 1995.

○ *Carbon monoxide* emissions fell to 5.5 million tonnes in 1995 from 6 million tonnes in 1994, a decrease of 8 per cent. Road transport was the source of three-quarters (75 per cent) of all emissions in 1995 and the fall was the result of the introduction of catalytic converters.

○ *Lead* emissions were 1000 tonnes in 1996, half the level of 1990 and one-sixth that of 1985. This was the direct result of the introduction of lead-free petrol in 1986. Seventy per cent of petrol sold is now unleaded.

○ *Volatile organic compound* (VOC) emissions fell to 2.3 million tonnes in 1995 from 2.4 million tonnes in 1994, a decrease of 4 per cent. Emissions peaked at 2.8 million tonnes in 1989. Solvent use (30 per cent) and road transport (30 per cent) were the main sources of emission during 1995.

○ 'Poor' air quality, as a result of *ground-level ozone* concentrations, was recorded at 22 of the 32 monitoring sites on at least one occasion. The more stringent World Health Organization (WHO) guidelines were exceeded at 30 sites in 1995.

○ *Rainfall* in Great Britain during 1995 was 14 per cent below the 1961–90 long-term average.

○ Fifty-one *drought* orders were made in 1995, compared with none in 1993 and 1994, and this was the most since 1990.

○ In 1995, almost one in ten (91 per cent) of samples in England and Wales failed to make the grade of 'fair' or 'good' *drinking water* chemical quality content.

○ In 1995, about 97 per cent of the total length of designated *rivers* in the UK complied with the EU Freshwater Fish Directive standards. This compares with 98 per cent in 1992, and 96 per cent in 1989.

○ In 1995, 97 per cent of the 4000 *sewage treatment works* in England and Wales complied with the conditions of their discharge.

○ During 1996, one in ten (10 per cent) of the identified *bathing water* beaches in the UK failed the EU Bathing Water Directive on mandatory coliform standards.

○ *Total nitrogen* increased by 12 per cent between 1985 and 1995, but there were reductions in heavy metal contents, *lead* by 75 per cent and *mercury* by 77 per cent, in river waters.

○ Around the UK, the total number of *oil spill incidents* reported in 1995 was 8 per cent more than in 1994, but 26 per cent less than the peak of 1991.

○ In 1995, *Diuron* and *Isoproturon* were the pesticides most commonly found in marine water samples.

○ Nearly half the *fish stocks* fished in EU water during 1996 were calculated to have a spawning biomass below the minimum biological acceptable level, the level below which there is a risk of stock collapse.

O   Some 85 per cent of the average total *radiation* dose to UK individuals comes from natural radiation sources.

O   Most of the remaining 15 per cent of radiation does comes from medical sources (mainly X-rays).

O   Less than 1 per cent of radiation does comes from radiation discharges from nuclear plants.

O   *Noise* complaints in England and Wales rose by 22 per cent between 1993–94 and 1994–95.

O   Noise complaints from domestic premises, two-thirds of the total, rose by 300 per cent between 1983–84 and 1994–95.

O   Although, during 1994–95, noise abatement notices rose by 17 per cent, noise prosecutions fell from 502 in 1993–94 to 465, a decrease of 7 per cent.

O   At 26 million tonnes, *waste from mining and quarrying* was almost one-quarter (24 per cent) less than in 1990.

O   On average, each *household* produces 21 kg of waste per week.

O   *Landfill* accounts for 83 per cent of disposal methods for municipal waste during 1995–96.

O   1.5 million tonnes, or 6 per cent, of household waste was collected for *recycling* or *composting* during 1995–96.

O   In 1994, 57,000 tonnes of *waste was imported* into the UK from 27 countries (three-quarters from Germany and Ireland).

O   The use of *recycled aluminum* rose from 39 per cent in 1994 to 53 per cent in 1995, mainly due to the 'save-a-can' scheme (1900 million collected in 1995; eight times that of 1990). But for other metals (e.g. iron, copper, zinc and lead) there was no difference.

O   The amount of *waste paper* used in newspapers rose by 58 per cent between 1990 and 1994.

O   *Bottle banks* rose four-fold from 1988 to 14,998 in 1995.

O   Total *forest cover* in the UK increased by 17 per cent between 1980–81 and 1995–96.

O   The areas designated as *Sites of Special Scientific Interest* (SSSI) in Great Britain increased by 41 per cent between 1985 and 1996 (to over 2 million hectares).

O   In 1995–96, 2000 hectares of SSSIs were affected by short-term damage and 3000 hectares by long-term damage.

O   There are 247 species of British breeding *birds* (the most common being the wren).

O   One hundred and forty-two British breeding species have been identified to be of special concern. For 76 of these declining species, more than 20 per cent of the Western European population are found in Great Britain.

O   The number of *grey seals* has increased by 75 per cent since 1986.

○   There are 54 species of *butterfly*, 34 species of dragonfly and 23 species of grasshopper. Whilst almost one-third (29 per cent) increased in geographical distribution, just over half decreased.

○   There were significant declines in the *diversity of plant species* in Great Britain in arable fields and woodlands between 1978 and 1990.

This book is concerned about what can be done at the workplace, in a relatively simple way, and I will therefore concentrate on some of the key issues that can be practically addressed by workplace action.

GLOBAL WARMING

Certain gases that are naturally present in the atmosphere trap some of the heat that reaches the earth from the sun to give a 'greenhouse effect' on the earth. This is a natural effect which keeps the earth warm enough to support life. Indeed, without it the earth's surface would be around 30°C colder than it is now! But human activities, especially in industrialized countries, are causing an increase in these 'greenhouse' gases, especially carbon dioxide (CO_2). Carbon dioxide is produced from burning fossil fuels – coal, oil and natural gas – to generate electricity, provide heat and power transport.

The average global temperature of the earth reached 15.39°C in 1995, breaking the previous record of 15.38° in 1990. Depending on air pollution trends, it is predicted that human activity will warm the earth by 1–3.5°C by the year 2100. This may not sound much, but the last time temperatures substantially exceeded current levels, 125,000–115,000 years ago, hippopotamuses were living in what now is Britain. The global temperatures trend[11] for the past 130 years has been upwards. The ten warmest years in the past 130 years have been in the 1980s and 1990s, with the three warmest years being in the 1990s.

Among other things, the continued rise in the burning of fossil fuels – up from the record 6 billion tonnes in 1991 to 6.1 billion tonnes in 1995 – indicates that most governments of industrial societies are failing to reach the carbon emission levels set at the 1992 Rio summit. Ironically, because of the run-down of the UK coal industry, the UK is one of the few countries to reach this target. The more immediate and obvious effects of global warming will be an abrupt change in weather conditions, including storms and droughts; there is some evidence of the storms already appearing. In addition, there could also be rising sea levels if the polar caps melt; the average global sea level has already risen about 18 centimetres over the past century. But the biggest threat may be drought, with Spain and Greece loosing 85 per cent of their inland wetlands. Spain has lost two-thirds of its inland wetlands since 1965.

A warmer world is likely to be a more disease-prone world for both humans and non-humans. Even the insurance industry is worried. As Franklin Nutter, president of the Reinsurance Association of America, says: 'The insurance industry is first in line to be affected by climate changes ... it could bankrupt the industry' (Brown, 1996, p. 118).

THE DEPLETION OF THE OZONE LAYER

About 30–40 km above the earth there is a thin, diffuse layer of ozone gas – the so-called ozone layer. This layer filters out harmful ultraviolet (UV) rays from the sun, protecting plant and animal life, including us. Since 1985 there has been convincing evidence that synthetic chemicals – in particular chlorofluorocarbons (CFCs), which were commonly used in refrigerators and aerosol sprays – are damaging the ozone layer. Holes in the ozone layer have appeared, at first above the South Pole, and now elsewhere. In March 1997 the ozone layer above the Arctic fell to a record low. It was 40 per cent thinner than the average between 1979 and 1982. Although not yet a 'hole', it continues the downward trend; last year the March level was 24 per cent down on the 1979–82 levels. Excessive levels of UV light can cause skin cancer and cataracts on the eyes, and can also damage plant growth. In November 1996 an expert panel told the government that 8000 extra skin cancer cases would be caused in Britain by increased UV exposure. At present, there are 80,000 cases annually in Britain, so this is a 10 per cent increase. Children are especially at risk.

Yet the depletion of the ozone layer may yet turn out to be a very significant turning point in world collaboration to improve the environment. In 1987 negotiators from 24 of the major nations (it was subsequently ratified by more than 150 countries) signed a historic document – the Montreal Protocol on Substances that Deplete the Ozone Layer – that placed far-reaching restrictions, and even bans, on production of some of the key chemicals that are damaging the ozone layer. A recent review of the impact and working of the Montreal Protocol found that, whilst it was not perfect, 'The ozone treaty and its successive amendments represent the most advanced attempt to date to give concrete form to the abstract notion of global partnership advanced at the Rio Summit.'[12]

ACID RAIN

Rain is naturally slightly acidic, but emissions of sulphur dioxide (SO_2) and nitrogen oxides (NO_x) are combining with moisture in the air to increase this acidity. These pollutants are emitted by power stations, industry and motor vehicles. The main problem is the burning of fossil fuels, especially coal and oil. Acid rain damages forests, streams, lakes and hence crops and fish. It also attacks buildings and materials. For many years, because of acid rain, the emissions of these gases has been drastically reduced in both Europe and North America. Yet the damage to lakes, streams and forests continues, possibly because of atmospheric dust levels, and it appears that 'Simple solutions do not always work in complex ecosystems'[13]

SOLID WASTE

The UK generates around 400 million tonnes of solid waste each year. All of this waste goes somewhere, and the environment is being put under increasing pressure. The traditional way of disposing of solid waste has been to bury it in the ground, in so-called landfill sites, although some waste has been burnt to generate power and some, more toxic, waste has been burnt in specially designed high-temperature incinerators. But burial has led to two major problems: (1) the waste leaches out of the landfill site and pollutes the water table; and (2) the waste decomposes to methane, and other gases, that are both explosive and harmful to the environment. Some people (and animals and plants) do not like living near high-temperature toxic waste incinerators, and several have closed because of human fears and/or claims of animal or crop damage by farmers.

As I write, a few streets away from where I live in North London, the local residents are up in arms about the redevelopment of the site of an old metal-plating factory that closed down in 1984. In the 1970s, green liquid containing lead and cyanide had oozed into local people's back gardens and they were told not to eat anything grown in the soil. A much larger public debate has opened up around the 200-year old Royal Ordinance factory in Enfield, maker of the famous .303 Lee-Enfield rifle that was used in two world wars. The 100-acre site closed in 1987 and is heavily contaminated with what looks like much of the periodic table of all the known chemical elements: cadmium, lead, mercury, copper, selenium, nickel, zinc, chromium, arsenic, phenols, cyanide, products of a gas works and asbestos. Again, as I write, there is a major battle going on between the council, an action group and various consultants as to whether it is safe to build 1300 homes on top of this 'toxic waste dump', with a one-metre cap of clay to seal the toxics in, or whether the whole site should be cleaned up and treated to render or remove the toxics, a much more expensive process. It should also be remembered that a major reason for the Lloyds insurance crisis was their underwriting, at far too low cost, of insurance for asbestos companies and toxic waste sites in the USA.

Although the last Conservative government backed off from a UK 'contaminated site' register, it is clear that the problem of the many known, let alone unknown, landfill and former industrial sites in the UK has only just begun. The Labour government, under Prime Minister Tony Blair, has promised to build 14,000 new council homes a year. Many of these will be built on land reclaimed from previous industrial use; so-called 'brown field' sites, just like the Enfield one cited above.

Waste disposal in the UK is becoming an increasing problem for companies and organizations in the UK as available landfill sites are rapidly running out and there is more pressure for strict environmental controls on incinerators, making waste disposal much more expensive. The recently introduced landfill tax will add to the pressure to eliminate, reduce and recycle waste. Companies doing this have found that waste is just waste profit (see page 29).

CASE STUDY 4: BURNING WASTE IN CEMENT KILNS

The downturn in the construction industry has, fortunately for the cement industry, coincided with the discovery that cement kilns, which operate above 1500°C and are highly alkaline, can be used to burn all manner of waste. In the UK, several already have permission from the Environmental Agency (EA) to burn waste solvents from the chemical and pharmaceutical industry. There are already experiments in burning old tyres, and even burning BSE-infected cows has been proposed. Everything can be burned, it seems, at a price.

Needless, to say, this new use of cement kilns has proved controversial, to say the least. People who live near cement kilns, and who have suffered cement dust over their gardens and cars for years, do not feel that the cement industry can be trusted to burn safely more toxic substances. On the other hand, more environmentally conscious countries – like Luxembourg, Germany and the USA – allow and even encourage this use of cement kilns.

What is certain is that the EA has not come out of the current 'trials' in UK cement kilns with much credibility, according to a recent report from the Environment Committee of MPs. Equally, when I helped organize a meeting for the safety representatives from all the key UK cement plants, to hear all sides of the argument (Cement Industry, EA, HSE and Friends of the Earth), the cement industry did not come out too well either. However, it appears that the cement industry is in the process of change and I have been invited to become an 'environmental stakeholder' for Blue Circle cement, the second largest UK cement company. They appear to be taking on board much of the comment and criticism of the environmental, parliamentary and, indeed, trade union observers. Only time will tell. But the future of waste disposal in the UK, and elsewhere, will be much greater waste reduction, recycling and low-temperature and/or biological waste neutralization or re-use.[14]

WATER POLLUTION AND SCARCITY

Water is a vital and, until very recently, underestimated resource in the UK. It is vital to life. Pollutants from various sources can find their way into inland waters and seas. Since most of the UK's drinking water is obtained from reservoirs, groundwater and rivers, these waters in particular need to be protected, especially from dangerous chemicals. Until very recently, my drinking water, in London, was contaminated with two pesticides – atrazine and simazine – that had been used by councils to rid the paths and kerbs of weeds. The weeding is now done by hand or better planning. In September 1996 the Environment Agency (EA) made the first ever attempt[15] at a national survey of groundwater contamination and found more than 1200 sources of pollution in England and Wales. Forty-nine of 472 (10 per cent; it was 11 per cent in 1995) major beaches in the UK failed[16] to reach the EU coliform standard

FIGURE 1.6   Three stages of water purification at Beckton Sewerage Works in London – the second largest in Europe

in 1996. In March 1997, in North London 300,000 people had to boil their drinking water because it had become contaminated.

In 1995 a drastic water shortage in Yorkshire, normally a very wet county, caused massive upheavals and came very near to being a national disaster.[17] In the first few months of 1997 the country was overcome with fear of a massive water shortage because of the exceptionally dry start to the year. The period of 1995-7, said the Institute of Hydrology, was the driest in England and Wales since reliable records began more than 200 years ago. Although the summer of 1997 turned out to be a wet one, in November 1997 the Environment Agency, in a report to the government, said that only in eight of the previous 30 months had there been above average rainfall in England and Wales (see 'After a wet summer, Britain heads for a winter drought', *The Independent*, 4 November 1997, p. 16). Globally,[18] almost half the present world population suffers from water shortages and droughts. Global warming and population growth seem set to make the situation worse.

Domestic demand for water has doubled in the past 35 years; we are taking more baths and showers, watering our gardens more often, using dishwashers and so on. The British Medical Association, in a recent report,[19] has pointed out the health hazards of the rising number of water disconnections and rising prices since water privatization. Others feel that only a public water system can deliver safe water, reliably and at a reasonable price.[20]

The UK Round Table on Sustainable Development has recently[21] carried out a detailed study on UK fresh water, and their key conclusions, from 13 main recommendations, are as follows:

○   The government should publish a national strategic framework for fresh water policy, with long-term sustainable water plans for each water supplier that take into full account demand management measures.

○ There should be a review of the regulatory structure of the water industry and an explicit duty on all regulators to take account of sustainable development.
○ There should be a licensing of all significant water abstractions (water users).
○ There should be a phased programme for the widespread measurement by meter of piped water supplies. Where metering is to be used as the basis for charging for water, the tariff structure must safeguard the essential needs of consumers whilst providing an incentive to reduce water wastage.

CASE STUDY 5: WATER POLLUTION FROM CYPRIOT DYE FACTORY

Cyprus is the third largest island in the Mediterranean, with a population of around 700,000 and a civilization at least 8000 years old. It has an excellent climate and short winters and is a favourite tourist resort, at the upper end of the market, with around 2 million visitors a year. Agriculture is an important part of the economy – with two crops a year – as are clothing, textiles, wine and footwear. This style of economy requires a large amount of water and there are frequent water shortages in the summer months. Since 1974 about one-third of the island has been under Turkish occupation. In 1992, as a senior lecturer at the Centre for Industrial and Environmental Safety and Health (CIESH) at South Bank University, I was asked by the cypriot 'Akaki Association' of north London to advise on a water pollution problem from a textile plant near their small home village of Akaki (population 4000), which is 20 minutes' drive from the capital of Greek Cyprus, Nicosia.

The pollution arose from a cotton dyeing and bleaching plant called 'The Rainbow Factory'. Built in 1975, this factory employs about 80 people and works a six-day week, 24-hour production cycle. It supplies much of the dyeing needs of the dress-making branch of the Cyprus cotton industry, and there was great political and economic pressure to keep it open. To carry out the dyeing and bleaching process around 90,000 litres of water per day are required.

Textile plants are well-known water polluters and the effluent from such plants is complex and often difficult and expensive to clean up. By 1987, sampling at boreholes around this plant had begun to show high levels of pollution. At one time, the water in this area had supplied part of the water supply to Nicosia, although this was stopped in 1987. The polluted water from the plant, which was in a poor state both inside and out, appeared to have very little treatment and was just pumped into unlined lagoons and allowed to diffuse into the surrounding water table. The water was used to irrigate local crops and, in the hot and dusty fields, local workers drank from the boreholes at times.

Many different scientific studies had shown that there was gross water pollution from this plant and there had been several specialist reports, dating back to 1988, recommending a variety of water-treatment methods to clean up the effluent. However, none had been implemented at the time of my visit. Gross water pollution from the plant had been demonstrated by the highly qualified

FIGURE 1.7   Protesters against the Rainbow Dye factory that is causing water pollution, near Nicosia in Cyprus, 1992.

and well-equipped Cyprus State General Laboratory (CSGL) as early as 1989. Their methods and analytical figures had been – for reasons I could never understand – attacked by members of the Cyprus Water Board (CWB). In the end, political pressure apart, I could only conclude that it was because the analysts of the CSGL were women with doctorates and the men of the CWB were graduates only. At times, in this investigation, I felt that I was on the set of Ibsen's famous 1882 play *An Enemy of the People* (about telling the truth about water pollution at a local baths), with Greek-Cypriot sexism added to spice the occasion!

I took samples from five representative boreholes and, with the help of the university analytical chemist Dave Walsh, analysed the water samples. It was clear that, compared to UK tap water, there was gross water pollution and that the main, if not only, source of that pollution was the Rainbow effluent (it had been suggested that the water pollutants could have come from a local piggery and/or a wood-treatment plant). The publication of my two reports received considerable press publicity in Cyprus and they were debated in the Cypriot parliament. Friends of the Earth, in Cyprus, demonstrated outside the plant and the issue was raised at a shareholders' meeting of Bayer Chemicals in Germany (who supplied most of the dyes used at the plant) and the publicity and pressure hopefully resulted in an improvement, although I was not convinced that this plant could operate safely at all and a 1989 report on the Rainbow plant by Dr Sewekow of Bayer AG, entitled 'Clarifications on the study of the effluent treatment plant required by the district officer', concluded: 'We can already now estimate that further treatment (to reduce water pollution) will be very expensive and not economic.' This case study gives an indication of the difficulty of resolving water pollution problems even in a relatively wealthy and advanced country like Cyprus.

With the election of a Labour government in May 1997 there was an immediate new initiative on water conservation and clean-up under the directorship of John Prescott, deputy prime minister and minister for the environment and transport. Speaking to a special 'Water Summit' in May 1997, he noted that:

> An average of nearly 30 per cent of the water companies provide leaks away before customers can use it ... Most of the leakage comes from water companies' own pipes. But up to 20 per cent of the total leakage is from the pipes which run from the stopcock to the customer's own building ... There are things that all of us as consumers can do as well:
>
> O Don't run the tap needlessly;
> O Don't water the garden endlessly;
> O Don't run the shower for half an hour before getting in.
>
> It is simple common sense.[22]

He then went on to require the water companies to respond to him on a ten-point action plan for a better water industry within three weeks. The key points of this ten-point plan were as follows:

O Tough mandatory targets for total leakage enforced by the director general of Water Services.
O Water companies should provide a free leakage detection and repair service for the supply pipes of domestic owners.
O There will be a legal duty on water companies to preserve water.
O Water companies must carry out with 'vigour, imagination and enthusiasm' their duty to promote the efficient use of water (e.g. by providing free a simple device to reduce toilet flush volumes; to offer a free water efficiency audit to customers and to encourage water-efficient gardening).
O Water companies should work with the government's Environment Task Force.
O The government will pass new laws on water efficiency and encourage 'best practice' techniques similar to those in the energy sphere.
O The government will review the charging system for water (including the use

of rateable values, metering, pre-payment units and disconnection policies).

O   The compensation system (e.g. for water contamination outbreaks) and the provisions of current licences to water companies will be reviewed.

O   Easily understandable and local performance information (e.g. on quality of drinking water, leakage targets, water supply, investment, benefits to the environment) should be published by all water companies.

O   The water abstraction and bulk transfer system will be reviewed to ensure the environment is fully taken into account. Each water company will produce a detailed, publicly available drought contingency plan with the EA. This will be made law when the opportunity arises.

By July 1997 John Prescott could report 'a positive response to the Water Summit Challenge', with, for example, all the water companies agreeing to offer their household customers a free leakage detection and repair service for supply pipes. Other items on the checklist were progressed by varying degrees.

TRANSPORT

Launching a green consultative document on an integrated transport policy in August 1997, Deputy Prime Minister John Prescott pointed out that 'Forecasts suggest that in 20 years' time traffic levels will be between 36 per cent and 57 per cent higher than now, and by 2025 there will be 10 million extra cars on the road.' The irony of him launching the green paper just before the late summer bank holiday was not lost on the media. The RAC spokeswoman advised people to 'stay at home' because of the traffic jams. Further, in Paris, because of high traffic pollution during August, the prices of public transport had been drastically cut.

Although Mr Prescott made a point of saying that his strategy was not anti-car, something will have to be done about the company car perks and free and subsidised company car-parking. Tax incentives for firms to provide public transport vouchers, together with an improved public transport system, may provide one answer.

A recent detailed study[23] of the economic and environmental consequences of road transport concluded forcefully, 'Road transport is one sector of the UK economy in which almost everything has gone wrong.' Companies and organizations have a major responsibility to support the 'green paper' with: reduced vehicle use, the use of cleaner vehicles and fuels, the encouragement of public transport and walking or cycling, and so on.

NOTES

1.   John Rimington (1995) *Valedictory Summary of Industrial Health and Safety Since 1974*. The Electricity Association, April.

2.   Ann Elvin (1995) *Invisible Crime – the True Life Story of a Mother's Fight Against the*

Cover-up of Workplace Manslaughter, £5 from Ann Elvin, 11 Glandford Road, Stroud, Rochester, Kent, ME2 2QP. This book is the source for this case study.

3. Carl Zenz (1994) *Occupational Medicine*, 3rd edn., St Louis: Mosby Books. W. R. Rom (1992) *Environmental and Occupational Medicine*, 2nd edn., London: Little, Brown and Co.

4. J. Jeyaratnam (ed.) (1992) *Occupational Health in Developing Countries*, Oxford: Oxford University Press.

5. Neil Davies and Paul Teasdale (1994) *The Costs of Workplace Accidents and Work-related Ill-Health to the British Economy*, London: HSE.

6. Health and Safety Executive (1993) *The costs of accidents at work* HSE, HMSO, HS(G) 96.

7. (1997) *More Isn't Always Better* London: The New Economics Foundation.

8. Sarah Boseley (1997) Parties' problem in making the polluter pay, *Guardian* 25 April; Nicholas Schoon (1997) May all our tax rises be green, *The Independent*, 2 April; D. R. Roodman (1996) Harnessing the market for the environment, in *The State of the World*, London: Earthscan.

9. D. L. M. Roodman (1997) Environmental taxes spread, in L. R. Brown, C. Flavin and H. Hane (eds), *Vital Signs 1996–1997*, London: Earthscan, p. 115.

10. *Digest of Environmental Statistics* (1997) Department of the Environment, Transport and the Regions, 11 July.

11. Charles Arthur (1997) The sun is changing the way we live *The Independent*, 10 April.

12. F. F. French (1997) Learning from the ozone experience, in L. R. Brown (ed.) *The State of the World 1997*, London: Earthscan, p. 170.

13. L. Hedin and G. E. Likens (1996) Atmospheric dust and acid rain, *Scientific American*, 56-60, 60.

14. *The Environmental Impact of Cement Manufacture* (1997), House of Commons, Environment Committee, 26 February. *The Safety, Health and Environmental Implications of Burning Alternative Fuels in Cement Kilns* (1996) London: The Transport and General Workers Union. H. M. Freeman (1990) *Hazardous Waste Minimisation*, London: McGraw Hill Publishing.

15. Fred Pearce (1996) Dirty groundwater runs deep, *New Scientist*, 21 September, 16-17.

16. Department of the Environment, press release, 20 November 1996.

17. Brian Cathcart (1996) The wrong kind of water; drought, Yorkshire and civil unrest, *The Independent on Sunday Review*, 23 February, 10-12.

18. Water Crisis, eight-page special report, *The Independent*, 21 March 1997.

19. British Medical Association (1994) *Water – a Vital Resource*. London, BMA.

20. *Against the tide or going through the motions? A Public Interest Report* (1996), Manchester University: Department of Accounting and Finance.

21. *Fresh Water* (1997) UK Round Table on Sustainable Development, Portland House, Floor 23, Stag Place, London, SW1E 5DF.

22. Department of the Environment, Water Summit – action on leakage is the top priority, press release, 19 May 1997.

23. David Pearce, David Maddison, Olof Johansson, Edward Calthorp, Todd Litman and Eric Verhoef (1997) *The True Costs of Road Transport*, London: Earthscan, p. ii.

2

WHO IS RESPONSIBLE FOR SHE HAZARDS AT THE WORKPLACE?

MANAGEMENT'S RESPONSIBILITY

> Trade union safety representatives are becoming so well trained that they will know more about shopfloor health and safety than some of their own managers.
> Mr Jim Hammer, Chief Inspector of Factories, 1978

That statement was made 20 years ago, when The 1977 Safety Representative and Safety Committee Regulations (SRSC Regs) had just become law. Since that time I have been teaching managers of large and small organizations about SHE issues, and I am afraid to say the same is true today! Rarely, if ever, are managers and supervisors given as much time as the 10-day, one-day-a-week, TUC-approved courses for trade union safety representatives. If they are very lucky, it is a three- or five-day block and, more often, a single day and sometimes just a Friday afternoon! Of course, there are many one-day, extensive 'song and dance' acts available from a variety of management training companies and consultants on specific topics and these are increasing in number, and price, daily. The best have some value in an informative way. But there is no substitute for an in-depth look, with real-life case studies, at the organizations where the hazards originate. That is what the TUC courses do. Further, the TUC-approved course, in running one day a week for 10 weeks, allow safety representatives to try out suggested solutions to problems and to bring them back to the classroom to discuss whether they worked or not and why. The education is small group (classes are normally 15–20 people), case-study orientated and participative.

But it is not just in the educational area that managers are lacking. Often, and especially in the current climate, production or service delivery comes first and all else – including safety, health and the environment – a very big second. This was a common complaint from many of the 450 or so safety representatives who replied to my 1994–95 safety representatives survey.[1] For example:

○ 'I have to say in my short time as a safety rep I have noticed that, in general, the management have no idea about health and safety. In find this very alarming as very senior management do not see this as a problem. So they do not train people to know the law and their moral obligations.' (Alan Parker, a Rail, Maritime and Transport (RMT) safety representative at Exel Logistics, North London Freight Terminal, which employs about 250 people.)

O 'I am at this time trying to organise a safety committee, regular inspections and to make management aware of their responsibility for the health and safety of their employees. I am amazed at their lack of knowledge about health and safety and their lethargic attitude ...' (Mr S. Page, United Road Transport Union (URTU) safety representative at Allied Bakeries, Sheffield.)

O 'Of late, however, I have noticed that even in our industry the pressure is there for individual managers, because of the purse strings, to cut corners or by-pass the system if they can, on health, safety or even environmental issues.' (Mr D. R. Ward, GMB safety representative/branch secretary, Anglian Water Authority.)

O 'I don't think that the competent people appointed by management are fully trained to know, at this moment, the full extent of safety policies and the rights of safety representatives.' (Alan Footer, UNISON safety representative, St Edmund Arrowsmith RC High School, Ashton-in-Makerfield.)

However, change is in the air. The Health and Safety Executive (HSE) has made a point of saying that it is now looking for effective 'management systems', and not just whether a guard is on a machine or the exposure levels for a certain chemical are being exceeded. The 1992 Management of Health and Safety at Work Regulations are crucial here. It is significant that in 1995–96 there were 31 convictions under these regulations, one of the highest number of HSE prosecutions under a single set of regulations, with an average fine of £2892. Even more significantly, 943 enforcement notices were served, the third largest number served under any one set of regulations.

The introduction to the very important Construction (Design and Management) Regulations 1994 – Approved Code of Practice, which became law in March 1995, says quite forcefully, 'Poor management is the prime cause of the unacceptable accident and occupational record of the construction industry.'

In August 1997 the HSE succeeded in a 'landmark' case against the Swindon and Marlborough NHS Trust. No accident or injury had occurred at the Trust, which employs 3000 people with an annual budget of £69 million. The Trust was fined £4000 with £1720 costs for failing to have 'effective management systems' in place and enforced on health and safety. This, as Swindon magistrates confirmed, 'placed undue risk, in particular on members of staff and also for the patients and members of the public'. The HSE now plans to 'blitz' the other 40 NHS trusts throughout the next year.

CASE STUDY 6: THE EMERGENCY SERVICES

The emergency services (i.e. ambulance, fire and police) have always been a difficult group of organizations to get to be concerned about health and safety issues, let alone environmental ones. It is easy to see why; they are often at the 'cutting edge' of society and concerned about saving life in a very blunt, and often brutal, way. They deal with situations that many of the rest of us just do not want to know about. As 'uniformed services' they are often run on semi-military lines. The niceties of health, safety and environmental issues often seem to have no place. All of this encourages a very macho culture, and it is no accident that there have been some very highly publicized cases of sexual and racial discrimination in both the fire and the police services.

A few years back I was a part-time employee of the Camden and Islington Occupational Health Project. A large part of the job consisted of interviewing people in the general practitioner's (GP's) waiting room, before they saw a doctor, about their working conditions and whether this had any relation to their health problems. One GP's surgery was very near a block of rented accommodation for police officers. The police are encouraged to report all bruises, injuries and accidents, and one of the GPs, a Tory councillor, was pretty sympathetic to their 'health' problems; for all except one, post-traumatic stress disorder. There were quite a few policemen, and women, who said to me that they were under stress, but could not admit it (even to the GP) because 'failing to cope' was not an injury the police management recognized. In fact, the police have recently set up a confidential counselling service; but many officers thought that if they went for such counselling, somehow, management would get to know.

Some years ago I was involved, at the Old South West London College (now part of South Bank University), in teaching London ambulance officers and, to a lesser extent, London Fire Brigade (LFB) officers health and safety. It was, in the main, hard work for the reasons discussed above and we had some strong clashes with higher management. I well remember having to rescue a younger lecturer from some baying fire officers who had pinned him to the wall and reduced him almost to tears!

It came as no surprise to me, then, that the HSE had to take action against the LFB in the early 1990s. The LFB is the largest fire brigade in the UK, employing 20 per cent of the total number of firefighters in the UK. It is the largest fire brigade in Europe, and the third largest in the world, employing around 7900 people. The incident that provoked the HSE enforcement action was the deaths of firefighters Terry Hunt and David Stokoe in 1991. They ran out of compressed air when fighting a warehouse fire in east London. An inquest jury returned a verdict of 'unlawful killing'. Two improvement notices (INs) were served on the LFB in 1992 as a result, relating to management safety systems and training. The LFB appeared to be dragging its feet, so, in January 1994, a further notice was served, under

Section 2(1) of the 1974 Act and the Management of Health and Safety at Work Regulations 1992, giving the LFB until the end of March 1995 to complete the requirements (see Schedule to Notice, pages 30–1). As a result, the LFB chief fire officers has set up a special management team to monitor LFB training.

Of course, the LFB is not alone. In 1993 two other firefighters, Mr Morris and Mr Davies, were killed fighting a fire at Sun Valley Poultry Ltd, in Hereford. Subsequently, two INs were served on the Hereford and Worcester Fire Brigade in 1994 that related to the inspection of premises to investigate potential fire risks at those premises and the correct use of and training with breathing apparatus. In early .1997, Tayside Fire Brigade was fined £5000 over the death of 43-year-old firefighter, Roderick Nicolson. He had heroically saved two men's lives at British Fuels, when he was buried alive in highly toxic soda ash. As Sheriff Kenneth Forbes noted, when passing sentence, 'There ought to have been a proper control over his entry into the silo. The emergency services are no less entitled to safe working practices than those in industry.'

A special Home Office committee on training of experts concluded, in December 1994, that the training of firefighters had changed little in the past 25 years and that the health and safety training 'leaves much to be desired'. Dave Matthews, national health and safety officer for the Fire Brigades Union, and a member of the Home Office committee, said that part of the problem was less time for training of firefighters due to cash curbs and fire officers having to spend too much time on paperwork and budgeting instead of training. The key point is that the HSE is now looking at, and enforcing, the law on the management systems and not just the hazards of a workplace. (Dalton, 1995.)

THE CONTENTS OF A TYPICAL IMPROVEMENT NOTICE SERVED REQUIRING MANAGEMENT SYSTEMS

To implement a systematic approach to the management of health and safety based upon the work already started and presented to me at our meetings since the Notices London Fire Brigade (LFB) 1 & 2 were served in March 1992.

In particular:

A   Provide an information system to support the management of health and safety.
     The system should:

   i.   provide the information needed by managers at all levels and the Authority, in order that they can discharge their responsibilities in relation to health and safety and associated training and resource issues.
   ii.   develop methods for ascertaining the training provided to all ranks, particularly in relation to the health and safety aspects of operational

performance, and recording this to accurately reflect the subjects covered, competence reached and the dates it was carried out.

B   Ensure that the development of risk assessments concentrates upon risks arising from:-

(1) The system of command;

(2) The system of tactical firefighting and

(3) The use of personal protective equipment including the support systems for breathing apparatus.

C   Prepare a programme to implement the audit topic areas identified in the "AUDIT PROTOCOL" and associated "GUIDE" which were produced to comply with LFB 2 and carry out such audits on at least 2 topic areas.

D   Ensure that training for command which officers receive in the revised programme fully addresses the health and safety implications; and

(1) At least 25% of staff serving at sub-officer level and above, and

(2) Not less than 80% of officers of Divisional Officer Rank, have received it.

Notes not forming part of the NOTICE

This Notice requires you to implement the planning undertaken in complying with the earlier Notices. It sets out the organisational arrangement & supervisory control systems needed to demonstrate the continuing and appropriate development of the approach to systematic management of health and safety and the training which supports it.

In particular:

O   A management information system designed to support the development of systematic management of health and safety is required.

O   A health and safety policy, organisation and control system which clearly articulates health and safety objectives and provides sufficient performance standards and measures is required.

O   Appropriate methods of hazard identification & risk assessment of operational incidents & training must be derived.

In the preface (produced in September 1993) to the current health and safety policy, there is a recognition of the need for changes to the existing policy statement (produced in 1977). We accepted this arrangement as compliance with Schedule to the Notice LFB/2 because the major changes you are introducing to the policy would otherwise require its frequent rewriting. We accept that it is often easier to reflect such changes in this way but we expect you shortly to produce a programme to implement longer term changes in the policy. This programme should include the setting of clearly defined health & safety objectives along side a broad time scale for their implementation.

You have started developing your understanding of risks and will need to carry out further work in developing and revising your approach, to risk & performance assessment and on management systems. Methods of hazard identification and risk assessment for operational incidents and training must be derived from the standards framework and competencies which you have developed since the serving of the earlier notices and in the context of the risk model you are currently developing.

HUMAN RESOURCE MANAGEMENT/TOTAL QUALITY MANAGEMENT (HRM/TQM) AND HEALTH AND SAFETY MANAGEMENT SYSTEMS

Following on from their analysis of why accidents and major disasters happen (see page 34), in 1991 the HSE produced detailed guidance entitled *Successful Health and Safety Management*. As HM Chief Inspector of Factories, Mr A. J. Linehan, said in his introduction to the HSE guidance, 'Much of the guidance involves the application of the principles of total quality management (TQM) to health and safety … HSE inspectors will be using this publication as a guide when judging the adequacy of health and safety management and compliance with statutory requirements.' The principles of this are illustrated in Figure 2.1. A vital aspect of the HRM/TQM approach is the co-operation of the workforce. In an important section on co-operation, the HSE report (emphasis in original) says:

> However, successful organisations are not satisfied with mere legal compliance and *they actively encourage and support safety representatives* in their role, recognising the valuable contribution they can make. Safety representatives are provided with training which, in common with all employees, enables them to make an informed contribution on health and safety issues. They also enjoy the positive benefits of an open communications policy and are also closely involved in directing the health and safety effort by the nature of the issues discussed at health and safety committees. Effective consultative bodies are involved in planning, measuring and reviewing performance as well as their more traditional reactive role of considering the results of accident, ill-health and incident investigations and other concerns of the moment.[2]

The HSE guidance goes on to suggest other methods of involving all the employees of an organization in health and safety issues (e.g. 'quality circles', 'team briefings', 'tool box talks') and notes that 'The involvement of employees may, in the short term, increase the potential for conflict and disagreement about what constitutes safety and healthy working.' However, it suggests that as long as supervisors and managers are supported by procedures for resolving problems and disputes. 'In the long term the potential for conflict is reduced as the participants develop constructive working relationships and shared objectives.'[2]

In 1990 the employers' organization, the Confederation of British Industry (CBI), published the results of its survey into the 'safety culture' of 266 companies.

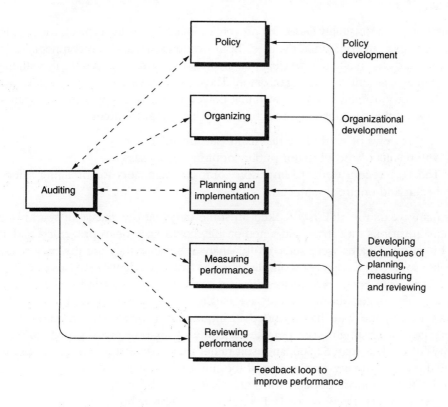

FIGURE 2.1   Key elements of TQM

The survey, entitled *Developing a Safety Culture*, noted:

> All the companies studied agreed that involving employees in an active way in health
> and safety was an important part of developing and sustaining the company's culture
> ... A second major factor in gaining participation was establishing health and safety as
> a joint venture. Safety committees which are required by law when requested by
> recognised trade unions are used extensively. (p. 36)

The 1996 British Standard BS 8800: 1996 on *Occupational Health and
Management Systems* is fully compatible with the HSE approach of successful
health and safety management, as outlined above. An alternative approach is
outlined in BS 8800, based upon BS EN ISO 14001, which is the environmental
systems standards (see also page 246). The standard, in outline only, links both of
these approaches to the general principles of good management as required by
BS EN 9001: 1994, *Quality Management Systems*. The approach of BS EN ISO
14001 also requires that, 'The organisation should establish and maintain
arrangements, where appropriate, for employee involvement and consultation'
(paragraph 4.3.3.(b)).

THE LAW

Where does responsibility lie for the prevention of all this death, ill-health, accidents, suffering and environmental damage? Both occupational and environmental law, criminal and civil, make it quite clear that the major responsibility lies firmly with the senior management of the organization. Those who have the power clearly also have the responsibility that goes with that power. In the area of workplace hazards, the proof of this responsibility has come from three main sources:

○   HSE reviews of workplace deaths in various industries
○   The results of recent major public inquiries into disasters
○   The very recent trend to imprison company managers for breaking safety, health and environmental law

For many years the HSE has looked, in some detail, at the causes of workplace deaths in various industries and whether they could have been prevented and, if so, by whom. Deaths were selected for analysis because they are the only really reliable source of data; most workplace deaths from 'accidents' (but this does not apply to death from workplace diseases) are in fact recorded. Additionally, because of their serious nature, they are usually fairly well investigated by the HSE. However, anyone who has attended in inquest of a loved one or friend on a workplace death might consider the outcome of an HSE investigation, often a paltry fine of less than £2,000, an insult rather than a deterrent. To be fair to the HSE, the responsibility for the size of the fine rests with the courts; but the HSE could campaign more publicly for higher fines (see also p. 35).

Over the years, many major HSE studies have shown the following:

○   About two in three deaths in the manufacturing industry could have been prevented by management action (HSE Annual Report, 1982).
○   In nearly seven out of ten deaths during maintenance, positive management action could have saved lives (HSE Annual Report, 1985).
○   Management are responsible for nearly six out of every ten farm deaths (HSE Annual Report, 1986).
○   Management action could have prevented seven of every ten construction site deaths (HSE Annual Report, 1988).

In addition, over the past ten years there have been several detailed public inquiries into public health and safety disasters, such as Zeebrugge (1987, 193 dead), King's Cross (1987, 31 dead), Piper Alpha (1988, 167 dead) and Clapham Junction (1988, 33 dead). In each and every case the senior management of the organization was heavily criticized.

○   'From the top to bottom the body corporate (of P&O at Zeebrugge) was infected with the disease of sloppiness' (the Sheen Report, Department of Transport, 1988).
○   'In truth London Underground (at King's Cross) had no system which

permitted management or staff to identify, and then promptly eliminate, hazards' (the Fennel Report, Department of Transport, 1988).

○ 'It appears to me that there were significant flaws in the quality of Occidental's management (of Piper Alpha) of safety which affected the circumstances of the events of the fire' (the Cullen Report, Department of Energy, 1988).

○ 'In BR (at Clapham Junction) ... there was a distressing lack of organisation and management on the part of some ... The result was that the true position in relation to safety lagged frighteningly far behind' (the Hidden Report, Department of Transport, 1989).

Manslaughter convictions for workplace deaths

These reports, coupled with increasing public concern over safety and the environment, and the pressure from relatives' support groups, trade unions and groups like the Construction Safety Campaign, the National Hazards Campaign and the media, have led to a wider public debate on corporate responsibility, and to calls for a change in the law to allow individual company directors to be prosecuted.

The state did prosecute the senior management of P&O European Ferries, the owner of the Herald of Free Enterprise that sank at Zeebrugge. Whilst the prosecution failed, it did establish that a company director – the guiding mind of a company – could be properly indicted for manslaughter. In December 1989, Norman Holt, company director of Holt Plastics, was prosecuted for manslaughter over the death of an employee, 25-year old George Kenyon. He was given a one-year term of imprisonment but it was suspended for two years. The leniency of the sentence caused an outcry locally. This was the first ever charge of manslaughter for a general health and safety offence. In 1994 the Law Commission produced a consultative paper on 'involuntary manslaughter' which included a discussion and some proposals, on the crime of 'corporate manslaughter'. In December 1994 the Trades Union Congress (TUC) submitted a dossier of grossly negligent workplace deaths, where no criminal prosecution had taken place, to the Law Commission. The TUC in their submission asked that

> a new offence of 'Manslaughter at Work' be created, with imprisonment as the ultimate sanction ... Responsibility for deaths at work must be borne by Directors unless they have clearly devolved both the responsibility and the power over health and safety matters to an individual manager.

In June 1997 Ms Jenny Bacon, director general of the HSE, told me[3] that a total of 47 potential manslaughter cases had been referred to the Crown Prosecution Services (CPS) in the past five years by the HSE (before 1990 there were practically none referred to the CPS by the HSE). The CPS has launched prosecutions in ten of these cases. Four were subsequently withdrawn or dismissed, and two resulted in convictions both of an individual director and of the company concerned. Several recent legal cases have advanced the law on corporate responsibility and manslaughter.[4]

The first concerned the crucial questions how far the senior management of a company can, in fact, delegate health and safety responsibility. In 1990 a subcontractor to British Steel plc was killed by an unsafe work method. It was agreed by British Steel that Section 3(1) of the 1974 Act had been broken. However, its counsel argued that the directing mind, or senior management, of British Steel had delegated the safety supervision to a Mr Crabb, a British Steel section engineer who was responsible for the supervision of the work. In December 1994 the Court of Appeal dismissed British Steel's claim, saying: 'It would drive a juggernaut through the legislative scheme if corporate employers could avoid criminal liability where the potentially harmful event was committed by someone who was not the directing mind of the company'.[4] It appears, then, that the managing director and the board cannot escape responsibility.

The second concerned the deaths of four teenagers who died on a canoeing trip in 1993. In the first ever conviction for corporate manslaughter in a British court, in December 1994, 45-year-old Peter Kite, managing director of the activity centre, was jailed for three years. Sentencing Kite, Mr Justice Ognall said, 'The potential for injury and death is too obvious for safety procedures to be left to inadequate vagaries of self-regulation ... You were more interested in sales than safety.' In addition, in a landmark ruling, the company, OLL – formerly Active Learning and Leisure – was found guilty of four charges of manslaughter and fined £60,000. A commentary on this case in the January 1995 issue of Lloyds List concluded that it 'should serve as a warning both to senior executives and to shareholders of corporations, whatever their size, that they could bear the ultimate responsibility if their corporation ignores safety concerns.'

There have been four recent cases of managers being imprisoned for direct health and safety offences, and the trend for more manslaughter charges seems here to stay.

O   In January 1996, 22 years after the 1974 Health and Safety at Work Act became law, the first ever managing director was imprisoned for a health and safety offence. The managing director of a building company, Roy Hill, was sentenced to three months in prison and ordered to pay costs of £4000 after he admitted to exposing his employees and the public to deadly asbestos dust. Judge Rupert Bursell said, when sentencing Hill, 'The greatest effect of this custodial sentence upon you will be when you hear the clang of the prison doors behind you.'

O   In March 1996 Joseph O'Connor, the operator of the trawler Pescada, was jailed for three years for manslaughter. The trawler sunk in 1991, with the loss of six lives, and was shown to be completely unseaworthy, and equipped with faulty live-saving equipment; the crew were inexperienced. However, in February 1997, Mr O'Connor was freed by the Court of Appeal on a technicality.

O   In April 1996 the managing director, Colin Barker, and the production director, Knox Kerr, of Calder Felts Ltd, were sent to prison for four months each. The HSE had served a prohibition notice on several high-speed roller machines at several of the company's premises. The two directors allowed their continued use in a dangerous state. As a direct result, at one of the banned machines 19-year-old Michael Pollard had his arm ripped off from the shoulder and shredded.

O In August 1997 Marck Litchfield was sentenced to 18 months. He was the captain of the tall sailing ship the Maria Asumpta. Two years before he had filled the ship up, against advice, with contaminated fuel, sailed her too close to the dangerous Cornish coast, and then failed to heed the advice of the Padstow harbour master to take the ship further out to sea. Even when the engines failed due to dirty fuel, and the ship was doomed, he failed to order all the crew to don the plentiful supply of lifejackets. The ship struck the rocks and three crew members died. The judge, Mr Justice Butterfield, said that the jail sentence was required because of 'profound disregard for the lives of the crew, – (and because of) his reckless and negligence'. In December 1997, Mr Litchfield lost his appeal against the sentence as three Court of Appeal judges confirmed the sentence of manslaughter (Skipper must serve jail sentence, *Guardian*, 13 December 1997).

Environmental pollution

With regard to environmental pollution, the UK courts, in recent years, have been seen, in general, to give much higher fines for pollution offences than for health and safety offences; typically tens of thousands of pounds rather than thousands. In the first three months of 1995 alone, three men were imprisoned for breaking environmental laws:

O In January, a Surrey man was sent to jail for three months for keeping large amounts of hazardous waste in his garden shed.

O Mr Michael Gray, an asbestos stripper, was sentenced, in February 1995, for two years and two months for leaving drums of toxic waste in a residential street.

O Mr Brian Morrell, the director of a licensed landfill business, carried on dumping waste after the site was full, so some of the waste spilled onto adjoining land, and he carried on an unlicensed waste transfer operation on the site. He was sentenced to 18 months in prison, in February 1995.

And during 1997 two other cases occurred:

O In September John Moynihan, Director of Green Environmental Industries, was sentenced to 18 months in jail for what has been described as the UK's worst clinical waste case. He was charged under Section 33 of the Environmental Protection Act 1990 (when up to five years is possible on indictment).

○ In November Suffolk businessman Frank Allum was jailed for three months after pleading guilty to two charges of unlawful management of asbestos waste.

In summary, it is clear that there is a slowly growing legal trend, fully backed by society's views, to view breaking safety, health and environmental law as a true criminal offence and to imprison serious offenders.

CASE STUDY 7: THE TRANSNATIONAL MINING COMPANY RIO TINTO

Rio Tinto is the world's largest mining company, with 51,000 employees worldwide and copper, gold, iron, coal, aluminium, salt, lead, nickel, diamond, boron, titanium, talc and uranium mines and smelters in many of the world's countries. Without realizing it, I had known of Rio Tinto (formerly the UK mining giant RTZ, and for the last year a UK–Australian mining giant RTZ–CRC) since I was a student at Bristol College of Advanced Technology (to become Bath University whilst I was there) in the 1960s. There were many local students on our chemistry degree course; quite a few came from the 'lead smelter' in Avonmouth, Bristol, and we did an 'industrial visit' there. By the early 1970s the very high levels of lead pollution inside and outside the plant had been the subject of a special government enquiry due to public concern and pressure. Later on, in the 1980s, there was to be similar, if more muted, concern about cadmium levels in the lead and a possible rise in cancer in the local community (this was confirmed for the workforce).

But my real SHE interest in RTZ, as it then was, came during the 1970s. First, I was contacted by a very concerned worker, Glyn Jones, at RTZ's massive aluminium-smelting plant in Anglesey, North Wales. In the 1960s the Labour government built a nuclear power station just to feed the enormous energy requirements of an aluminium smelter. By the 1970s there was a great deal of worker concern about possible hazards inside the plant and community concern about fluoride and other pollution outside the plant. But RTZ dominated the community, the local council, the GPs and the local solicitors, and there were job losses already, so little was done. By advertising in the local press for ex-employees to tell the truth and by a close examination of the published evidence it was clear that the plant was a major polluter, both inside and out. Threats were made of closure, but eventually a multi-million pound investment cleaned up the plant.

At around the same time the 1976 'tin crisis' happened. Having a long-term interest in Cornwall,[5] where the UK tins is mined, and RTZ were the dominant owners, I wrote about this in some detail. Now there is just one tin mine, about to close, in Cornwall. Various other RTZ plant pollution problems became apparent (tin smelter in Hull, the lead plant, again in Bristol, and one or two other plants) and a UK view of RTZ was added to Partizans' (People Against Rio Tinto Zinc and its Subsidiaries) previously mainly international coverage and campaigns.

One of Partizans' actions was to bring 'indigenous people' from all over the world, wherever RTZ was operating, to the London RTZ AGM and let them speak to the shareholders and the media. RTZ executives hated this! I well remember a very articulate aborigine giving a very moving and passionate speech to, for once, silent shareholders. It did not, of course, change the views or voting of the shareholders present at the AGM. However, the 1996 Annual report of RTZ–CRA had a very large SHE section with targets, reductions in pollution and energy use, independent environmental audits in the public domain, set-aside money for site restoration and all the signs of a company that is, at long last, recognizing its vital responsibility as a steward of the earth's crucial resources.

Although various environmental groups and others (e.g. Partizans) demonstrated at RTZ's 1997 AGM, calling these claims 'greenwash', I am sure that the indigenous people who spoke to many AGM's over the years, and the campaigns of Partizans and many other local and international environmental and community groups, have played a big part in forcing Rio Tinto to acknowledge the importance of SHE issues. Now, of course, it must be held to its promises and its green claims must be independently verified.

If this can be done with previously hidden and relatively immune mining company, what can be done with more public companies? An example is the turnaround in Shell after the Brent Spa fiasco in 1995.[6]

THE GOVERNMENT

Whilst most authorities, including industry, agree that it is the employer that is fundamentally responsible for controlling and eliminating SHE hazards from the workplace – as exemplified by the well-known slogan, 'the polluter must pay' – the government has always had an important role in setting the SHE standards and in inspecting and prosecuting those companies and organizations that do not, or will not, care about workplace SHE hazards. However, and especially since the advent of the EU, there is another very important role for national, European and – hopefully in the not-too-distant future – international governments and agencies: the setting, and enforcement, of a 'level playing field' of SHE standards. The world is increasingly becoming a 'global village', and the existence of the Internet is rapidly hastening that process.

Of course, this is really nothing new. Imperialist nations for thousands of years have had an international view as they conquered and pillaged other countries, and, in their own selfish way, set a 'level playing field' of exploitation, slavery, and often brutal repression. Karl Marx was perhaps the most famous social scientist and political theorist to point this out and it is no accident that he lived in the UK and used the UK as the most important model of imperialism of the day. Nowadays, of course, it is the multinational, or transnational, corporations that often play the role of imperialist national states. it is they who hold even relatively large countries to ransom. For example, the managing directors of Ford and Nissan are more important to UK prime ministers than the leaders of most other countries. However, the power of these transnationals should not be over-estimated. They are amenable to pressure at the most local level, let alone the national and EU level, and there are recent signs that even at the international level, governments, trade unions, community groups and non-governmental organizations (NGOs, like environmental pressure groups and charities) are, at last, waking up to the need to organize internationally. This is one of the positive spin-offs of global warming!

THE EUROPEAN UNION (EU)

Whilst the dream of international SHE standards is still some way off, the Montreal Protocol excepted, the fact of common European SHE standards is very much a reality. In this section I will briefly outline the situation as regards EU health and safety law. Slowly, since the 1980s, more and more health and safety law has its origins in Directives from the European Union (EU), formerly the European Economic Community (EEC). After some discussion, debate and a referendum the UK became part of the EU in 1973. Until 1987 the introduction of EU health and safety law into the UK was slow and piecemeal. Directives were made and passed into UK regulations on such subjects as: safety signs, vinyl chloride, carcinogens (cancer-causing agents), lead, asbestos, the control of substances hazardous to health (COSHH), noise, the labelling and notification of dangerous substances and the control of major hazards.

All of this was to change in 1987 with the passing of the Single European Act (SEA). In particular, the SEA modified the original Treaty of Rome with a new Article 118A. This amendment reflected a change in the EU, which was now to reflect the 'social dimension' of the new 'internal market' that was to be fully operative by 1992. The Social Charter gave a prominent place to health and safety. The ideas behind it were formed from a humanitarian ideal, partly because of trade union pressure; political forces and, significantly, larger EU employers and governments were determined to create a 'level playing field' without 'social dumping' (i.e. to undercut competitors).

Before passing on to the details of the SEA, it is worthwhile briefly examining the attitude of the UK government and the HSE to the EU. I think that it is fair to describe it as schizophrenic, under the Tory government of 1979–97. It was Conservative Prime Minister Edward Health, in 1973, who took the UK into the EU. Apart from a brief keenness in the late 1980s and early 1990s, when positive government-funded EU hoardings were even seen in the UK, I think that it is fair to say that the Conservative Party, as a whole, has never been very keen on our membership of the EU. In recent years, and even during the 1997 general election, this subject even threatened to split the party.

Of course, this has been reflected in the attitudes of the HSE. Although the HSC

Annual Report for 1991–92 rightly remarks that European and international developments, 'continue to set the agenda for developments in health and safety standards' it cannot be said that the HSE has been overkeen on EU standards and directives. As Frank Davies, chair or the HSC, says in the HSC's 1994–95 report (p. xv),

> We have continued to argue for a period of consolidation in European health and safety legislation, following the peak in the numbers of directives at the end of the 1980s ... we have doubts on grounds of risk, costs and scientific evidence (about the EU's fourth health and safety action programme).

Perhaps of most significance is the HSE claimed success (page 45) in getting the UK's 'so far as is reasonably practicable' phrase inserted in EU law as 'risk assessment'. In most European countries the preference is for more definite, or prescriptive, standards, directives and laws, and the European Commission has so far favoured the more general European view. However, with the election in May 1997 of the Labour government, and its promise to sign the EU Social Charter, we should now see a more positive view on the EU in government and thus in the HSE.

The SEA of 1987 did two things relevant to health and safety:

○ It moved the EU away from single-issue directives (e.g. lead, noise) towards general directives that laid down general duties and minimum standards, with the aim of harmonizing standards across the member states.
○ It set up a mechanism of qualified majority voting (QMV) on measures concerned with 'improvements', and especially those in the area of the health and safety of workers.

Under QMV a majority of two-thirds (i.e. 62 votes) is enough to agree in principle a common position at the powerful European Council of Ministers, and 23–5 votes constitute a blocking minority. The votes allocated are roughly according to a country's size and *now no single country, or even two countries, can block proposals*. This has been very important for the UK, for there is no doubt that the UK would have blocked many, if not all, EU health and safety directives if it could have.

The votes are as follows:

○ ten votes each – France, Germany, Italy and the UK
○ eight votes – Spain
○ five votes each – Belgium, Greece, Netherlands and Portugal
○ two votes – Luxembourg
○ four votes each – Sweden and Austria
○ three votes each – Finland, Denmark and Ireland

Total votes: 87.

The most important health and safety directives to come out of the new system in the UK have been the so-called 'six-pack' in 1992:

1. The Management of Health and Safety at Work Regulations 1992 (the EU Framework Directive).

2.   The Workplace Health, Safety and Welfare Regulations 1992.
3.   The Display Screen Equipment Regulations 1992.
4.   The Work Equipment Regulations 1992.
5.   The Personal Protective Equipment Regulations 1992.
6.   The Manual Handling Regulations 1992.

The HSC in its Annual Report for 1991–92 made it quite clear that with regard to the enforcement of these new EU-inspired regulations,

> employers will need time to take sensible action when requirements are completely new. Formal enforcement measures are not likely unless the risks to health and safety are evident and immediate, or what needs to be done is not knew, or employers appear deliberately unwilling to recognise their responsibilities.

As we shall see in the rest of this book, it is one thing to pass a health and safety law, but quite another to enforce it!

THE ROBENS REPORT

I have discussed in more detail elsewhere (Dalton, 1991) the social and political background to the 1974 Health and Safety at Work Act (the 1974 Act), of which the 1970–72 Royal Commission on health and safety, chaired by Lord Robens, was crucial. Recently, more information has become available about the lack of concern for safety issues that Lord Robens, then head of the National Coal Board (NCB), showed at the time of the Aberfan disaster. Thirty years ago, in 1966, a NCB slag heap engulfed a South Wales school in Aberfan and killed many children. The subsequent enquiry lad the blame squarely on the NCB's shoulders, and on Lord Robens in particular, who showed no remorse. It seems strange that with this record he should be selected to chair a Royal Commission on health and safety.

Be that as it may, my view and that of many other health and safety professionals, such as Professor Theo Nichols of Bristol University (one of the few UK academics to maintain a sustained interest in the issue of workplace health and safety), is that the conclusions of the Robens Report were fundamentally flawed (Nichols, 1997). In essence, Robens thought that there was too much law and that this, and other issues, led to an 'apathy' about workplace health and safety issues. Leading the Labour Party opposition to the report in the House of Commons debate, in 1973, was MP Neil Kinnock, who said that, 'to suggest that the law is the main cause of apathy is a distortion of reality. It is like saying the crutch has made the cripple.'

I make no apology for briefly surveying the Robens Report, as his philosophy has had, and has even more today in a 'de-regulatory climate', a great influence on HSE thinking and action. Recently John Rimington, the director general of the HSE for its formative years of 1983–94, in a 'valedictory summary' of industrial health and safety since the 1974 Act, concluded: 'The Roben's Report was visionary. Its analysis – which at the time I thought rather sketchy – stands up impregnably to a re-reading twenty-three years on.'[7]

His successor, Ms Jenny Bacon, is even more direct when she says that the Robens seminal report changed the UK's whole philosophy towards regulating health and safety around four main propositions:

1. The UK approach, based on Robens principles, has had many successes ... Robens 'big idea' (was): that the most effective way of ensuring health and safety was to design an effective system of self-regulation in which all key players were engaged.
2. Robens advanced the business case for health and safety and the importance of managing health and safety as an integral part of the business process, and not an add on.
3. Legislation should be goal, not rule, based. Prescriptive, rule-based regulation is inflexible, has built-in obsolescence, and encourages duty holders and the regulators to focus on symptoms, not causes.
4. The need for consistent approach in terms of standard-setting, legislation and enforcement, across industry.[8]

With propositions 2 and 4, I have no arguments: proposition 2 is just the principles of using HRM/TQM techniques to integrate SHE issues with quality management and service delivery (see page 32). One might ask why it took the HSE 20 years to rediscover these principles. And, of course, proposition 4 is just the EU's 'level playing field' argument.

But propositions 1 and 3 are the really dangerous ones. 'Self-regulation' so often means no regulation, or, in the current terminology, 'de-regulation'. Based on no evidence, the Conservative government's 'Deregulation Unit', under the direction of Deputy Prime Minister Michael Heseltine, made a great fuss of getting rid of a few silly laws (e.g. you cannot drink all day) and many out-of-date ones (e.g. The Mules, Self-acting, Spinning by Means of, Regulations, 1905; the last mule spinning was carried out in the 1930s). But, in the area of health and safety, they misdirected a lot of time and effort – on behalf of the HSE, employers and trade unions – in 1992–94 in a fruitless 'de-regulation' enquiry that set up numerous industry-specific committees, to produce a massive amount of paperwork and a large report in 1994 saying, essentially, that everyone, employers included, was pretty happy with the HSE and current laws. As I have quoted elsewhere (page xix), US right-wing economists came to this conclusion several years ago and, indeed, see them as stimulating the capitalist economy!

On the face of it, 'general SHE laws', and not specific SHE laws, seem quite commonsense. But are they really? Consider a 'simple' issue like the temperature of a workroom. Should the law say it should be 'a reasonable temperature'? Or is it really more useful to the employer, the employees (and their safety representatives) and, especially, the enforcement officer to have a set temperature, as at present: 16°C for most work and at least 13°C for work involving 'severe physical effort'? I think the latter is much more useful for nearly all interest groups.

The group in society that might be thought to be most opposed to SHE laws, and to specific SHE laws in particular, is the growing area of small and medium-sized enterprises; the so-called SMEs. There are some 3.6 million businesses in the

UK; 99 per cent of businesses employ less than 50 people, over half the workforce work in SMEs, and they are the growth area of the economy. But their employees have a 50 per cent greater risk of death or serious injury than employees in larger organizations. The HSE is trying to reach SMEs. In February 1997, the HSE launched the results of its largest, by far, consultation exercise.[9] It received some 2700 responses to its consultation document, *Health and Safety in Small Firms*, 2100 of which came from firms employing 50 people or less. In addition, it held 18 breakfast meetings, up and down the country, which about 3000 small business people attended.

The HSE found that SMEs thought the following:

O   Almost nine out of ten (89 per cent) of HSE/EHO inspectors have 'useful or practical' advice.
O   Over nine out of ten (94 per cent) did not think HSE/EHO inspectors took action over 'trivial' matters.
O   Almost all SMEs (97 per cent) thought that health and safety controls should be based on the risk and not the size of the firm.
O   Over eight out of ten SMEs (86 per cent) wanted to be told exactly what they needed, and did not need, to do.
O   Over nine out of ten SMEs wanted easily available, relevant, easily readable HSE publications that told them what to do.

In summary, from what might be expected to be the most critical group of employers, there was full support for the work of the HSE and environmental health officers, and of local councils, and massive support for prescriptive law! Let us hope that this survey spells the death of 'de-regulation' and general, goal-based law.

THE 1974 HEALTH AND SAFETY AT WORK ACT (THE 1974 ACT) – AN INTRODUCTION

As mentioned before (page 42), the 1970–72 Robens Report was the basis for the 1974 Health and Safety at Work Etc. Act (the 1974 Act). The etc. is important, in that the Act covered not just employees, as had previous Factory Acts, but people who could be affected by work hazards, such as students, visitors to premises, passers-by, children etc. The 1974 Act was, in fact, introduced as a Bill by the Conservative government headed by Prime Minister Edward Heath, but by the time it became law in 1974 it was the Labour government of Prime Minister Harold Wilson that actually passed the law through Parliament. It is important to note that, with just two exceptions, the Labour law is the same as the Conservative Bill.

The first point was on agriculture. The Conservatives adopted the view of their farmer supporters, and wanted the Agricultural Inspectorate to remain in the old Ministry of Agriculture. The Labour party took the view of the agricultural workers union, and the agricultural workers, and they became part of the new Health and

Safety Executive. Writing now in 1997, and representing 25,000 farm workers as I do, it is clear to see that, with all the current BSE and food scandals, the Labour Party was right. Yet in 1997, agriculture has the highest death rate of any industry (higher even than construction) and a worker in a farm of five or less employees will see an HSE inspector, on average, once every 30 years. Clearly, from this example, there is more to improving workplace SHE issues than to which government department the enforcement officers report.

The second point relates to 'safety representatives'. The Labour Act required that they are only appointed by trade unions, where they are recognized for negotiation purposes (i.e. over wages, hours of work, sick pay, discipline, pensions etc.), whereas the Conservatives wanted them to be elected from all employees, whether in a trade union or not (see also page 78). Looking back in an in-depth review in 1981 John Locke, the architect of the 1974 Act and director general of the HSE from 1974 to 1983, concluded that:

> Some would assert that the main advances in protection – certainly of workers and perhaps also of the general public – are likely to be made by 'radical' or 'leftwing' Governments rather than by 'conservative' or 'rightwing' Governments … However, in Britain at any rate, one would be hard put to it to show that such a distinction had existed over the past century and a half.[10]

The 1974 Act covers *all* employees at work, with the exception of domestic servants, for the first time ever. With the recent rise in domestic servants, this omission may yet prove to be significant. So, at a stroke, around an extra 8 million working people gained the benefits of health and safety laws, although in some areas, like the National Health Service (the NHS is, with around one million employees, the biggest employer in Western Europe), the protection was watered down by 'crown immunity', whereby the NHS could not be prosecuted. This was removed, after several serious accidents and after a campaign by health service unions in the late 1980s, but the police had to wait until the 1990s for crown immunity to be removed (see also case study on emergency services, page 29).

'SO FAR AS IS REASONABLY PRACTICABLE', 'COST–BENEFIT ANALYSIS' AND 'RISK ASSESSMENT'

Many of the duties in the 1974 Act are qualified with the phrase, 'so far as is reasonably practicable'. This is a legal term which means that some balancing of the risks versus the benefits can be made. The leading case that is usually quoted is that of Edwards versus the National Coal Board in 1949, where the judge, Lord Justice Asquith, said:

> 'Reasonably practicable' is a narrower term that 'physically possible' and seems to imply to me that a commutation must be made by the owner in which the quantum of risk is placed in the one scale and the sacrifices involved in the measures for averting the risk (whether in time, money or trouble) is placed in the other, and that, if it is

shown that there is a great disproportion between them – the risk being insignificant to the sacrifice – the defendants discharge the onus upon them.[11]

However, the preamble to the 1989 EU so-called 'Framework Directive' on health and safety (nearly fully implemented in the UK as The Management of Health and Safety at Work Regulations 1992) specifically provides that health and safety at work 'is an objective which should not be subordinated to purely economic considerations', a principle which John Hendy QC – co-editor of the 25th edition of the 'factory inspector's Bible' by Redgrave[12] – considers 'inconsistent with the element of cost present in the assessment of what is "reasonably practicable" … (and therefore) … open to challenge'. The HSE has made no secret of its dislike for the EU's preference for definite health and safety law, and frequently boasts in its annual reports of its success in influencing the EU in this respect. Ex-HSE director general John Rimington is very honest in this respect (Rimington, 1995: 14):

> During the very hurried negotiations on the framework directive, the UK found itself in a collapsing minority in defence of its main principle – that health and safety law should be founded on reasonable practicability, involving a balance of cost against risk. We contrived to substitute for it the principle – which we consider equivalent – that health and safety measures should be based on an assessment of risk.

Indeed, John Rimington is widely regarded as the architect of the philosophy of the HSE approach of the 'tolerability of risk' that has encouraged the application of risk assessment. He says of risk assessment:

> It has its limitations, since it depends on the use of judgement and discretion. But it does provide a valuable *lingua franca* for the treatment of risk on an economic and professional rather than a purely emotional or an engineering basis, and is highly characteristic of HSE's approach to its job. Its influence worldwide is increasing. (Rimington, 1995: 18)

Other important, and perhaps surprising, people are in favour of risk assessment, such as ex-Prime Minister John Major. He says in his preface to *Regulation in the Balance – a guide to risk assessment*, DTI (1993), 'Common understanding of the principles of risk assessment would help to ensure that we get the balance of regulation right to everyone's benefit.'

In the USA there is a big debate raging about the use of risk assessment (RA) and cost–benefit analysis (CBA) to neuter the government's Environmental Protection Agency (EPA) in a form of 'paralysis by analysis'. Those in favour of RA/CBA conclude that, if properly done, benefit–cost analysis can be of great help to agencies participating in the development of environmental, health and safety regulations and it can likewise be useful in evaluating agency decision-making and in shaping statutes.[13] Currently, the EPA's duty to protect public health takes priority over its obligations to assess risks.[14] Therefore, the EPA relies on risk estimates that are conservative from the point of view of public health. Where there is uncertainty, it veers on the side of caution. Republicans in both houses of Congress want to tighten up EPA risk assessment practice and make the EPA do both worst-case and best-case RAs and take the 'centralized' estimates. This has been opposed by President Clinton's administration and now seems stuck in the Senate.

In early 1997 a huge two-volume report[15] on 'environmental health risk management' was issued by the Presidential/Congressional Commission on Risk Assessment and Risk Management. The report, based on a massive amount of commissioned research and public discussions over three years, proposes a six-stage approach to 'risk management (see Figure 2.2) that is pretty similar to many other 'risk management' approaches, e.g. the HSE and BSI (page 33). Perhaps what is really new about the approach is the central role given to 'stakeholders'.

According to the report, a stakeholder may include:

○   community groups
○   representatives of different geographical regions
○   representatives of different cultural, economic or ethnic groups
○   local governments
○   public health agencies
○   businesses
○   labour unions
○   environmental advocacy groups
○   consumer rights organizations
○   religious groups
○   educational and research institutions
○   state and federal regulatory agencies
○   trade associations

FIGURE 2.2   US Congress report on Risk Assessment 1997 – framework for risk management

The guidelines for stakeholder involvement are:

O   Regulatory agencies or other organizations considering stakeholder involvement should be clear about the extent to which they are willing or able to respond to stakeholder involvement before they undertake such efforts. If a decision is not negotiable, don't waste stakeholders' time.

O   The goals of stakeholder involvement should be clarified at the outset and stakeholders should be involved *early* in the decision-making process. Don't make saving money the sole criterion for success or expect stakeholder involvement to end controversy.

O   Stakeholder involvement efforts should attempt to engage all potentially affected parties and solicit a diversity of perspectives. It may be necessary to provide appropriate incentives to encourage stakeholder participation.

O   Stakeholders must be willing to negotiate and should be flexible. They must be prepared to listen to and learn from diverse viewpoints. Where possible, empower stakeholders to make decisions, including providing them with the opportunity to obtain technical assistance.

O   Stakeholders should be given credit for their roles in a decision, and how stakeholder input was used should be explained. If stakeholder suggestions were not used, explain why.

O   Stakeholder involvement should be made part of a regulatory agency's mission by:

  –   Creating an office that supports stakeholder processes.
  –   Seeking guidance from experts in stakeholder processes.
  –   Training risk managers to take part in stakeholder involvement efforts.
  –   Building on experiences of other agencies and on community partnerships.
  –   Emphasizing that stakeholders involvement is a learning process.

O   The nature, extent, and complexity of a stakeholder involvement should be appropriate to the scope and impact of a decision and the potential of the decision to generate controversy.

In a quieter, and much less public and typically British way a similar debate is starting to happen in the UK. In March 1997 one of the leading UK safety organizations, the Royal Society for the Prevention of Accidents (RoSPA), invited a leading US critic of risk assessment, Professor Ellen Silbergeld, to give a lecture on its limitation at its annual exhibition and conference in London. After examining the American experience in some detail she concludes:

> Risk assessment has become the dominant policymaking method for safety and health regulations in many countries, following its introduction in the US in the late 1970s. Nevertheless, public acceptance of its increasingly complex methods is far from complete.
>
> Scientific controversies have increased with practice, despite the increasingly detailed guidelines and regulatory only requirements, major issues in safety and health remain poorly characterised by conventional methods. In practice, the use of risk assessment has not improved US policy making, which has become increasingly expensive in use of resources for testing, analysis and government process.[16]

In February 1997 the Department of the Environment quietly published a consultative paper on the wider costs and benefits of environmental policy. The discussion paper admitted that the

> discussion of the costs to business tends to become the chief driver of any debate on an environmental proposal ... for a variety of reasons, neither Government nor business always take the wider benefits into account ... The market opportunities for suppliers of environmentally-beneficial goods and services tend similarly to be left out of the equation.[17]

The leading environmental research and consultancy organization, Environmental Data Services (ENDS), immediately saw the significance of this publication and gave it a full analysis, concluding:

> It would be premature to suggest that the paper marks the beginning of a swing back against deregulation and all its accoutrements ... (but the) discussion document on the wider costs and benefits of environmental policies and business ... has now blasted that methodology to smithereens – though by implication, rather than direct attack.[18]

Finally, the Dutch government, as part of its Presidency of the EU, organized a conference on costs and benefits in health and safety in May 1997.[19] It seems that the intention of the conference was 'de-regulatory', but as the conference went on the mood changed and there seems a long way to go to get an EU consensus on this contentious issue. A keynote paper was given by a very senior, and well-respected, American academic, Professor Nicholas Ashby of Massachusetts Institute of Technology, who said that most 'cost–benefit analyses' estimate only the cost of health and safety measures and not the true benefits, and we should be very wary of catching the 'American disease'.

In conclusion, the theory and discussions about cost–benefit analysis, risk assessment and even the 'risk society' – as postulated by Professor Ulrich Beck of the University of Munich[20] – range far and wide. There are both right-wing (e.g. Bate, 1997) and left-wing[21] views on the subject. I have said enough to indicate some of the political ideology behind the apparently simple and 'common sense' idea of risk assessment, as applied to the workplace in the UK. That is not to say that the practical, and serious, application of risk assessment at the workplace level cannot be very useful in the SHE area (see p.128).

THE BASICS OF THE 1974 HEALTH AND SAFETY AT WORK ETC. ACT (THE 1974 ACT) AND THE 1990 ENVIRONMENTAL PROTECTION ACT (1990 EPA)

Introduction

There are many valuable and detailed studies of the 1974 Act and the 1990 Environmental Protection Act, to be found in any good bookshop under 'law', 'health and safety' or 'environment'. Some are listed in the Recommended Reading. The summary below concerns the main practical parts of both Acts, their administration and enforcement. It is convenient to deal with the Acts separately, the 1974 Act first, although, in practice, there is considerable overlap with regard to enforcement, especially by environmental health officers (EHOs) from local councils.

The 1974 Act is a 'framework act' that sets out some general principles and structures and the detail of the law is provided for by the many regulations made under the 1974 Act. The 1974 Act was debated in Parliament, where (as noted on page 70) there was really very little difference between Conservative and Labour, except with regard to trade union safety representatives. The regulations, made under the 1974 Act, are usually, these days, the direct result of an EU Directive and are the subject of considerable consultation. They are discussed by a committee of MPs in Parliament, but are *not* the subject of a full parliamentary debate. In the early 1990s, a major set of new EU Directives was introduced, the so-called 'six pack', including the key EU 'Framework Directive' – implemented in the UK as The 1992 Management of Health and Safety at Work Regulations. Twenty-four years after the 1974 Act, and especially in view of the growing influence of the EU, there is now a good case for a detailed review (a Royal Commission?) on the working of safety, health and environmental law and a full parliamentary debate on these important issues. There are few signs that this will happen in the near future. Although most of the general duties of the 1974 Act have now been spelt out more fully in other regulations, the HSE, when it prosecutes, often does so under the original 1974 Act, as well as a more detailed regulation.

Brief outline of the 1974 act

Section 2(1) essentially requires employers to ensure, so far as is reasonably practicable (see page 45), that they protect the safety, health and welfare of all of their employees and other persons from any health and safety hazards arising out of the work that they control.

Section 2(2)(c) is very important in that it requires the employer to provide 'such information, instruction, training and supervision as is necessary to ensure, so far as is reasonably practicable, the health and safety at work of his employees'. This section has been reinforced by various regulations made under the Act and, in particular, The Management of Health and Safety at Work Regulations 1992. Recently the HSE has produced some excellent, free, guidance on the regulations that have this requirement, of which there are 12.[22] There is also a free HSE 'five-step guidance' to the provision of information, instruction and training:

1.   Decide who needs information.
2.   Decide what information is needed.
3.   Decide when information is needed.
4.   Decide how you are going to provide the information.
5.   Check that the information has been effective.

Section 2 also requires employers to have a 'safe system of work' and, where they employ more than five employees, to have a 'written safety policy' and to bring this policy to the attention of all their employees. It also makes provision for trade union safety representatives and safety committees (page 78).

Section 3 introduces a new concept: the protection of people *not* in the employment of the employer (e.g. visitors, passers-by, students, children, subcontractors) from the health and safety hazards of work activity. There has been a great growth in the use of contractors in recent years. As a result, the HSE has produced an excellent guide/workbook[23] for anyone who has to deal with contractors from a health and safety point of view. It looks in detail at the control of contractors under five headings:

1. *Policies* – health and safety policy, including arrangements for contractors.
2. *Organizing* – involving those working in the organization, in-house staff and contractors; lines of communication and authority.
3. *Planning and doing* – practical arrangements and methods of working used; contracts/agreements, whether written or not.
4. *Monitoring* – keeping track of what actually happens.
5. *Reviewing and learning* – checking on how the company is getting on with contract management, deciding what needs to be improved and how to go about it.

Section 3 also covers the self-employed, who often feel that they are beyond any laws; they are also under a duty not to endanger themselves or other people by their work. There is a duty on the main contractor and any subcontractors and any safety specialists to conduct their work safely.

Section 6 is still under-used and under-enforced, yet it is very fundamental. It requires designers, manufacturers, importers and suppliers of any article or substance for use at work to ensure that it is safe and healthy for use.

Section 5 contained some general air pollution requirements, which were really never enforced, and which were repealed, and are now part of the Environmental Protection Act 1990.

Sections 7 and 8 concern for the first time, the responsibilities of employees and they are worth spelling out in full, as they are so limited as compared with those of the employer.

Section 7: 'every employee when at work shall take reasonable care for themselves and other people who may be affected by their acts or omissions'. If a joke or 'horseplay' goes wrong at work and someone is injured, then the law is being broken. When there is a legal duty or requirement on the employer, then the employee must co-operate with the employer as far as is necessary to ensure the employer can perform or comply with that duty or requirement. If, for example, an employee is working in noise levels above the legal limit, the noise cannot be reduced at source or by other means of protection, and the ear muffs supplied are clean and comfortable, then they must be worn by law.

Section 8: 'no employee should intentionally or recklessly interfere or misuse anything provided for in the interests of safety, health or welfare'. If a fire extinguisher is set off for a laugh, then the law is being broken.

Section 9 states that the employer cannot charge employees for anything done or provided for when it is required by a health and safety regulation. For example, by law, safety helmets are required to be worn by all employees (and visitors) on all building sites, so they must be supplied free of charge by the employer.

Sections 36 and 37 are very important, in that they allow for the prosecution of the managers and directors or a company, or organization (e.g. local council, hospital trust), as well as the company or organization itself, for an offence, 'committed with the consent or connivance of, or to have been attributable to any neglect on the part of any, director, manager, secretary or other similar person of the body corporate'. An early, and famous, 1976 case, where a council employee fell to his death whilst painting a bridge in Scotland, determined that a 'Director of Roads' was a senior manager in this respect and he was fined for failing to prepare a safety policy. Since that time many managers have been fined under this section. But imprisonment and manslaughter charges (page 35) are, generally, a more effective way of changing 'the management culture of risk'.

Finally, section 28(8) is important in that it allows – for the first time, amazingly – employees, and their representatives, to see copies of any letters or notices served on employers by EHOs and HSE inspectors that concern health and safety issues at their workplace. Prior to the 1974 Act, such information was restricted under the Official Secrets Act.

The rest of the 1974 Act is concerned with administrative details, two of which are important and will now be considered: the role of the Health and Safety Commission and Executive and HSE/EHO inspectors and the enforcement procedures.

The Health and Safety Commission (HSC) and Health and Safety Executive (HSE)

The 1974 Act established the tripartite, employer–government–trade union, Health and Safety Commission (HSC). The chair of the HSC is appointed by the secretary of state, and the other members of the HSC are approved by the secretary of state. Originally there were three members of the HSC nominated by the employers' organization, the Confederation of British Industry (CBI), three nominated by the trade union organization, the Trades Union Congress (TUC), and a representative of local government. Under a Conservative government, the TUC membership was weakened somewhat over the years and the small business interest grew. In fact, the HSC remains the only tripartite body to have survived the 1979–97 Conservative government.

It is not clear whether this has really made any difference, since a 1985 academic study that compared the American and British government health and safety systems (Wilson, 1985) concluded of the HSC, 'The relations between the

TUC and the CBI are particularly close. The unions have voluntary accorded the employers a veto over health and safety regulations; officials of the CBI and TUC refer to each other as "our colleagues".'

CASE STUDY 8: HSE DROPS ASTHMA CODE UNDER INDUSTRY PRESSURE

Asthma is a large and growing problem in society, and in workplaces too. Exposure to 'respiratory sensitizers' at work causes at least 1000 new cases of asthma a year and the HSE estimates that workplace asthma costs the economy around £50 million a year. In 1997, research suggested that up to one in five adult cases of asthma may be work-related. In 1992 the HSC issued a consultative draft HSC 'Approved Code of Practice' to control workplace sensitizers (substances that cause asthma). For years there had been HSE guidance, but it had proved ineffective in controlling the hazards of the growing number of workplace sensitizers – as witnessed by the steady rise in occupational asthma cases. An HSC approved code of practice is stronger than HSE guidance, but weaker than HSE regulations. Its power is something like that of the well-known Highway Code and it can be, and is, quoted in a court of law. Regulations are drafted by lawyers and are often difficult for non-legal people – employers, employees and even enforcement officers at times – to understand. An HSE approved code of practice is supposed to be readable, yet authoritative, so it was an important step in controlling workplace respiratory sensitizers to propose a code of practice.

During this time I was a senior lecturer in SHE issues at South Bank University and, as part of my job, I was supervising student projects. One, in 1993, related to measuring high exposures to a known respiratory sensitizer, in an internationally known pharmaceutical company. The company was simply using new labourers and, when they developed asthma, as they invariable did, it either moved them on to safer jobs or sacked them.

However, we were in there measuring *just* because they were aware of the proposed draft HSC approved code of practice, and knew that they would have to do something about the dust sooner or later, a clear indication of the value of a code of practice, as opposed to guidance. As part of his background research the student rang up the HSE, in late 1993, and asked when the draft code of practice would become a *full* HSC approved code of practice. He was told that the HSC had decided to drop the idea of a code of practice. Why?

The truth only came out when I met the person who was the senior HSE inspector behind the draft code. He told me that the CBI representatives on the HSC had been lobbied hard by the flour industry to block the code. This is ironic, since up to one in three bakers may develop asthma because of their exposure to the well-known respiratory irritant in flour dust! The CBI objected and the code fell. He told me that he had resigned from the HSE in disgust. But he would not go public on the issue, as he was now in private consultancy and feared that he would lose work (almost certainly true). The protests from the trade unions, the

TUC and others, like the National Asthma Campaign, were inadequate and because of this thousands of workers are doomed to develop totally preventable workplace asthma.[24]

There have certainly been no great public disagreements between the CBI and the TUC on health and safety issues. During the great de-regulation review of 1992–93 they were united in favour of most existing health and safety regulations. Recently, through a Parliamentary Ombudsman complaint of mine, under the government's Code of Practice on the Freedom of Information, the agenda of the HSC, and those of other key HSC/HSE committees, have become available for 1996 onwards. They are even on the Internet now! However, they are not very exciting documents. They do reveal, however, that the HSC's main activity appears to be rubber-stamping the HSE committee work and draft regulations; there is very little discussion of the HSC's role and functions. The only signs of HSC life, in recent years, was the leaking of a draft letter from the part-time, CBI nominee chair, Frank Davies to John Gummer MP, the former Secretary of State for the Environment, in March 1996. The TUC nominees deny vehemently that they leaked it and, given their past performance (or lack of it), we should believe them. The letter concerned the contentious issue of the lack of resources for the HSE. Davies said in part of his letter:

> We cannot meet all the expectation and requirements that Government, Parliament and the Courts are placing on us with the resources now available ... (HSE staff) have fallen from their historical peak of some 4,250 in late 1993 to around 3,900 now, with a further planned reduction to less than 3,400 by the turn of the century – a reduction of 20% ... We must therefore ask the government to make available additional running cost resources, totalling £5 million, £6 million and £7 million (in the next three years).

This leak did cause some public debate at the time.

We know that the HSE budget will be cut by 9.2 per cent by the turn of the century. That is, in real terms, it will be £158 million in 1999–2000 as compared with £178 million in 1996–97. The HSE budget has been slashed during the past six years. This is, of course, not new. At the start of the industrial revolution the British government was forced, by public opinion and Chartist agitation, to pass *some* laws to protect working people. However, Karl Marx noted, 'Parliament passed 5 labour laws between 1802 and 1833, but was shrewd enough not to vote a penny for the requisite officials' (1867: 264). The first four Factory Inspectors, to enforce the laws, were only appointed in 1833.

In 1976, when the International Monetary Fund (IMF) wanted the Labour government to drop the draft regulations for trade union safety representatives, and they were going to agree, the HSC issued a press release attacking the government's proposals, saying, 'We wish to express our unanimous and strongly held view that the (safety representative and safety committee) regulations should be laid before Parliament without delay.' Why was there no such HSC press release over de-regulation and decreased HSE funding in the 1990s?

The Health and Safety Executive (HSE)

The key UK health and safety agency is the Health and Safety Executive (HSE). It is a central inspectorate, under the control of the Department of the Environment, Transport and the Regions (DETR) which is responsible for inspecting the more dangerous workplaces such as chemical plants, North Sea oil platforms, hospitals, coal mines, railways, quarries, farms, construction sites, schools, local councils and so on. The so-called 'less dangerous' workplaces – such as offices, shops, zoos, public houses, churches etc. – are inspected by the environmental health officers (EHOs) of a local council. EHOs have the same powers as an HSE inspector. The HSE has 4150 staff and an annual budget of £216 million in 1995–96 (provisional). This is around 0.05 per cent of total public expenditure or around £10 per head of the working population of around 22 million. The HSE is responsible for enforcing health and safety law in over 650,000 workplaces. The HSE has a key role in the transposition of EU health and safety laws, now about 50 per cent of the total, and also in framing new and revised health and safety regulations, codes of practice and guidance notes.

All major new health and safety law is the subject of consultation. In recent years the submissions to the consultative process have been made available to the public, and it is clear from these submissions that, where there is disagreement, the employer's view dominates. Nevertheless, some very useful guidance has come through this process. This is especially true of the more active tripartite – employer, government, union – industry/sector guidance. Sometimes there is agreement by the employers, unions and HSE inspectors on a committee and it is the HSE at the top – under de-regulatory pressure from the previous Conservative government – which has blocked or delayed guidance. A recent example of this was the very good HSE guidance on *Slips, Trips and Falls* in the food and drink industry that was delayed by at least at year. It is to be hoped that a new Labour government will not act in this manner.

Workplace inspections

As important as the production of guidance and regulations is, the real role of the HSE is to inspect workplaces: for hazards, to give guidance and check compliance with the law and, where appropriate, to enforce the law by means of letters, enforcement notices and prosecution. As Ms Jenny Bacon, director general of the HSE, told the Environment Committee of MPs in 1997, 'Inspection remains central to enforcement'.[25] Yet she also admitted that workplace inspections had fallen from 150,000 in 1995 to around 100,000 in 1997. Whilst some larger and dangerous workplaces (e.g. nuclear plants, large chemical plants) still receive

FIGURE 2.3   An HSE inspector (centre) inspects a workplace – the key work of the HSE that has been cut drastically in recent years. (Photo: HSE)

regular attention from the HSE, the average workplace will see an inspector about once in ten years. On one of the many small farms with less than five employees, it will be once in 30 years. As far as can be ascertained (Dalton, 1991), it was the Factory Inspectorate's aim from 1928 to 1954 to inspect the more important factories and workshops at least once a year and the less important at least once every two years. A 1956 government committee of enquiry more or less legitimized the once every four years inspection cycle. In the 1990s it appears to be once in ten years and falling rapidly. Where is the 'level playing field' that both employers and employees seek?

Fines

One of the most contentious issues over many years has been the low level of fines for breaking health and safety law. Concern over the level of fines is not new. In April 1975, three months after the 1974 Act fully became law, when giving the prestigious 'Redgrave Memorial Lecture' (Alexander Redgrave was one of the first factory inspectors), Bill Simpson, the first chair of the HSC, said:

> In the past the price for negligence has been far too low. In welcoming higher fines I am not being punitive or emotional, but simply recognising that there is some measure of deterrence in higher fines. It devalued the work of inspectors, employers,

trade unions, researchers, policy makers and Parliament if, on conviction, safety miscreants were fined 'piddling amounts' that had more in common with a dog fouling the pavement than the breaking of the law of the land by employers which could result in the killing and maiming of workers. (HSC, 1975: 1)

By 1976 the Minister of State for Employment, Harold Walker, was publicly calling for the courts to use harsher penalties. He noted that the average level of fine, in 1976, was only £75 and gave the following illuminating case study. 'Recently, a firm had two tenders to remove asbestos. They accepted the lowest, were prosecuted because of a dangerously high level of dust in the atmosphere, paid the fine and still showed a saving on the job of up to £2000.' Almost 30 years later, in 1995, a property developer got £50,000 knocked off the price of some laboratories because of asbestos contamination, removed the asbestos danger-ously, got caught by the HSE, got fined £8000 plus £650 costs and still made a handsome profit![26]

Unfortunately the courts and judges have paid no attention. The current chair of the HSC, Frank Davies, wrote about this problem in the *Magistrates Journal* a few years ago and he recently admitted that it had no effect. In the 1997 Environmental Committee of MPs enquiry into the work of the HSE, the Lord Chancellor's department told the MPs that 'There can be no question of the Department, or the Lord Chancellor himself, seeking to direct or influence the way in which magistrates or judges exercise their discretion in sentencing matters.'[25]

The HSE only prosecutes for serious offences, when the health and safety law is obviously broken and life, safety or health is clearly at risk. In 1994–95, the latest year for which figures are available (HSE, 1996), there were 1429 successful convictions with an average fine of £2514. Elsewhere (page 35) I have discussed the trade union and other campaigns for the imprisonment of managing directors who seriously break health and safety laws; the real answer to effective safety, health and environment law enforcement.

HSE/Environmental Health Officer (EHO) Inspectors' powers

It is worth remembering that an HSE (and EHO) inspector has very wide powers, stronger than those of a police officer with regard to workplace entry. These are given to her or him by virtue of section 20 of the 1974 Act and are:

○ to enter and inspect premises at any time if there is danger. They will have an official warrant with them
○ to take a police officer with them, if they feel they will be obstructed
○ to take with them such people and equipment as will be necessary for the purpose of investigation etc
○ to require any part of the premises or equipment to be left undisturbed for as long as is necessary
○ to take measurements, photographs and samples

○   to seize, render or destroy any items that may cause danger
○   to take possession of articles and examine them
○   to get information, ask questions and take statements (under caution if necessary)
○   to inspect any relevant documents

From time to time a stupid employer is prosecuted for obstructing an EHO or HSE inspector in their line of duty.

Taking enforcement action

Of course, safety, health and environment law, like any other law, operates mainly through just existing. We do not steal from shops because we know it is against the law and if we did there would be some chance of being prosecuted. But many people do exceed the speed limit often, because the chance of being caught and prosecuted, for minor speeding offences, is rare. In general, however, most people obey the law: seat belts are worn in front seats (but much less so in the back seats) and people rarely smoke in buses or tubes.

However, health and safety law must be enforced. The following outline is the general procedure. An enforcement officer, HSE or EHO, is *not* obliged to follow it and, in serious cases, may well shorten the procedure and/or use two procedures together (e.g. serve a prohibition notice and prosecute).

If the offence is minor, the enforcement officer may just talk to the appropriate manager or supervisor (or much more rarely employee) either over the telephone and/or by making a workplace visit. There is no requirement on the enforcement officer to write anything down and if talking resolves the problem, with the minimum of bureaucracy and paperwork, that is all to the good for the employer and enforcement officer.

It is quite common, however, especially if there has been a workplace visit, for the enforcement officer to put down her or his concerns for workplace hazards in letter form. If this is done, the enforcement officer is obliged by law – section 28(8) of the 1974 Act – to give a copy of the letter to the employee's representative (normally a safety representative, but can be a shop steward or staff representative). It is a matter of some surprise, and concern, that employees were not informed of the hazards at their workplace by enforcement officers until the 1974 Act!

Should the enforcement officer be more concerned about offences against health and safety law and/or any immediate hazard, then she or he can serve one of three types of notice:

1. An *improvement notice* where health and safety law is clearly being broken but there is no immediate threat to life or health. The law(s) being broken will be specified; the remedial actions to be taken are often specified on an accompanying schedule and the time allowed for the remedial work (at least

21 days, but can allow months). During 1995–96, HSE and EHO inspectors issued 16,632 improvement notices (down from 25,134 in 1994–95 and 31,932 in 1993–94). Three-quarters (74 per cent) of all notices served are improvement notices.

2. An *immediate prohibition notice* can be served if there is risk of serious personal injury, this stops the work activity to which it applies immediately. In 1995–96, 5602 prohibition notices were served by HSE/EHO inspectors (5791 were served in 1994–95). This is the lowest number served since 1986–87.

3. A *deferred prohibition notice* may be served that stops the work named after a specified time, in the small proportion (6 per cent) of work processes where the stopping of work immediately would cause danger itself (e.g. a blast furnace, chemical process). In 1995–96 364 such notices were served (1994–95, 324).

Clearly, improvement notices remain the main way by which HSE and EHO inspectors enforce health and safety law.

Finally, or in addition to any of the above, an EHO or HSE inspector may decide to prosecute an employer (or very rarely employee). This may be carried out in the magistrates court (maximum fine £20,000) or at the Crown Court where, for some offences, there is an unlimited fine and/or up to two years imprisonment possible as a sentence. There is also, as noted before (page 35), an increasing tendency to refer the more serious cases to the CPS for the consideration of manslaughter charges.

'Minded-to' letters

As part of their de-regulation exercise, the Conservative government introduced, during 1995, the requirement for enforcement officers to inform an employer before they were going to serve an improvement notice with a so-called 'minded-to' notice. According to recent research commissioned by the HSE, this new system has not led to any less enforcement and is working well. According to the Institute of Environmental Health Officers, and the enforcement officers I know, it is another piece of unnecessary bureaucracy, more added paperwork that gives them less time to actually inspect workplaces. Both the HSC and the HSE have agreed to drop this 'bureaucratic procedure' on 1 April 1998, at the request of the new Labour government.

Appeals against enforcement notices

The employer can appeal to an industrial tribunal about the terms and conditions, or even the very serving, of an improvement or prohibition notice. With regard to an improvement notice, it is lifted until the appeal is heard. However, a prohibition notice stays in force until the industrial tribunal has heard the appeal. This is really a little used procedure, where employers often lose.

Crown immunity

Historically, the Crown cannot be prosecuted. At the time of the 1974 Act, the most important workplace covered by Crown exclusion was the NHS. After trade union campaigns and several serious incidents – the NHS is as dangerous, if not more dangerous, than many other workplaces – Crown immunity was removed in the late 1980s. Now, with the very recent removal of Crown immunity from the police force, only the armed forces remain protected from real health and safety law enforcement by the HSE, and this is to be removed soon. However, the relevant ministers have always said that their departments will meet the requirements imposed on non-Crown premises and there exists a system of non-enforceable 'Crown Notices'.

Environmental Health Officers (EHOs)

Local council EHOs have, since 1974, been taking over more and more responsibilities for health and safety inspections at mainly smaller workplaces, as well as food hygiene, the local environment, environmental noise pollution, safety in houses of multiple occupation and all the other responsibilities that they might have under various public health acts. In addition to their new responsibilities under the 1990 Environmental Pollution Act (around 12,000 processes under part B, air pollution only), they are now responsible[27] for enforcing health and safety law in some 1,274,000 'low-risk' workplaces employing about 8.5 million people; an increase of one-third since 1986–87. Typically, EHOs enforce health and safety law in shops, offices, churches, restaurants, zoos, cinemas and theatres, football stadiums and so on. There are around 1580 EHOs who carry out health and safety work (not all work full time on health and safety) and each one is responsible for around 806 premises (up from 790 in 1996). The average number of visits per full-time EHO was 311, a small drop from 1994–95. But workplace visits and inspections are said to be better now, with 64 per cent proactive, compared with 57 per cent in 1991–92.

The total number of deaths in this area fell from 51 in 1993–94 to 33 in 1994–95. This is due to a fall in the number of members of the public killed from 34 to 14. The number of deaths of people in employment rose by two. The number of injuries at work reported to local authorities in 1994–95 was 27,607. Of these, 2856 were major injuries to employees, a 16 per cent rise from the 2463 reported in the previous year. For members of the public there was an 8 per cent increase in reported major injuries from 1995 to 1996. In 1996 the number of three-day injuries to employees rose to 21,049, 5 per cent higher than in 1993–94, and continuing the upward trend of the last nine years. The HSE considers that some of this rise may be due to improved reporting, but Frank Davies, chair of the HSC said at the launch of the report, 'The rate of major injuries continues its upward trend. Every accident has a human cost in terms of pain and suffering. Improved

FIGURE 2.4   An Environmental Health Officer (EHO) from a local council inspects a
hazardous corrugated asbestos roof; EHOs have the same wide-ranging
powers as HSE inspectors

health and safety standards makes sound economic sense' (HSC press release, 24
June 1996).[27]

Despite this rise in serious accidents, the enforcement action by EHOs is down.
Could there be a relationship? The number of formal enforcement notices issued
during 1994–95 fell by 46 per cent from 1993–94 to 11,790. Almost nine out of ten
(86 per cent) were improvement notices. The *1995–96 Local Authority Report on
Health and Safety in the Service Industries* notes a substantial fall in the serving of
such notices in the previous two years and says that, 'a factor in this downward
trend is the move by inspectors towards an advisory rather than punitive role'. In
1994–95 a total of 494 prosecutions were undertaken, of which 413 (84 per cent)
were successful. The total fines imposed were £572,495; or £1386 per conviction
(22 per cent higher than in 1993–94). As with the HSE, these prosecutions will
only be for serious offences – including death and serious injury – and this level of
fine is an insult to those injured or dead and no deterrent to the employers who
are responsible for the increases in serious injuries and over three-day off work
injuries.

The Environment Agency (EA)

The Environment Agency was formed in 1996 from the old National Rivers Authority (NRA), Her Majesty's Inspectorate of Pollution (HMIP) and the waste regulation functions of local authorities. In September 1997 the EA issued its first annual report[28] (summarized in *Environmental Information Bulletin 73*, November 1997, pages 11–13). After the record fine of £1 million against Shell UK for polluting the Mersey with crude oil in August 1989, hopes were high that fines would match the environmental crimes and that there would be strong enforcement of environmental law. This hope has not been fulfilled. A report released by Friends of the Earth (*Independent*, 16 September 1997), to coincide with the EA's AGM, showed that there were 1,573 breaches of the water pollution regulations at 830 sites in the year starting October 1995. During that period the EA launched only 17 prosecutions for water pollution incidents.

Speaking at the EA's AGM in September 1997, chief executive Ed Gallagher said:

> In the US, fines for environmental offences can run into millions of dollars. In this country they are often less than the cost of hiring the monitoring staff. Even the largest fines represent negligible costs to the largest companies. The Agency's largest fines last year represented the equivalent of a £15 fine on someone earning £30,000 a year.
>
> These fines are really small change to these large companies. They send the wrong signal to boardrooms and the public at large. To be realistic, fines have to bear more relation to the financial strength of the offending company as well as to the damage done to the environment. We look to the courts to award tougher penalties against repeated and blatant offenders.

Environment Minister, Michael Meacher, has been vocal on the low level of enforcement and fines, and he has raised the possibility of guidelines for courts on the sentencing of persistent polluters.

However, the EA claims that the number of prosecutions should not be used as an indicator of environmental performance. The true-level indicator should be a reduction in the number of significant pollution incidents and through real improvements to key environmental indicators of air, water and land pollution. Some of the key indicators from the EA for 1996/97 were:

Water
○ 20,158 substantial pollution incidents in 1996, a fall of 14 per cent compared with 1995
○ 114,284 water quality inspections
○ 32,409 water pollution incidents in 1996, of which fewer than 1 per cent (229) resulted in a successful prosecution; 91 formal cautions were issued
○ Total fines for water pollution offences during 1996 came to £863,950; the highest fine was £175,000 against Severn Trent for polluting the River Elan with ferric sulphate and causing the death of 35,000 fish
○ Of designated bathing water in England and Wales, 89.1 per cent met or exceeded the EC Directive in 1996; the figure for 1995 was 89.2 per cent

○ There were 47,692 water abstraction licences in force in 1996/97 and the EA carried out 16,070 licence inspections
○ 45 successful prosecutions were brought for breaches of abstraction licence conditions with total fines of £78,400

Integrated Pollution Control (IPC)
○ There were 1987 IPC authorizations in force in 1996/97, of which 175 were new authorizations
○ The EA carried out 6003 inspection visits of IPC premises
○ 846 pollution incidents from IPC premises were recorded, of which 8 resulted in successful prosecutions; 34 improvement or prohibition notices were issued; total fines were £110,00, with the highest being £50,000

Waste regulations
○ A new system to track 'special waste' resulted in over 500,000 notifications of special waste during 1996/97.
○ Over 2200 visits to waste producers were made
○ There were 123,008 sites licensed under the Waste Management Regulations 1994
○ The EA brought 241 successful prosecutions for waste offences during 1996/97, resulting in total fines of £272,890.

The EA had 9563 full-time posts during 1997/98 (up from 9450) in April 1996). With new environmental requirements, such as the EU Directive on Integrated Pollution Prevention and Control, the EA warns that it 'cannot, and should not, commit to further staffing reductions'. The real budget of the EA of £564 million (45 per cent of which goes on flood defence, 14 per cent on water resources and only 30 per cent pollution prevention and control) will fall in future years. The EA is seeking government approval for raising its income-generating activity. Without additional funding the EA says it will not be able to complete its planned work programme, and that this would have a detrimental effect on the environment.

The essence of the 1990 Environmental Protection Act[29] is two systems of control, depending on the levels of pollution expected from the plant or process:

Part A: Around 2000 of the most 'seriously polluting' plants will be covered by integrated pollution control (IPC), which covers air, water and land pollution and which will be policed by EA inspectors. There will sometimes be a balance struck, when the control of pollution from one medium (e.g. air) could increase the pollution in another medium (e.g. land or water).

Part B: Around 12,000 or so 'less polluting' processes or plants will be covered by air pollution standards only and the pollution levels policed by EHOs from local authorities – local authority air pollution control (LAAPC).

CASE STUDY 9: LOW LAAPC PRINT INDUSTRY POLLUTION STANDARDS

Printing companies produce pollution in all forms: air, solid and waste (land). During 1992–95, whilst at South Bank University, I was involved in an EU-funded project, called SUBSPRINT, which was set up to promote the substitution of organic solvents with safer vegetable oil-based solvents. Organic solvents, such as common 'white spirit', harm the body's nervous system and cause headaches etc. They are also harmful to the environment.

As part of this project I investigated the DoE LAAPC standards for air pollution from print works. By chance the DoE was reviewing its LAAPC standards during this period, and I was invited onto the 'informal' print industry DoE working party (so 'informal' was it that the Graphic Paper and Media Union's (GPMU) health and safety officer was only allowed on as an 'observer' after much persuasion).

One of the first items on the agenda was a proposal to raise the amount of organic solvent permitted to be worked with, for registration for LAAPC, from 5 tonnes per annum to 25 tonnes. This had the effect of excluding about 90 per cent of all print works from LAAPC control at the stroke of a pen! I objected on the grounds that we were supposed to be reducing pollution and not increasing it. The DoE chair told me firmly that the subject was not up for debate. That set the tone of the whole standard-setting process for LAAPC: the employers deciding on what standards they wanted, and the DoE officials agreeing.

To be fair, there was a very good EHO on our committee who had worked with a large local employer who had successfully introduced the vegetable oil cleaners we were promoting (but only after the threat of enforcement action). He presented these results to the employer-dominated committee and it was then less dismissive of our control at source proposals. But, overall, this experience gave me little faith in the independence of the DoE standard-setting procedure for LAAPC air control standards.[30, 31]

Integrated pollution control (IPC)

A survey of the first three years of IPC produced mixed results.[32] The survey covered 145 processes on 120 sites. It was thought too early to assess the degree of environmental improvements arising from IPC, but the researchers were cautiously optimistic that there would be long-term improvements. However, they added that 'One major area of concern is that despite HMIP's efforts, much of the industrial focus continues to be on end-of-pipe abatement rather than waste minimisation at source' (p. xvi).

In July 1997 the Environment Secretary, Michael Meacher MP, announced a radical review[33] of the IPC regime to fulfil the requirements of the EU *Directive 96/61 on Integrated Pollution Prevention and Control* (IPPC). Mr Meacher said:

> I believe that IPC is a fundamentally sound framework. We do not need, and we would not want, to tear up IPC and start all over again to implement the new

Directive. However, IPC – and IPPC – are frameworks which leave a lot of room for the exercise of discretion by the pollution regulators. (p. xvi)

He went on to say that he expected high standards to be set and enforced by the EA. He added that education and co-operation would always be tried first.

But the most powerful weapons in the Agency's armoury – prosecution, prohibition and revocation – are there to be used if gentler measures fail. I will not countenance a system so laxly applied that one firm could clock up nearly 500 breaches of its authorisations on one single site!

The main features of the review are as follows:

O   Implementation by late 1999, although it will not affect most existing plant until 2007.
O   Extension from some 2000 installations currently covered by IPC to around 7000 (e.g. 3000 landfill sites, 1000 pig and poultry farms over 1000 firms in the metal industry, 400 installations in food and drink).
O   IPPC will take into account a wider range of environmental impacts, such as emissions, noise, energy efficiency, the use of raw materials, accident prevention and site restoration.

It may be far worse with the Local Authority Air Pollution Control (LAAPC) if my experience of an attempt to reduce air pollution from print works is typical (see case study 9, page 64). Central to LAAPC is the guidance on air pollution standards given to industry and on which EHOs rely for enforcement. These standards are set by 78 or more 'informal' committees. It was surprising to find that many of these 'informal' DoE committees were totally dominated by industry, with just a few DoE officials.[30] In some cases there were EHOs sitting on the committees, but there were no environmentalists and not many other independent experts. Of course, some of these standards may be more than adequate, but can it really be right for British industry to set its own air pollution standards in the late twentieth century?

The EA inspects and enforces environmental law in some 2150 industrial processes and over 8200 permissions for sites where non-nuclear radioactive sources are held and used. In the first half of 1995–96, inspectors carried out 4344 regulatory visits and investigated 1174 reported pollution incidents. During this period 41 enforcement notices, seven prohibition notices and seven improvement notices were served, and one prosecution was undertaken. Compared with the HSE and EHOs, the level of enforcement action appears minimal. The first really big challenge for the EA, which it appears to have failed, has been the major issue of the burning of toxic waste in cement kilns (see case study 4, page 20), which has been the subject of much public concern, parliamentary debates and reports. A report from the Environment Committee of the House of Commons on this issue was very critical of the EA's role in this major pollution problem. The MPs noted that 'During our visit to Castle Cement at Clitheroe it appeared that the Agency had a close working relationship with the cement company. It is the Agency's normal practice to prenotify the company of many of its visits.[34]

The committee of MPs was very forceful in its conclusions on the role of the EA:

> This Inquiry has brought to light examples of inefficiency and lack of foresight on the part of the Agency, both in its local enforcement role and central decision making functions ... The introduction of Secondary Liquid Fuel (toxic waste) at Clitheroe appears to have been handled clumsily and without adequate forethought by Her Majesty's Inspectors of Pollution ... The Environment Agency must act to restore confidence in its regulation of the cement industry ... Wherever practicable, inspections should be unannounced. Inspectors should not automatically believe what they are told by the industry.[34]

In September 1997 the LAAPC standards came under attack for their weakness from a report by the Environmental Industries Commission (EIC) (see *ENDS Report 274*). The EIC is the trade body representing the UK environmental technology business. Formed in 1995, it now has 200 member companies. The report surveyed 30 EIC members who supplied air pollution control equipment: 3 out of 4 said that LAAPC had no effect on the demand for their products, and only 1 in 5 said that orders had increased. The companies were very critical of the lack of enforcement by local authority officers. In 1995–96 just eight firms were prosecuted for LAAPC offences, and only ten enforcement notices were served. There are 12,000 LAAPC-'approved' processes. However, the EIC is dominated by 'end-of-pipe' companies (e.g. extraction and after-burner manufacturers), and air pollution reduction methods (e.g. alternative non-air polluting processes, water-based products and vegetable oils replacing organic solvents) would not be reflected in such a survey.

Complaining about HSE/EHO/EA inspectors

As explained above, the HSE, local council EHO inspectors and EA inspectors are overworked and are often being told to 'lay off' in a de-regulatory climate. This is no reason, of course, why someone or some group suffering from a work-related SHE hazard should accept the law on SHE issues being broken or remaining unenforced. Indeed, the HSE inspectors' union, IPMS, has said that it wants the public to complain when the SHE law is not enforced, as this will lead to more pressure for better resources and an increase in staffing levels. There must be, of course, some bad or even corrupt inspectors. However, the latter are rare in this area since there is little money around to corrupt inspectors with. Yet there must be some, and they may yet increase in number, since there are large amounts of money riding on some increasingly stringent SHE decisions.

The procedure to follow is pretty much common sense, until it comes to a complaint to the ombudsman. The most important rule in making a serious complaint about the actions, or inactions, of an HSE/EHO/EA inspector is to keep a copy of all letters, date them and send them by recorded delivery; keep a copy of all replies and ensure that they are dated (or keep envelope); keep a note, or better a tape, of the main points of any telephone conversations and the time and date; and keep a note, or better tape (or even video) of any meetings, with the date, time and place, with enforcement officers. I have made too many complaints, and helped people with too many, not to know that you must not trust anyone when making the complaints, and the higher you go, the more this is true.

○   First, make a formal complaint to the enforcement officer, in writing, if a verbal complaint is not responded too. Send it by recorded delivery. Give them time to respond, ensure that they are not on holiday, etc.
○   If this fails, do the same to their 'area director' (HSE), director of environmental health (EHO) or director of the EA office that you are dealing with.
○   If this fails then go to the director general of the HSE or the chair of the relevant local council committee dealing with the environmental health department, in the case of an EHO, or the director of the Environment Agency – enclose copies of all your correspondence and replies so far. Give them a few weeks to reply.
○   If this fails, you can write to the minister responsible for health and safety (about the HSE), the Environment Minister (about the EA), both at the House of Commons, or the leader of your local council (about EHOs) at your local council town hall.
○   If this fails, or the answers are unsatisfactory, you should enclose copies of all the correspondence to your local MP (HSE/EA) or local councillor (EHO), whose names and addresses will be found at your local library or Citizens Advice Bureau. Ask them to investigate for you.
○   Should this all fail, your last formal resort is the Parliamentary Ombudsman (HSE/EA) or local council ombudsman (EHO). The first you have to contact through your MP, and the second you can contact directly yourself. The big problem is that they both deal with something called 'maladministration'. This means that you cannot complain, for example, of too low a fine or some other enforcement procedure. You can only complain about the time delay or where they have blatantly not followed official guidelines or the law.

The whole complaints process is very slow (several years), long-winded, detailed and often unsatisfactory. I would like to say that it changed something. But, freedom of information apart, I do not think that it does. For example, I have detailed knowledge of the three major ombudsman complaints, fully upheld, taken against the HSE during the past 20 years: asbestos in Hebden Bridge, 1987; lead in a battery plant, 1990; and pesticides in the home, 1992 (I helped prepare the last two). Despite massive publicity, I could detect no change in HSE actions or attitudes as a result of the ombudsman criticism. I also helped with a local council ombudsman complaint in 1994, over the 1992 'Pesticides in the Home' case (see case study 13, page 153). Again. although fully upheld and much better than the parliamentary complaint, it had no noticeable effect either. The 1967 Parliamentary Ombudsman complaint was one more nail in the coffin of asbestos, but it took another 20 years and many more nails and coffins for any real action (see case study 17, page 178). Both the lead and pesticides complaints vindicated the sufferer and may have helped improve actions internally, but not in any obvious way.

THE TRADE UNIONS

> Thus, in the Trade Union world of today, there is no subject on which workmen of all shades of opinion, and all varieties of occupation, are so unanimous, and so ready to take combined action, as the prevention of accidents and the provision of healthy workplaces. (Beatrice and Sidney Webb, *Industrial Democracy*, 1902)

It could almost be said that one of the major reasons for the formation of the trade unions was to protect the health and safety of the workers. Elsewhere (Dalton, 1981) I have outlined in more detail the early history of the involvement of trade unions in health and safety: the push for protective legislation for women and young children (which also created more jobs for male workers), the first workingman's inspectors in the coal mines in the late nineteenth century, the fight to control lead poisoning and silicosis among pottery workers, the experiment with worker's inspectors around the time of the First World War, and so on.

However, when the late John Williams (Williams, 1960) came to review the situation in the 1950s, in his highly detailed, but much neglected, *Accidents and Ill-health at Work*, he found that for all the efforts of the trade union, there really had been little change. He found that one in every 15 working people could be expected to be injured in some kind of industrial accident each year, the Factory Inspectorate was understaffed and demoralized, the average fine for breaking the Factories Act was £14 (it was £8 in 1938) and that voluntary organizations, compensation, research and safety committees were all ineffective in reducing this workplace carnage. He concluded:

> The outstanding features of the British system are that its growth over 150 years has been piecemeal, uncoordinated, anomalous and limited ... another remarkable feature is the limited scope given to workmen who run the risks of industrial injury to take part in establishing safe standards at the workplace. (p. 31)

It is clear that William's book influenced what was to be the seminal book of workplace hazards (from the workers' point of view), Patrick Kinnersly's *The Hazards of Work and How to Fight Them*, (Kinnersly, 1973), which sold over 100,000 copies. It was the book that was to inspire many trade unionists and a few scientists and safety professionals, like myself, to take workplace health and safety seriously. There is no doubt that Kinnersly's book influenced many others at that time. For example, Michael Foot, Secretary of State for Employment, spoke the following words in a parliamentary debate when introducing the Health and Safety at Work etc. Bill for its second reading into the House of Commons, on 3 April 1974:

> I have also read an excellent book on the subject entitled 'The Hazards of Work and How to Fight Them' by Patrick Kinnersly, published by Pluto Press. Although the book was only published a week or two ago, I recommend it to all who are interested in this subject because I feel that the book should be set alongside the Robens Report. (Col. 1289, *Hansard* 3. iv., 1974)

Although Foot felt that Kinnersly's book adopted 'a more astringent approach to the subject' than the Robens Report, he went on to suggest that these two works should be bound together, 'since they make an excellent introduction to the whole Bill'.

But we have seen elsewhere (page 50) the subsequent 1974 Health and Safety at Work Act did not, in fact, follow the advice of Foot (let alone Kinnersly), but slavishly adopted the ineffective approach of the Robens Report. Had Kinnersly's approach been adopted in 1974 then many more working people would be alive today and much unnecessary, and preventable, suffering would have been avoided.

The 1974 Health and Safety at Work Act brought trade unions into health and safety at the highest level as members of the HSC. Everybody concerned with health and safety – including managers and safety professionals – would agree that the most important law, from a trade union perspective, was the 1977 Safety Representatives and Safety Committee Regulations (1977 SRSC Regs).

There are now around 70 union 'health and safety officers', according to the TUC, who bring these people together on a regular basis, and they produce some excellent briefings and materials on the subject. Of course, many of these people have other responsibilities and there are only around ten to twenty union people with full time health and safety responsibilities. Although I have been very critical of the trade union members who have sat on the HSC over the years, the same cannot be said of the many trade unionists who sit on the lower-level working parties and industrial trade group committees that have produced some very good guidance. With little technical support (especially as compared with the employers' representatives), and sometimes in their own time, lay trade union members have made an important input into many of these committees. But if they are to make a real input into the very many HSE, and, even more, the growing environment committees, not to mention important committees like those of the British Standards Institute (BSI), they need technical support, paid time off, more education and training and the time and resources to report back their actions and results to the trade union members they represent. Without such resources, the trade unions will often fail to take up their allotted places and be less effective when they do.

Ever since the time of David Gee, the TUC has run very good courses on health and safety, with the basic course being a ten-day, one day a week, course. There have also been many follow-on and short courses around specific subjects, e.g.

women's health and safety, COSHH, noise, repetitive strain injury (RSI), stress, risk assessment, and environmental management systems. In the early 1980s the TUC course materials were substantially rewritten and new course techniques of 'student and project centred learning' introduced, primarily by Andy Fairclough.

The 1977 HSE Annual Report noted:

> (HSE) inspectors have often seen supervisors, inadequately trained in safety, who have experienced a loss of authority and confidence when presented with well informed shop-floor representatives, and in one case this is known to have been an indirect cause of industrial action by senior staff.
>
> On one occasion, a senior supervisor was reduced to near despair by his inability to talk on equal terms with a safety representative who had established a comprehensive library of reference material with which to support his arguments. (p. 3)

The situation is little different today. The TUC courses, and many other union courses, are still much better than the expensive, one-day 'song and dance acts' that many management courses consist of. There is no substitute for real-life, workplace case studies around which the general laws and approach can be tested. The ten-day, one-day-a-week TUC format allows safety representatives to try out suggestions and methods at their workplace to see if they work and to report back on successes and failures. The TUC has, since 1974, produced some very useful materials on health and safety issues. In fact, the latest edition (TUC, 1997) of its best-selling *Hazards at Work* was produced in early 1997. Also, in recent years, the TUC has organized campaigns (such as an excellent one on RSI), research, conferences and media interest in health and safety issues like never before.

THE ENVIRONMENT

There is one major area where the TUC, and most other trade unions, are doing very little: the environment. Whilst it is true that at the beginning of the 1990s there was a little flurry of trade union interest in the environment, with the TUC producing an excellent guide, *Greening the Workplace* (TUC, 1991) and one or two other unions (e.g. GMB, Manufacturing, Science and Finance Union) trying to generate some interest, it must be admitted that, for reasons not fully understood, there was no real interest from the union membership in the subject.

In the early 1990s Ruskin College and the Labour Research Department (LRD) carried out a large, EU-funded, two-volume survey[35] into the involvement of trade unions in environmental issues throughout Europe. The results were pretty depressing and they concluded that:

> The fact remains, however, that even in industrial relations systems where involvement and participation are highly specified, there appears to be a reluctance to allow employee representative organisations (whether works council or trade union) to be involved fully in the critical areas of decision making. The wider environmental impact of an enterprise is still seen largely as a management responsibility. (vol. 1, p. 5)

This EU conclusion is in broad agreement with the UK experience. With very few exceptions, despite some effort, the trade unions have had little real say in environmental issues. They neither sit on DETR industry committees, nor are they consulted at workplace level. There have been no 'model agreements', as suggested in some of the TU environmental packs, with employers signed. Andrea Oates, of LRD, who surveyed the UK for the above-mentioned 1993 EU-funded report, concluded:

> The integration of environmental issues into the system of industrial relations is in the very early stages in the UK. It is unclear at present how far employers will enter into voluntary agreements with unions, and indeed how far unions at workplace level are attempting to negotiate on these issues. (vol. 2, p. 226)

To determine whether this was still the case in 1994–97 I carried out several studies from both the employer's point of view and from the trade union perspective (Dalton, 1995).

The employers

First, in late 1994, in connection with some other work, I surveyed around 70 of the larger organizations of the 150 or so organizations signed up to the CBI's Environment Business Forum (EBF). The only requirement of membership is to be open with information: as the CBI says, 'The EBF requires the production of a publicly available report.' Only about 25 organizations replied, thus failing the one and only definite requirement of membership! Second, I asked the companies about the extent of trade union involvement with their environmental policy statement. With only one exception, they all said there was little or no union involvement, although a few said that the completed environmental report was 'discussed' with the unions.

The trade unions

I included several environmental questions in my 1994–95 *Hazards* survey[36] of around 450 safety representatives representing almost 250,000 employees. The result was both good and bad. The bad news, as expected, was that very few of the safety representatives were involved in anything remotely environmental. The good news was that the vast majority (nine out of ten or 92 per cent) of respondents wanted to be involved in environmental issues, with rights similar to those they have as safety representatives.

Some typical comments from that survey were:

○ 'Management only consider the environment when we raise issues, such as the disposal of fluorescent light tubes, the use of Bromochloroflourine (BCF) in fire extinguishers' – Mick Shaw, FBU safety representative, London Fire Brigade.

○ 'Presently in discussion with management regarding the venting of fumes from the film processors' – Pauline Robinson, safety representative Society of Radiographers, Inverclyde Royal NHS Trust.

○ 'We do not have any effect on the public or the surrounding countryside/environment' – Anthony O'Malley, Union of Construction and Allied Trades and Technicians safety representative, Swift Construction Group of Companies.

○ 'Complaints were received from the public about the smell of tobacco and this led to the EHOs visiting the factory. We are involved in every stage of their visits and the outcome was an air scrubbing plant to clean the atmosphere' – R.J. Hudson, GMB safety representative, Imperial Tobacco Ltd, Notts.

○ 'HMIP came on site regarding an ammonia leak and I was refused access to him by a British Steel Manager' – D. Lascelles, GMB safety representative, Rebate Contract Organization.

○ 'We negotiate over the recycling and disposal of toxic and infectious waste' – Tig Davies, UNISON safety representative, Cefn Coed Hospital, Swansea.

○ 'The environmental audit is done solely by an auditing body and British Gas management. I would like to be involved' – a UNISON safety representative at a British Gas Depot, Dundee.

○ 'I would very much like to be involved in environmental issues!' – Carol Lee, UNISON branch health and safety officer, Worthing Priority Trust (Health Care).

Clearly, then, safety representatives *are* keen to take on new environmental responsibilities, provided, of course, they are given the paid time off (with adequate cover for colleagues), the relevant trade union-based training, and powers to achieve results. This makes sense, as the more responsible UK organizations often include 'traditional' health and safety issues – such as accident statistics, COSHH information, risk assessment and safety case studies – as part of their annual environmental reports. There are several recent developments that suggest that 'safety representatives' may indeed become 'safety, health and environment representatives' towards the end of the 1990s. Some of these are described below.

During 1994 some college tutors in Lancashire ran the first ever TUC-approved course for safety representatives on environmental auditing and British Standard 7750, on Environmental Management Systems (EMS). East Lancashire has been selected as one of two areas targeted by the government for an increased 'environmental awareness' experiment and 25 companies have signed up to an EMS system. Dr Charlie Clutterbuck, one of the TUC tutors, told me that 'Safety representatives were able to get paid release because the course was dealing with EMS', whereas it would be very difficult to get release for something as general as 'trade unions and the environment'. The course concluded that trade unions should have:

○   consultation rights regarding the organization's environmental policy
○   similar rights during environmental audits as for safety inspections
○   involvement in negotiations on environmental targets (as these could affect job prospects)

In March 1995 the Manufacturing, Science and Finance (MSF) union launched a pathmaking new report entitled, *Clean Production – from Industrial Dinosaur to Eco-efficiency*.[37] At the press conference to launch the report were the director of a water board and the then head of HMIP, which gives some idea of the weight behind the report. It was written by David Gee, former head of the GMB's health and safety department and a former director of Friends of the Earth. However, the union input is pretty thin, and this is a pity, since one example at Coca-Cola shows it making £1.6 million a year by 'waste minimization' – from which the unions negotiated a £1,000 a year 'eco-bonus'. More examples like this would make other unions envious and advance the cause of clean technology no end!

FIGURE 2.5   David Gee, formerly Director of Health and Safety at the GMB, briefly Director of Friends of the Earth, and now an EU Environmental person

CASE STUDY 10: UNIONS HELP REDUCE ORGANIC SOLVENTS IN PRINTING

Organic solvents, such as 'white spirit', are derived from non-renewable petroleum oil resources and are polluting the planet by contributing to global warming and the destruction of the ozone layer and more locally, towards the formation of ground-level ozone (which causes or exacerbates asthma). The government has signed an international protocol to reduce these organic solvents – more generally known as volatile organic compounds (VOCs) – from the 1988 levels, by 30 per cent by 1999.

The print industry is a major user of VOCs, and the government's target for reduction by 1999, for this industry, is 50 per cent. A major use of VOCs in the print industry is for 'wash-up', when the old ink is washed off the rollers in the print machine. This is still a rather crude process, and is often done with a rag and scraper, on rollers that are warm and moving slowly. Operator exposures are high, as is the pollution to the atmosphere. In Scandinavia, and increasingly in other countries, it has been recognized for over ten years that exposure to organic solvents can cause damage to the nervous system of the body (especially brain damage). Therefore, in industries like construction, over 90 per cent of the paints used are water-based. Printers, too, suffered from a large amount of government-compensated brain damage and, inspired by the long-known fact that butter removes grease from clothing, the printers looked for alternatives to VOCs and found vegetable oils. After much experimentation and chemical modification, the vegetable cleaning agents (VCAs) were found to work. By 1990, one in three Danish printers were said to be using these products.

At this stage the EU stepped in and part-funded a 'technology transfer' programme to other EU countries, including the UK. Since 1993, a research team (of which I was a member) has been researching and trialling these VCA products in the UK. In a traditionally conservative, but also very advanced, printing industry in the middle of a recession, this has not been easy! A key to VCA use has been the publication of the results of successful trials of five VCA wash-ups at Her Majesty's Stationery Office (HMSO) printers. HMSO consists of five big printing works, which print the parliamentary reports, (e.g. *Hansard*), all the government laws and reports and many other items. As a government agency, it wanted to set an example and go 'green', but not at any price. On the verge of being privatized, HMSO is under a great pressure to make a healthy profit, and this pressure almost ruined the trials from the start.

The production manager at the Oldham HMSO plant was clearly not going to give the new VCAs a fair trial (different cleaning methods are needed, and slightly more time) until a key meeting with the GPMU safety representatives convinced him otherwise: they were going to give the VCAs a fair trial, as it was their health, as well as the environment, at risk. This, plus successful trials at the Express Printers, Manchester and elsewhere, plus recent DoE guidance on

FIGURE 2.6   Rose Tilley, a campaigner against the pollution from the giant News International printing plant in Wapping, London

substituting VOCs in cleaning, has kick-started the UK VCA market. A lasting memory I have is the comment from an in-house printer at the large charity Save the Children, who, when using VCAs for wash-up for the first time on his printing machine, remarked, 'This is the first time in seven years I have not had a headache when doing this job'.[38]

In 1994 the Labour Party produced its well-received policy document on the environment entitled, *In Trust for Tomorrow*. In a short section on environmental rights at work, the policy document says, 'Too many companies do not consult their workforce on environmental matters ... A Labour government will therefore introduce a statutory obligation for companies to consult their workforce on health and safety matters; indeed, the two areas are often hard to distinguish.'

During 1996, with the aid of EU funding, I helped organize and run at the Transport and General Workers' Union (TGWU) two three-day European-wide courses for trade unionists, and others: eco-auditing and trade unionists, and SHE issues and European works councils. The reports of those conferences are available.[39] As a direct result of the eco-auditing conference, a delegate from the chemical industry put a resolution to his local TGWU branch, which eventually worked its way up the union to be agreed as TGWU policy at its top policy-making body, the General Executive Council (GEC), in September 1996. The TGWU GEC agreed:

○ to campaign within the EU and UK for the voluntary Eco-Audit Scheme (EMAS) to become compulsory
○ to put EMAS on the negotiating agenda at the workplace
○ to incorporate environmental training into the TGWU training of safety representatives

This is a tall order for any trade union and makes the TGWU, at least on paper, the greenest UK trade union. At the same time the TGWU released the results of its survey of 1000, of its safety representatives.[40] Three out of four (75 per cent) said that they would like the legal right to be involved in environmental issues at the workplace. Already TGWU tutors in the regions are running one-day, 'top-up', environmental auditing sessions to supplement two-day risk assessment training in the chemical industry, and the one-week, national TGWU environmental course has seen considerable expansion. In some companies, like London Brick, the TGWU is running 'add-on' one-day environmental auditing sessions to its standard two-day risk assessment course for safety representatives and others.

The case study of the use of alternative fuels in the cement industry (page 20) is one example of how a union can tackle even an environmental issue that is by no means clear-cut and that does not have easy answers. This was followed by an EU-funded 'pesticides conference' in December 1997, at which all the interested parties – industry, regulator and victims – spoke. The TGWU, uniquely brought together trade unionists making pesticides and those using pesticides. (A report of the conference, *Pesticides – Production, Use and Protection*, is available from the T & G Health and Safety Section of the TGWU.) These conferences can be confrontational, but it is better to have a 'controlled' confrontation at a conference than one at a workplace, on a demonstration against a plant or in court.

At the TUC conference in Brighton in September 1997 the Environment Minister, Michael Meacher, announced that he was to set up an 'Advisory Committee on Trade Unions and the Environment' along the lines of the well-established government Advisory Committee on Business and the Environment. With the right people on this committee, a budget and a good secretariat, this may well be the kick-start the trade unions need to take the environment seriously. In the twenty-first century, we may see trade unions becoming full 'stakeholders' in workplace environmental auditing (see also page 246).

THE 1977 SAFETY REPS REGULATIONS – INTRODUCTION

The trade union movement is already involved in this area (health, safety and the environment) and should continue to take an active and responsible role. They well understand the difficult balance between reducing risk and maintaining a viable operation. (Hickson Interntional PLC, evidence to the Tory-dominated 1994 Employment Select Committee enquiry on The Future of Trade Unions.)

There are now an estimated 200,000 trade union safety representatives in UK industry and organizations. When you consider that the trade union movement has fallen from around 12 million members in 1979 to less than 8 million currently, this is quite surprising. In 1979 around one in two working people were in trade unions, and now it is about one in three. Yet, of the UK's top 50 companies, 47 are unionized. This is because survey after survey has shown that what trade union members are concerned about most of all – above even wages in some cases – is workplace health and safety and, increasingly, the environment.

Thus, in 1995 the TUC commissioned the National Opinion Poll (NOP) to survey 1002 people about their attitudes to trade unions and what trade unions should do. The results were very revealing. The question asked was: Do you think people at work should or should not have the right to be represented by a trade union if they want to on the following issues:

Issue	Yes %	No %	Not sure %
Their pay?	93	5	2
Health and safety?	98	1	1
Conditions of employment?	95	4	1

Clearly then, health and safety issues top the poll with regard to trade union activity with the general public. More specifically, in 1992, the TGWU commissioned Warwick University to survey new TGWU members as to what they thought were the important issues for the union. Top of the poll as 'very important' came 'improved health and safety at work' with 80 per cent, beating even 'improvements in pay', which scored 77 per cent. Even a 1992 CBI Gallup Poll survey found three out of four people (75 per cent) questioned felt that 'protecting workplace health and safety' was the key issue for trade unions, the next being 'negotiating pay and conditions', for two out of three people (66 per cent). So there is no question that health and safety is the principal issue for trade unionists.

THE SRSC REGS 1977

Nearly all trade unions, and the TUC,[41] produce comprehensive guides on these regulations. I have written, in more detail, on these regulations elsewhere (Dalton, 1995). The HSC provides a guide[42] that contains the regulations, code of practice and guidance notes, sometimes known as the 'brown book', and it is not always easy reading. The regulations are law, the code of practice may be used as evidence in a court of law (compare the well-known 'Highway Code') and the guidance is the lowest legal right. In practice, employers, trade unionists, HSE and EHO officers and industrial tribunals make little distinction between the three documents. There is, amazingly, after over 20 years, still no simple free HSE guide to these regulations, as there is to virtually all the other important regulations. Even when the SRSC Regs 1977 first became law, the name was already out of date: health issues were of equal concern to safety. With the increased concern over the environment they should now be updated to safety, health and environment, or SHE, representatives.

First, it is very important to note that the essential role of the trade union safety representative is to audit and check up on management's action or inaction over safety and health (and sometimes environmental) issues at the workplace. Representatives are not part of management (although some may be managers and supervisors) and they are not unpaid safety officers, although some may act in that way.

They are appointed, and removed, by their trade union or its members, and the SRSC Regs 1977 specifically state that a safety representative has functions under the SRSC Regs 1977, not duties. The regulations make this quite clear: 'Without prejudice to sections 7 and 8 of the 1974 Act, no function given to a safety representative ... shall be construed as imposing any duty on her or him.' (Regulation 3). Sections 7 and 8 of the 1974 Act are concerned with taking 'reasonable care' at work for yourself and other people and not interfering or misusing 'anything provided in the interests of health, safety or welfare'. The HSC has said quite clearly in SRSC Regs 1977, Guidance 11, that there will be no possibility of any criminal proceedings against a safety representative for 'any act or omission' by her or him in performance of the SRSC Reg. 1977 functions.

A trade union that the employer recognizes in negotiation over other issues (e.g. wages, sick pay, discipline, holidays, pensions), may appoint safety representatives from among the employees in all cases where one or more employees are employed by that employer. The 1996 Health and Safety (Consultation with Employees) Regulations were brought in, under pressure from the EU, to cover workplaces where the trade union was not recognized and therefore no safety representatives could be appointed (see page 105). In nearly all cases the safety representative is elected from the members he or she represents, although there have been a very few cases where a union head office has appointed or removed a safety representative as is clearly their right by law. But the appointment or the removal of a safety representative, if against the local union members' wishes, is not a very effective recruitment tool for national unions and therefore only happens in very rare instances.

There are two exceptions to this rule: when the employees are members of the British Actors' Equity Association, or Equity, with 44,000 members, or the Musicians' Union, with 33,000 members. Safety representatives representing actors and musicians, by the nature of their work, which means they work at many different workplaces, are allowed by Regulation 8 to be appointed by the union and not from employees employed by an employer. This regulation actually introduces the principle of 'roving safety representatives', or safety representatives representing workers at other than their own workplace, in other areas, such as the pilot farms project (see page 106).

Regulation 3.4 suggests, 'so far as is reasonably practicable', that a safety representative should have been employed by an employer for two years or at least have had two years experience in similar employment. Since the 1974 Act first came in, trade unions, and some employers, have been very critical of how many of the requirements in the 1974 Act are prefaced with the words, 'so far as is reasonably practicable' (see page 45). In essence, this phrase allows for a balance of risk and costs (whether money, time or trouble) by the employer. However, in this case, it actually works in favour of the trade unions, for if it is not 'reasonably practicable' for an employee to have that two years experience, and someone with far less experience is appointed by the unions, there is nothing an employer can do. Interestingly, in my 1994–95 survey I noticed that a fairly large proportion of the respondents had been safety representatives for a year or less (although I did not ask them how long they had been an employee of that organization).

As soon as a safety representative is appointed, he or she, or their union, should inform their employer in writing with the groups of employee that they represent (e.g. all the cleaners, the technicians in building 201, the lecturers in department A or, simply, all the employees in union X). Some unions provide documents for this process and keep a copy so that they have a record of the safety representative for their files, to send information to and so on (Regulation 3.2).

An employee ceases to be a safety representative when the trade union which appointed (or elected) her or him notifies the employer in writing that the appointment has been terminated, he or she is no longer employed at the workplace (but if representing employees at more than one workplace, if still employed at another, shall continued to be one) or he or she resigns (Regulation 3.3).

A question often asked by a manager, and safety representatives, is what is a workplace? The definition in the 1977 SRSC Regs is in fact very broad: ' "workplace" in relation to a safety representative means any place or places where the group or groups of employees he is appointed to represent are likely to work or which they are likely to frequent in the course of their employment or incidentally to it'. Clearly, then, a safety representative can inspect almost any part of a workplace that her or his members work at and the areas in that workplace that they frequent (e.g. toilets, corridors, canteen).

When I was a safety representative I frequently visited sites where my members worked, many miles away, to investigate complaints and accidents/near misses, and I carried out a regular inspection every three months of that same workplace.

One common question raised by safety representatives, and by managers, is how many safety representatives should a workplace/union have? There is no prescribed number and the 1977 SRSC Regs, Guidance, paragraphs 8 and 9, suggest that the following factors be taken into account:

○ The total number employed.
○ The variety of different occupations.
○ The size of the workforce and number of locations.
○ The operation of a shift system.
○ The type of work activity and its dangers.

As can be imagine from these criteria, and other considerations (e.g. will anybody stand as a safety representative?), there is a wide variety in the ratio of safety representatives to employees found, even in the same industry. In my 1984 survey the spread ranged from 1:9 in a school to 1:900 for various building sites. However, the average for a wide range of workplaces was 1:63, with the majority being in the range 1:30 to 1:150. The 1993 LRD survey showed little change, from 1:7 at a carpet factory to 1:300 at Zeneca Chemicals and a higher education college. The average was 1:70; slightly up from 1984 (but the sample was much smaller).

Functions

Again, as with appointment, the functions of a safety representative are very broad and recent EU legislation is extending them all the time. First, the 1974 Act makes it quite clear that:

> It shall be the duty of every employer to consult any such (safety) representatives with a view to making and maintenance of arrangements which will enable her or him and her employees to co-operate effectively in promoting and developing measures to ensure the health and safety at work of employees, and in checking the effectiveness of such measures. (Section 2.2.6)

It should be noted that there is no qualification to this phrase: it is a legal duty placed upon the employer.

It is also significant that the employer's duty to consult the safety representative has recently been extended by an addition to the 1977 SRSC Regs, known as Regulation 4A, detailed in The Schedule to the Management of Health and Safety at Work Regulations 1992. This requires the employer to consult, 'in good time', over;

○ the introduction of any measures which may substantially affect health and safety
○ the arrangements for appointing competent people (e.g. to carry out risk assessments) to assist with health and safety and implementing procedures for serious and imminent risk
○ any health and safety information the employer is required to provide

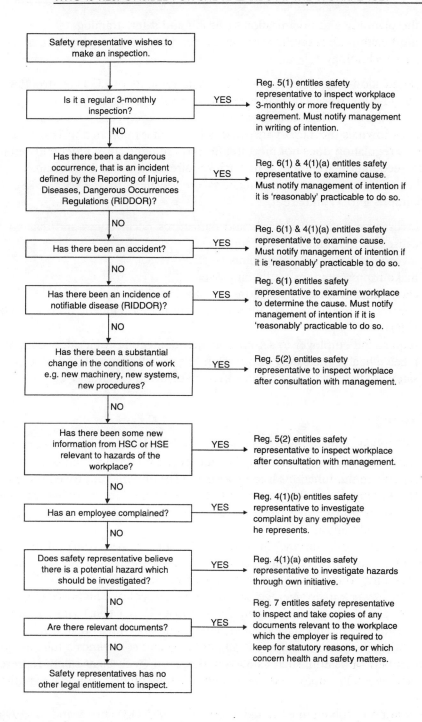

FIGURE 2.7   Legal rights of safety reps to carry out inspection and investigations

○ the planning and organization of health and safety training
○ the health and safety implications of the introduction (or planning) of any new technology

This Regulation was added to meet the requirements of EU Directive 1989/391 (Article 11); the so-called 'Framework Directive'. Hendy and Ford, in the 1993 edition of the authoritative *Redgrave's Health and Safety* (this is the 25th edition of what is known as the 'factory inspector's Bible', first published in 1878) consider that this regulation does not meet the EU requirement, since it depends on trade union recognition and there is no such requirement in the EU Directive.

The safety representatives functions are detailed in the 1977 SRSC Regs (paragraphs 4 to 7) and are to:

○ investigate potential hazards and dangerous occurrences and examine the causes of accidents
○ investigate members' complaints
○ make representations to the employer
○ carry out workplace inspections (at least every 3 months)
○ consult with and receive information from enforcement officers (HSE or EHO)
○ require the employer to set up, and attend, meetings of a safety committee
○ receive health and safety information (e.g. accident reports, hygiene surveys, safety audits, risk assessments, safety cases) from the employer

Time off with pay

The 1977 SRSC Regs require the employer to 'permit a safety representative to take such time off with pay during the employee's working hours' as are required to (a) perform the functions listed above and (b) undergo approved trade union or TUC training. Normally, the amount of time required for these two activities is decided by negotiation between the employer and the safety representative (or her or his trade union).

In my 1994–95 survey, over half (214, or 53 per cent) of the safety representatives surveyed said that they were satisfied with the paid time off arrangements. The time allowed off varied from 'as required' to nothing, with a few hours a week in an 'average' workplace being typical. This was confirmed by the 1993 LRD survey, which, again, found most (71 per cent) safety representatives saying they did not have trouble getting time off, with a range from none (18 per cent), to as much as required (30 per cent) and sometimes a full-time safety representative position; such as Massey Ferguson (with eight safety representatives and over 500 employees). Commonly, the time off was around two hours per week.

A common problem mentioned in both the 1993 LRD survey and my 1994–95 survey was that there were often staff shortages (especially in the NHS and education), lack of cover or large workloads so that safety representatives felt guilty when taking time off as their colleagues had to carry an extra load; or else the safety representatives work just piled up for them when they returned from their safety representative work or training. The 'guilt' feeling, of leaving your colleagues, was especially mentioned by the NHS safety representatives at a Royal College of Nursing (RCN) safety committee meeting that I spoke to in early 1995.

On the other hand, a National Association of Teachers in Further and Higher Education (NATFHE) safety representative at a technical college told the LRD in 1993, 'Since we negotiated one hour off teaching timetables some two years ago – no problems.' One problem arises with shiftworkers, when they have to attend meetings (or carry out other duties) outside of their normal shifts. In many workplaces the unions have negotiated extra payments or time off in lieu for such activity. The LRD's 1994 survey of the time off for union representatives, in 165 organizations, gave a table of around 50 named organizations with such agreements, such as Lucas Flight Control Systems, which pays or allows time off in lieu for meetings outside normal working hours, and Chesterfield Cylinders, where shiftworkers are paid a minimum of four hours for meetings outside of their shift.

However, where there is a disagreement between management and unions, there is the provision (Regulation 11) for the issue to be taken to an industrial tribunal (IT), within three months of the date of when the refusal took place. However, in practice, the number taken is very small, averaging less than 20 a year (compare IT cases for 'unfair dismissal', of which there around 30,000 a year). IT decisions are not binding on other ITs, but employment appeal tribunal (EAT) decisions usually are. ITs are given a code number, XXXX/year of tribunal sitting, so that the original decision can be obtained, for a fee, from the Central Office of Industrial Tribunals (COIT). Several interesting IT/EAT decisions are given below.

○ In an EAT case, Hairsine v. Hull City Council 1991, a shiftworker whose shift ran from 3 pm to 11 pm (eight hours) attended a training course from 9 am to 4 pm (seven hours teaching plus three hours of work), and carried out his duties until 7 pm. However, the EAT said that he only had to be paid from 3 pm to 7 pm (only four hours' pay).

○ Where more safety representatives have been appointed than there are sections of the workplace for which safety representatives could be responsible, it is not unreasonable to deny some of the safety representatives paid time off in order to carry our their functions (IT 0732-3/89).

○ Risely Remand Centre refused a prison officer, Norman Townson, a safety representative appointed by the Prison Officers' Association, time off for inspection of the laundry and main stores area of the centre. An IT found in his favour and instructed local management that the legal requirements must be fulfilled (IT 24773/79).

○ George Dowsett, a TGWU safety representative at Ford's Dagenham, had to visit an injured employee at home to gain his version of an accident at work. Ford's refused payment, claiming that the 1977 SRSC Regs only required payment for workplace investigations. An IT disagreed, saying that there was no qualification to the word 'investigate' and adding that, 'The representatives of employers and employees may have different theories and both may wish to question the injured man accordingly' (IT 1812/80E).

Training

The 1977 SRSC Regs are quite clear on training, in that it is a function of the safety representative to 'undergo such training in aspects of those functions as may be reasonable in all the circumstances' and it is the legal duty for the employer to allow the safety representative time off with pay (Regulation 4.2.b). A mercifully brief approved code of practice, which is included in the 1996 edition of the 'brown book', spells out the requirements in more detail. The main points of these are as follows:

- 'As soon as possible after their appointment safety representatives should be permitted time off with pay to attend basic training facilities approved by the TUC or by the independent trade union which appointed the safety representatives.'
- 'Further training, similarly approved, should be undertaken where the safety representative has special responsibilities or where such training is necessary to meet changes in circumstances or relevant legislation.'
- 'With regard to the length of training required, this cannot be rigidly prescribed ...'
- 'A trade union ... should inform management of the course it has approved and supply a copy of the syllabus, indicating its contents, if the employer asks for it.'
- 'It should normally give at least a few weeks' notice (to the employer) of the safety representatives it has nominated for attendance.'
- 'The number of safety representatives attending training courses at any one time should be that which is reasonable in the circumstances ...'
- 'Unions and management should endeavour to reach agreement on the appropriate numbers and arrangements and refer any problems which may arise to the relevant agreed procedure.'

There were some initial hitches in the late 1970s, where some local councils (full of hazards, even before contracting-out and the cuts), some office-based companies (this was 'before' stress, RSI, VDUs and sick building syndrome) and the NHS (with around a million employees, the biggest employer in Europe, and one of the most hazardous to work for after construction and agriculture) tried to argue, and failed, that a five-day TUC course was sufficient for their needs, instead of the now standard ten-day TUC-approved course. However, surveys, such as the 1993 LRD one, indicate that there are now few problems in this area, with the vast majority (70 per cent) of safety representatives attending a union course and/or a TUC stage I, or basic, course (55 per cent). However, fewer (almost one in three or 31 per cent) had attended a more advanced ten-day TUC course (stage II). But many had attended short, normally two-day, courses on: the COSHH regulations, new EU Directives (the 1992 'six-pack regulations'), risk assessment, noise and RSI (which the HSE calls, work-related upper limb disorders) and so on. A few employers had refused time off, because of pressure of work or shortage of staff, and it was clear that in these workplaces the safety representatives did not know their legal rights or chose to ignore them. A few of the comments from my 1994–95 survey were as follow:

- ○ 'I only got the time off after I quoted the SRSC Code of Practice regarding time-off, "as soon as possible after appointment", and with some pressure from the union' (Mark Burlington, Union of Construction, Allied Trades and Technicians (UCATT), safety representative, Aerostructures Hample Ltd, Hants).
- ○ 'I keep asking for time off (I've been a safety rep for six months), but the answer is, "as and when" and in practice I am usually too busy. I will have to get more insistent' (MSF safety representative in the Clinical Chemistry Department of a large London Hospital Trust).
- ○ 'Management do not want to give me time off' (Michael Thompson, Transport Salaried Staffs Association (TSSA), safety representative (one year), Waterloo Underground Station, London).
- ○ 'I was originally told my management that if I had to be covered by overtime, as I work 3 × 12-hour shifts, then I would not get paid ... I informed my union through my Father of the Chapel (union steward) and it was resolved by them' (Ian Mitchell, GPMU safety representative BPC Magazines, Leeds).

A big blow to TUC-approved training courses has been the withdrawal of the government grant to the TUC for all trade union training, of which around 40 per cent was spent on safety representative training. The TUC trains 14,000 new safety representatives each year at 84 colleges. The grant started in the 1970s and the announcement of the withdrawal was made in December 1992. The TUC received almost £1 million a year from the government, and in April 1996 it was abolished. No one at the HSE was consulted. Apparently, the union training grant was created to train trade union officials to improve industrial relations. Now that the strike rate is at an all-time low, it is no longer deemed necessary. It is possible that the HSE may help with some safety representative training in the future. It is also possible that EU requirements for the costs of worker training not to fall directly, or indirectly, on workers themselves may make the government think again. Again, it needs to be asked, what are the trade union representatives on the HSC doing about this withdrawal of funding for safety representative training?

This is an area where there have been the most applications to ITs, and some of the more interesting cases are summarized below:

○ Mr Denys Rama was a RMT union representative for South West trains. He applied, and gained, initial approval from his management for paid time off to attend a TUC stage two, 10-day health and safety training course at South Thames College, London. Then his employer withdrew the offer and he attended the course in his own time. He appealed to an industrial tribunal (IT) for loss of earnings. At the IT, South West Trains argued that the course might turn him into 'an agitator' and the IT found in the employer's favour, stating that stage two training was not 'necessary' for the safety rep. to be able to carry out his functions.

With the backing of his union, the RMT, Mr Rama appealed to the High Court. The hearing was heard on 5 November 1997 and the judge ruled the IT had interpreted the Code of Practice on time off, made under SRSC regulation 4(2), wrongly. The tribunal had wrongly placed the emphasis on what the employer felt to be 'necessary' training to carry out safety rep. functions as opposed to what was 'reasonable'. Costs, in the region of £30,000, were awarded against South West Trains and Mr Rama will be awarded his estimated £500 costs by a re-constituted IT. (Rama v South West Trains, High Court, 5 May 1977 (CO/310/96).)

○ Mr B. Owens was appointed a National Union of Public Employees (NUPE) (now the trade union, UNISON) safety representative for St Luke's Hospital, Bradford when he was a year away from retirement. The hospital refused him paid time off but an IT found for Mr Owens. Factors influencing the IT were: there is no mention in the regulations about the personal circumstances of the safety representative, the election of a safety representative is the union's responsibility and there is a fairly high turnover of safety representatives in any case (IT SR1/2821/1980).

○ Mr V. G. Croft was a Transport and General Workers Union (TGWU)-appointed safety representative at Heathrow Airport. Having been on a TUC day course, and being a fireman, he applied to go on a TUC-approved ten-day, follow-on course (stage II). Management refused permission and an IT found for Mr Croft, especially since he was the only safety representative in the fire service and the IT thought that management had 'no sense of urgency' in its negotiations with the trade unions. (IT 1417/82).

○ A safety representative was entitled to be paid as if he was doing his ordinary work, even though at the time he was attending his training course he had been laid off (Hendy and Ford, 1993, p. 318).

○ The London Borough of Sutton, because of 'financial stringency', said that it could only pay for time off for the training of one each of the teacher's union safety representatives per year. This meant that the National Union of Teachers (NUT), with 16 of 44 safety representatives, would have to wait 16 years to have all its representatives trained. The IT found for the NUT and that the council was disobeying its statutory duty (IT 38773/81/LS).

○ SW Garside, a woodworking company employing ten people, said it could not afford to pay safety representative Terrence Fanning to go on a TUC-approved ten-day course. They suggested that a non-TUC approved, British Safety Council three-day course would be sufficient. An IT disagreed and ordered the company to pay Mr Fanning his ten days' pay (IT 18410/79).

○ Staples Printers Rochester Ltd refused to pay the National Graphical Association (NGA '82) (now the GPMU) printing union representative Steward Murray to attend a TUC-approved five-day course on noise. The company argued that the noise was not a problem in its industry (even though printing is one of the most noisy industries). An IT disagreed and ordered the company to pay him for the days he was on the course (IT 27568/83).

○ Pork Farms management refused to pay a TGWU safety representative to attend at TUC-approved two-day course on RSI (the food industry has a high rate of RSI). An IT disagreed and found that the company had unreasonably refused the representative time of for training (*Health and Safety Law*, LRD, 1995).

○ A key EAT case, White v. Pressed Steel Fisher, found that a course run by the employer was not necessarily inadequate because it was not approved by the trade union. However, since the trade union or representational aspect was an important aspect of the course, if that was absent, the safety representative could be entitled to additional time off to be trained in those functions elsewhere (Hendy and Ford, 1993, p. 315).

○ East Hertfordshire District Council refused to allow a newly elected National Association of Local Government Official (NALGO) (now the trade union UNISON) safety representative, Kate Scarth, to attend a TUC-approved, ten-day course. The employers relied heavily on White v. Pressed Steel Fisher (above), but in fact had no idea about an appropriate three-day course, which, the IT said, they had simply 'plucked out of the air.' The IT ordered the employer to pay up (IT 8887/89).

○ The Drum Engineering Co Ltd. had a safety committee that consisted of eight members – five from management and three safety representatives. Because of COSHH, two managers had been trained and another was due training in COSHH. The union, the Amalgamated Engineering Union (AEU) (now the Amalgamated Engineers and Electricians Union, AEEU) wished to send its three safety representatives on a TUC-approved two-day, COSHH course. Management said that it would only pay for one of the three union representatives to attend the COSHH course. Mr Davage, one of the safety representatives attended the TUC-approved COSHH course, and Mr Galla-gher, one of the other two safety representatives, applied to an IT for a ruling on this issue. The IT found that although 'It is apparent that the company takes the COSHH regulations very seriously ... there has been a breach by this employer in not allowing Mr Gallagher to attend the TUC course on the COSHH regulations'. The employer agreed to pay for a second safety representative to attend the TUC-approved COSHH course (IT 13301/89).

Access to information

The 1977 SRSC Regs make it quite clear that 'A employer shall make available to safety representatives the information within the employer's knowledge, necessary to enable them to fulfil their functions' (Regulation 7.2). Some mention of the types of information is made, under functions (page 80); however, the 1977 SRSC Regs, Code of Practice, spells it out in more detail (C of P, 6):

○ Plans and performance and any changes proposed that may affect health and safety.
○ Technical information about hazards and necessary precautions, including information provided by manufacturers, hygiene measurements and so on.
○ Information and statistical records on accidents, dangerous occurrences and notifiable diseases.
○ Any other information relevant to health and safety at work, such as measures to check the effectiveness of health and safety arrangements (e.g. safety audits, consultants; reports).
○ Information on articles and substances issued to homeworkers.

Some of the newer regulations mention this requirement specifically. Thus the Construction (Design and Management) Regulations 1994, which became law on 31 March 1995, say 'the principal contractor needs to use the safety representatives and any committee they request to be set up, so far as he is able to ensure that consultation takes place and employees can offer advice on health and safety issues' (Regulation 18, C of P, 104).

In 1994 the Conservative government produced a Code of Practice on Access to Government Information, and whilst a survey of the first year of operation shows that it has not been very successful (many people do not even know it exists), it has prompted the HSE to produce its own *Policy Statement on Open Government* and to be more open with information. There are exceptions on information disclosure, under the SCSC Regs, and these are (1977 SRSC Regs, 7.2, a–e):

○ Where disclosure would be 'against the interests of national security'.
○ Where it would contravene a prohibition imposed by law.
○ Any information relating to an individual (unless consent has been given; however, anonymous aggregate figures in certain working areas – say on blood lead levels, or deafness as shown by audiograms, or personal dust levels – can be given).
○ Information that would damage the employer's undertaking.
○ Information obtained for the sole purpose of bringing, prosecuting or defending legal proceedings.

Ten years ago, in my 1984 survey, this was the one area where safety representatives were not achieving their legal rights: only just over one in three

(39 per cent) said that they were getting this type of information. By 1993, the LRD survey could report that the majority of respondents (70 per cent) said they did have adequate access to their employer's health and safety information. However, a large minority, over one in three (37 per cent), said that they did not have adequate access to information or what they did receive was not sufficient. Despite a changing climate of 'freedom of information', there is clearly still some way to go on the provision of workplace health and safety information.

Inspections and investigations

Again, the regulations are clear on this aspect:

> Safety representatives shall be entitled to inspect the workplace or part of it if they have given the employer or her representative reasonable notice in writing of their intention to do so and have not inspected it, or that part of it, as the case may be, in the previous three months; and may carry out more frequent inspections with the employer. (Regulation 5.1)

Clearly, the bottom line is a regular workplace inspection four times a year.

However, elsewhere in the 'brown book' there are rights to: inspect when there has been a 'substantial change' in the conditions of work; inspect when new information about hazards/equipment becomes available; act on complaints of members; inspect after accidents or dangerous occurrences; accompany experts and enforcement inspectors where agreed; and so on. So, in reality, a fairly flexible right is given to safety representatives to inspect the workplace at any time, for justifiable health or safety reasons, even though they have inspected routinely within the past three months. With regard to the three-monthly inspections SRSC Regulation 5(3) is clear:

> The employer shall provide such facilities and assistance as the safety representatives may reasonably require (including facilities for independent investigation by them and private discussion with the employees) ... but nothing ... shall preclude the employer or her representative from being present in the workplace during the inspection.

All in all, this is one of the more straightforward sections of the 'brown book' and some extra information is given in the guidance section (Paragraphs 16–22).

In my 1984 survey, this was not an area where most safety representatives had any problems. Nearly all did their three-monthly inspections, many inspected 'as required' and quite a few used versions of the recommended report forms. However, by the 1993 LRD survey, things appeared to have deteriorated somewhat, with only just over half (55 per cent) inspecting their workplace every three months or more, although there were variations, from monthly (one in 12; 8.5 per cent) to every three months (one in three; 32.5 per cent) and annually, (one in 14; 7 per cent). Significantly, the safety representative at Lothian Health Board remarked that staff shortages had led to inspections being cancelled due to 'exigencies of the service'.

HEALTH & SAFETY

HEALTH & SAFETY REPRESENTATIVE REPORT FORM – HS2

Date report submitted	Brief description of problem	Reply: Action taken or proposed (with date) or reason Management consider no action necessary.
Name of Safety Representative		
Name of Manager to whom submitted		

Instructions

1. **Safety Rep** fills in date, names, description.
   Safety Rep gives top two copies to **Manager**.
   Safety Rep and **Manager** agree time allowed for reply.
   Safety Rep retains 3rd copy for record, with note of time agreed for reply.

2. **Management** are asked to reply within agreed time.
   Management fill in reply section and return top copy to **Safety Rep**.
   Management keep 2nd copy for their record.
   Safety Rep should chase up reply.

Union of Shop, Distributive and Allied Workers
188 Wilmslow Road, Manchester M14 6LJ.

FIGURE 2.8   A typical safety rep's report form

Routine, and reactive, inspections of any workplace are a very important aspect of any organization's health and safety policy, and it is difficult to see how management can fulfil its legal obligations under the 1974 Act and The Management of Health and Safety at Work Regulations 1992 – not to mention the 1977 SRSC Regs – if this is not done. The value of 'another pair of eyes', such as the safety representative, during such inspections is well recognized and employers who fail to take advantage of this opportunity are missing a great chance for workplace health and safety prevention. And, of course, where they fail to meet the minimum legal requirements – as in the case of the Lothian Health Board – they are breaking the criminal law and leaving themselves liable to enforcement action.

The 'brown book' gives two examples of report forms that a safety representative might use to inform management: (a) an inspection report from and (b) a form to 'notify to the employer, or his representative, unsafe and unhealthy conditions and working practices and unsatisfactory arrangements for welfare at work, (pp. 29–30). Many unions have produced their own version of these report forms (see pages 90 and 92). In both types of report, the HSE suggests that the following words are included: 'This report/record does not imply that the conditions are safe and healthy or that the arrangements for welfare at work are satisfactory in all other respects' (pp. 29–30).

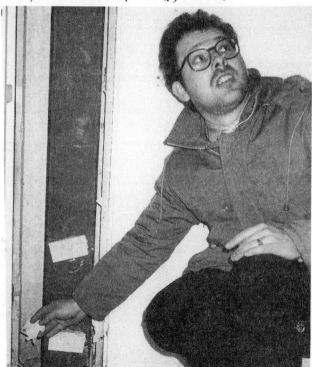

FIGURE 2.9   A school safety rep finds exposed asbestos on a routine inspection

HEALTH AND SAFETY

SAFETY REPRESENTATIVE'S INSPECTION REPORT FORM

ipms

Date and time of inspection	What is the hazard and where did it occur?	Safety rep's name	Remedial action taken (with date) or explanation if not taken. This information to be relayed to the safety representative(s).

Signature(s) of safety representative(s) _____

Record of receipt of form by the employer (or his/her representative) _____ Date _____

This report does not imply that the conditions are safe and healthy of that the arrangements for welfare at work are satisfactory in all other respects.

Signature of employer or his/her representative _____

Date _____

FIGURE 2.10   A typical safety rep's inspection form

Facilities

The 'brown book' only talks about the employer providing facilities to the safety representative for the three-monthly routine inspections. However, this requirement has been strengthened by the requirement in The Management of Health and Safety at Work Regulations 1992 which require the employer to 'provide such facilities and assistance as safety representatives may reasonably require for the purposes of carrying out their functions' (p. 19). Although no further details are given, both the 1984 and 1993 surveys have shown that most employers are not mean in this respect. Thus, the 1993 LRD survey revealed that most safety representatives are provided by the employer with the following facilities:

○ a room and desk at the workplace (71 per cent)
○ facilities for storing letters and reports (83 per cent)
○ ready access to a telephone (95 per cent)
○ access to typing and copying facilities (89 per cent)
○ use of internal mailing system (85 per cent)
○ time off with pay to meet other safety representatives (73 per cent)

In addition, a number of safety representatives had access to a fax machine, and other facilities mentioned included the following.

○ Dairy Crest: a computer and external mailing facilities.
○ Lothian Health Board: noise-monitoring equipment.
○ Royal Mail and BT: stationery.
○ Department of National Savings: a television.
○ Fife Regional Council: a vehicle for carrying out inspections on a very large site.
○ Davis Engineering, Coventry District Health Authority and Birmingham Health Service (from the 1984 survey): a camera for recording accidents, dangerous machinery and dangerous workplaces etc.

Safety committees

Although the regulations are called the 1977 Safety Representative and Safety Committee Regulations, what they say (Regulation 9) about safety committees is far less than that about safety representatives and very simple:

○ One shall be established by the employer if two or more safety representatives request one in writing, within three months of the written request.
○ The employer shall consult with safety representatives and trade unions as to how the committee shall function.
○ A notice shall be posted where it can be easily read by employees, stating the composition of the committee and the areas to be covered by it.

There is nothing in the 1977 SRSC Code of Practice about safety committees, but there are extensive Guidance Notes (25 paragraphs) on the terms of reference of committees, objectives, functions, membership, conduct and so on. The absence of more material on safety committees reflects, to some degree, a commonly held view (at least among trade unionists) that in the past, before the 1974 Act, safety committees were often used by management as 'tea and bun' talking shops to ensure that there was little real action on health and safety issues. When I was teaching on safety representative and management courses, it was common for safety representatives to bring in the past several years' safety committee minutes and the same, sometimes serious, items would appear time and time again.

It was somewhat surprising, then, that when I surveyed 400 workplaces in 1984, three out of four (314 or 78.5 per cent) had a safety committee. Even more surprisingly, almost three in four (225, or 72 per cent) of those who did have a safety committee said that it was effective in that 'it got things done'. However there were some notable exceptions even in 1984, when the safety representatives said that the safety committee was ineffective and they used more direct methods to get results. But, by the time of the 1993 LRD survey, things had clearly taken a turn for the worse. Although safety committees had been established in nearly all (86 per cent) of the 83 workplaces surveyed, almost one in three (31 per cent) of the safety representatives said that the safety committee did not work satisfactorily. The most common complaints appeared to be that the safety committee did not meet very often and that there were too many managers on the committee and/or they dominated the committee. The 1977 SRSC Guidance states clearly, 'The number of management representatives should not exceed the number of employees' representatives' (Paragraph 9). However, it was not all doom and gloom, as the safety representative from Fife Regional Council Water/Drainage Division remarked, 'The safety committee has set up a COSHH monitoring panel, consisting of two safety reps and two managers, and an accident sub-committee, which again consists of two managers.'

In 1990 the main employers' organization, the CBI, published a booklet, *Developing a Safety Culture*, that surveyed 'safety culture' in around 250 companies. It concluded that 'Safety committees which are required by law when requested by recognised trade unions are used extensively' (p. 36). Finally, the 1996 British Standard on *Occupational Health and Safety Management Systems* notes that 'Health and Safety committees provide one way of involving the workforce.'

Safety committees and occupational health staff

The position of the company doctor, nurse, safety officer and engineer, occupational hygienist etc. is not always an easy one, as the following case study will show. The names have been changed.

CASE STUDY 11: THE DOCTOR'S DILEMMA

Killing and cleaning turkeys and chickens for the dinner table is an unpleasant job. The workers suffer from a high rate of RSI and chest diseases (e.g. asthma) from the dust and droppings of the birds. They suffer from infections caught from the poultry and/or the microbiological spores in the air, and after from the stress of killing live creatures on a mass slaughter basis. In addition, the work is often wet, cold and dirty, low paid and involves long hours.

I was approached by the safety representative of a large plant and she showed me the results of a dust survey carried out by a university some six months before. The recorded dust levels were high and would clearly lead to cases of asthma. But the employees were frightened that they might lose their jobs and were afraid to push for the recommendations of the report to be implemented. I wrote to the well-respected occupational hygienist, asking him if he had done anything about the report and, in view of its seriousness, if he thought that his professional ethics required him to inform the HSE. He was not apologetic, he did not feel responsible, and, yes, if they had paid him he would have liked to have carried out a follow-up survey.

Some months later the company doctor resigned in disgust at the lack of care shown by the company for its employees. The doctor sent the union a copy of her resignation letter, which was very revealing. One the basis of this letter and the above report we were able to call in the HSE to carry out further medical and hygiene tests and enforce some health and safety law at the plant. But this case study does show the weak position of independent advisers, and even company doctors and nurses, if top management does not care.

The SRSC Regs 1997 Guidance, paragraph 11, suggest that 'In undertakings where a company doctor, nurse, occupational hygienist or safety officer/adviser is employed, they should be ex-officio members of the safety committee. Other company specialists, such as project engineers, chemists, organisation and methods staff and training officers might be co-opted for particular meetings when subjects on which they have expertise are to be discussed.'

In 1988 I conducted a survey[43] of safety representatives in nearly 500 safety workplaces and their views and experiences of occupational health staff (OHS), such as those mentioned in the guidance, paragraph 11 (but including first aiders, fire officers and safety engineers). Over half the respondents thought that the OHS worked for the benefit of the company and not the staff. This is not a view confined to trade unionists. A very detailed House of Lords enquiry into occupational health staff (House of Lords, 1983), when considering the fact that, 'trade unions and employees sometimes suspect occupational health services of being too closely aligned with management and not impartial' went on to recommend that, 'a great opportunity be offered to trade unions and employees to joining the management committees of occupational health service' (para. 8.44, p. 43). They were not alone; a leading occupational health doctor, Dr Cotes of the University of Newcastle, commenting on these problems in the *Journal of the Royal College of Physicians* in 1988, concluded that 'Health auditors and providers of occupational health services might be elected jointly by management and employees. In this way they would be identified with health, not with management interests within the company.'

In about half of the 500 workplaces surveyed there was *some* accountability to the joint management–union safety committee (Dalton, 1995) and there was a variety of companies where safety representatives had some say in OHS staff concerning appointment, what they do, the types of reports they give, and action taken or not taken.

The following list incorporates the CBI conclusions (CBI, *Developing a Safety Culture*, 1990) and a survey of 56 workplace safety committees (Beaumont, P. B. *et al.*, *The Determinants of Effective Joint Health and Safety Committees*, Glasgow University, 1990) that, although a bit long in the tooth, remains valid to this day (it is also the only specific published survey on safety committees that I am aware of).

O The committee must meet regularly.

O It must be seen to be a 'virile part of the safety organization'.

O In large workplaces (over 500 employees) there should be smaller departmental safety committees, co-ordinated by a central safety committee.

O If health and safety committees have endless agendas, then the fault lies in management organization, not in the committee. Each member of the committee should have an equal chance to contribute items to the agenda.

O While there is no clear optimum size, the general agreement was that the committees should be as compact as possible (5–12 members seems to work best).

O It is crucial that a senior manager is present on the committee.

O The most effective committees tend to be those which have relatively well-trained personnel on both management and employee sides.

O The health and safety officer's role in the committee should be an ex-officio advisory one.

O On the employee side of the committee there must be an agreed balance of representation between different trade unions in the organization and different working areas.

O In general, representation on the committee operates most smoothly through established union channels.

O It is important that all members of the committee are committed to the objectives of improving the organization's health and safety and see the committee as contributing to this end.

O Regularity of attendance at the committee is important for continuity and to show that members regard health and safety as a priority.

○ It is important to establish a two-way flow of information between the workforce and the health and safety committee. The results should be publicized (e.g. circular, notice board).

There have been several IT decisions on safety committees of interest:

○ Barclays Bank refused to set up a safety committee and was served an improvement notice, requiring it to do so within three months, by the local council EHO (LRD, *Health and Safety Law*, 1995).

○ NALGO (now UNISON) at the London Borough of Haringey had 66 safety representatives in 46 different locations and wanted a pre-safety committee meeting, without management present, to co-ordinate their efforts and discuss their views on safety committee agenda items. Management refused and the safety representatives took their complaint to an IT. The IT found their complaint to be 'well founded' and subsequent negotiation resulted in the union-only health and safety committee meeting once a month for three hours. (IT 1101-1109/82)

Victimization

For many years, trade union safety representatives, like other trade union officials, have been protected from victimization for their actions from the start of their appointment. An employee has to have two years of employment to qualify for legal protection against victimization or unfair dismissal. It is true to say that mot cases of victimization are dealt with by management–union negotiations, sometimes with the help of the union full-time officer.

Despite this – and especially in the current climate of recession and unemployment, short-term and casual contracts etc. – there have always been many accusations by trade union safety representatives of employer victimization when they have tried to do their job. Indeed, over the past 20 years, I have often been involved in backing safety representatives who have been victimized, with supporting technical evidence, at industrial tribunals, writing letters to the chair of the HSC/HSE, arranging media attention and on picket lines. Sometimes we have won, but more often we have lost and the safety representative has remained sacked, albeit with some small financial compensation on occasions.

In the early 1990s this all came to a head with some notable victimization of safety representatives, especially offshore in the North Sea oilfields. Under some public pressure and after debates in both Houses of Parliament on this issue, the government brought in the Offshore Safety (Protection Against Victimisation) Act 1992. Then, in 1993, they widened this protection to all workplaces in the Trade Union Reform and Employment Rights Act 1993, which was consolidated into the Employment Rights Act 1996 (ERA 1996). The ERA 1996 introduced protection not just for trade union safety representatives, but for any employees who take action or raise concerns about health and safety at work and are victimized. Unlike most

FIGURE 2.11   A successful strike to protect a trade union safety representative during the 1980s

unfair dismissal rights, for which two years of work are needed to qualify, health and safety rights are valid from the first day and apply to part-time employees too.

Employees, and safety representatives, who are victimized in any way, selected for early redundancy or dismissed can now take a case to an industrial tribunal regardless of length of service, hours of work or age, if the dismissal is due to:

O carrying out (or proposing to carry out) any health and safety activities for which they are designated by their employers
O performing (or proposing to perform) any functions as an official or recognized safety representative or committee member
O bringing to their employer's attention, by reasonable means in the absence of a representative or committee who could do so on their behalf, a reasonable health and safety concern
O leaving (or proposing to leave) the workplace or any dangerous parts of it in the event of danger which they reasonably believed to be serious and imminent and which they could not reasonably be expected to avert, or (while the danger persisted) refusing to return

○   in the circumstances of danger which they reasonably believed to be serious and imminent, taking (or proposing to take) appropriate steps to protect themselves from the danger

The employee, or safety representative, claiming a victimization or dismissal for health and safety activities must present their claim to a IT within three months of the original action. One big flaw in the law, and this is true for all unfair dismissal law, is that the IT *cannot enforce job reinstatement; it can only recommend it.* However, if an IT does recommend reinstatement, and the employer refuses, then the monetary compensation awarded to the victimized employee will be higher. In addition to compensation, when the IT finds that a complaint is 'well founded', it shall make a declaration to that effect. The resultant publicity in the media and to other employees may also harm the organization.

    There have been several interesting cases, using these laws:

○   In November 1994 a whistleblower, Bob Nortcliff, accepted an out-of-court settlement of £20,000 just before he was due to appear before an IT claiming unfair dismissal against his old employers, the drilling company Nabors. Mr Nortcliff was a drilling supervisor on the Elf-operated platform Piper Bravo. He had been with the platform from its origins, when it was still in the shipyard in 1991. By 1993 he was complaining to management about health and safety issues and, after nothing was done, he complained to the HSE in early 1994 and went public on these issues. In March 1994 an HSE investigation confirmed all his four detailed complaints, but no legal action was taken. Four months later Mr Nortcliff was sacked. (*Health and Safety at Work Magazine*, December 1994 and *Blowout 41*, Oil Industry Liaison Committee, OILC, Oct./Nov., 1994).

○   Francis McKenna had been a joiner with Marshall Construction Ltd, Alloa, Scotland for five years. In April 1992 he turned up for a job and was, in his words, 'given a bundle of scaffolding, with no expertise and no training and told to erect a tower scaffolding over 5m in height'. He refused and was sacked. The IT, after hearing evidence from the management, commented, 'We say immediately that we preferred his (Mr McKenna's) evidence.' The IT noted that the manager made no enquiries as to the complaint, gave no disciplinary hearing or interview and simply sacked him. With the help of his union, UCATT, Mr McKenna was awarded £11,417.50 for unfair dismissal in October 1994. (IT S/2590/92).

○   Thirty-year-old Mathew Harris, a timber frame worker, had worked for Select Timber Frame Ltd, Basingstoke, for seven years. In July 1993 he made a complaint to management about health and safety conditions at the factory, in particular with regard to the use of the pesticide Lindane, which was on the wet wood he was working with, without ventilation. He claimed that it caused him to suffer from mood swings, nausea and shaking. He even showed the firm a documentary video on the health effects of wood preservatives. On 1

September 1993 an HSE inspector arrived to inspect the workplace and arranged for a doctor from the HSE to examine Mr Harris. On 24 September 1993, Mr Harris was sacked. Supported by his union, UCATT, Mr Harris took his case to an IT. The IT concluded: 'We are driven to the conclusion that the dismissal was prompted by the complaints over health and safety ... We are firmly of the view, having heard the evidence, that it was the forthcoming medical examination, coupled as it was with the possible threat of litigation, which, prompted the dismissal.' In the first ever case of the new 'whistle-blowing' laws, the Trade Union Reform and Employment Rights Act 1993, Mathew Harris was awarded £8760 compensation in March 1994. (IT 59214/93)

○   During the RMT union's signal workers dispute in 1994, the train drivers' union, ASLEF, told its members that they could not be sacked for refusing to drive a train if they believed they were in 'serious or imminent danger' (the TURER Act 1993 wording). British Rail agreed that this advice was correct. (TUC, *The Future of Workplace Safety Reps,* 1995).

○   In mid-January 1994 labourers working for subcontractor Bomac Construction, on the refurbishment of St John's Hospital, South London, stopped work when they were told to work on a substance they believed to be asbestos. They were sacked. Being members of the building workers union, UCATT, they sat in the canteen and called their full-time officer, Mick Cummins. He told them that they were protected in law, under the TURER Act 1993, and tried to speak to Bomac Construction. This company refused to speak to him, so he went to the main contractor, Ruddy Construction, who insisted that the labourers be reinstated, with no loss of earnings. During the next few weeks UCATT received 50 new applications for memberships from other workers on the site. (*Hazards*, 46, page 3, 1994).

○   In 1997, an EAT found that a safety rep could take action, providing s/he was performing the functions of a safety rep acknowledged by the employer, without victimization, even if the safety rep intended to embarrass the company or s/he performed her/his functions in an unreasonable way. (Shillito v. Van Leer (UK), *Industrial Relations Law Report*, 455, 1997).

Enforcement

In the preface to the 1988 'new' edition of the 'brown book' (the 1977 SRSC Regulations, Code of Practice and Guidance) the HSC made it quite clear that:

> Disagreements which might arise between employers and trade unions on the issues should be settled through the normal machinery for resolving industrial relations problems. There are two circumstances in which safety representatives may present a complaint to a tribunal – if employers have failed to allow time off or failed to pay safety representatives while carrying out their functions or undergoing training.

This not quite as informative, or definite, as the guidance issues to enforcement officers (HSE and EHO) when the 1977 SRSC Regs first became law in October 1978. There, the HSE listed five problem areas that may require enforcement action:

1. Where the safety representative is not in a recognized trade union, enquiries should be directed 'firmly' towards the Advisory Conciliation and Arbitration Service (ACAS).
2. Where an employer refuses to recognize a legitimate safety representative, an inspector will need to consider enforcement action under Section 2 of the 1974 Health and Safety at Work Act.
3. Where the employer refuses to give time off with pay, either for duties or training, the appropriate course of action is a complaint to an IT.
4. An employer refuses to give health and safety information or facilities. If the complaint is justified, the serving of an improvement notice may be appropriate.
5. The employer refuses to set up a safety committee following a request by two, or more, safety representatives to do so. In this case it may be appropriate to issue an enforcement notice, requiring a committee to be established, or, as a last resort, to prosecute the employer for failing to carry out her or his duties.

In fact, in 20 years there has been very little enforcement action, by either HSE or EHO inspectors, on the provisions of the 1977 SRSC Regs. It is not clear why this should be the case, except that safety representative surveys have shown a wide ignorance of the role of the HSE and EHO in 'traditional' health and safety issues, let alone those that have an 'industrial relations' element. Of course, the same is true for enforcement officers who, if they are trained at all in health and safety (and many EHOs are not), will have had a training on the 'nuts and bolts' of health and safety and the law, but nothing, or very little, on the industrial relations-type issues that the 1977 SRSC Regs raise.

In general, the majority of the safety representatives who responded to my 1994–95 survey were unaware of the HSE/EHO. The minority who had an opinion were divided upon their value. Many found them useful for advice, especially on the telephone. However, quite a few mentioned that they were very busy and, or understaffed and consequently never had time to follow anything up properly. Others thought that the HSE, in particular, was only concerned with 'high-risk' organizations (e.g. chemical companies and construction) and was not very interested, or active, in areas such as hospitals, education, local councils and offices (mainly covered by EHOs in any case).

There were quite a few complaints that the HSE/EHO did not inform the safety representative when it was on the premises or carrying out a survey (this is not a legal requirement) and some others said they never even received copies of their letters etc. to management (this is a legal requirement). Some thought that the HSE/EHO were without value. Below is a sample selection of comments from my 1994–95 survey:

O 'Because EHO visits are far and few, when they do visit it is for the shortest time possible and they never request to see safety reps for their opinion. Thus management never inform us of their visit' (Leslie Whiteside, United Road Transport Union (URTU) safety representative, Lo-Cost Stores, Salford).

O 'Both times I have called the HSE they have come promptly, but due to their shortage of staff they have not always followed up the smaller details' (Sue Brooks, UNISON Safety representative, the London Borough of Hillingdon).

O 'The HSE are useful in giving weight to getting problems solved, after all other means have suffered delaying tactics' (Alan Footer, UNISON safety representative, St Edmund Arrowsmith RC High School, Ashton-in-Makerfield).

O 'The HSE are too overworked to be effective in a "low risk" premises such as an office – only seem to act when there is a major incident' (David G. Martin, UNISON safety representative, Borough of Merton).

O 'Useful as a backstop or threat. I've threatened building owners (not my employers) with the fire authority a few times: they take me and my Department seriously now!' (National Union of Civil and Public Servants (NUCPS), safety representative in a Water Authority).

O 'Very useful, like the HSE Inspector who wrote to us recently saying, "I refer to my recent visit to the factory at Brough when I met you and a number of your colleagues for a discussion of matters arising. This formed the basis for my inspection of a section of the site and I enclose a copy of the appendix which I have sent to the company containing a summary of the matters which now require the company's attention"' (Vincent Ponari, GMB TU Chair (all unions), British Aerospace, Brough, North Humberside).

O 'The HSE are of no use. I sent a draft of our new h&s procedures to them for their comments, marked it urgent, enclose an SAE and even phoned them. No response' (Mark Burlingham UCATT safety representative, Aerostructures Hamble Ltd, Hants).

O 'My local EHO is extremely helpful, but has been warned, "from the very highest level" to take a softly softly approach to the new 6-pack legislation. Since it is too early to have produced any test cases she feels very frustrated in her attempts to use this legislation effectively' (Joe Merrell, USDAW safety representative, Sainsbury's, West Sussex).

O 'The HSE are useful by issuing Improvement Notices and, when they investigate an accident, we can use their reports as a threat to management' (MSF safety representative, Lancaster University).

O 'HSE are understaffed and limited in their ability to visit farms and nurseries' (P. J. de Vries, TGWU safety representative, Horticulture Research Institute, Hants).

O 'We have just had a visit from the HSE. He took time to talk to me and listen to our side of the story. He appeared to be most helpful and interested, management appeared concerned' (Shaun Clarkson, GMB safety representative, AKZO/Nobel Coatings plc, Hull).

○ 'I think the HSE are the lackeys of the Tory government' (J. Graice, UCATT safety representative, Glasgow District Council).

○ 'The HSE are only interested in hazardous chemicals (e.g. cleaning agents). They are not interested in understaffing, stress, overcrowding or electrical safety. They did not notify the safety rep about their visit and there was no opportunity to talk to the HSE inspector' (Aird Hamilton, UNISON safety representative Kyle and Carrick District Council).

○ 'I am very impressed with out local HSE office. On the 6th December 1994, they issued two Improvement Notices (INs) on the council that were to be complied with by the 1st February 1995. One required a revised Safety Policy, and the other required "effective planning, organisation, control, monitoring and review of the preventative and protective measures", under Regulation 4 of the Management of Health and Safety at Work Regulations 1992 [see page 104]. Sylvia Dean, Acting Chief Executive for Tower Hamlets Council told the HSE, "I can assure you that the Authority views the current situation with the utmost concern ... (we will) ... Give the maximum priority to the preparation of a Borough-wide safety policy together with the development of suitable structures for ensuring delivery of health and safety throughout the Borough"' (Ian Cochran, UNISON, safety representative, London Borough of Tower Hamlets).

Safety representative agreements

Because of the complexity of the 1977 SRSC Regs, quite a few employers and unions have written agreements over the terms and conditions of safety representatives. Quite often this agreement will form part of the organization's safety policy. However, the HSC, in its preface to the 1988 second edition of the 'brown book', states:

> The Regulations and Code of Practice provide a legal framework for employers and trade unions to reach agreements for safety representatives and safety committees to operate at their workplace. There is nothing to stop employers and employees agreeing to alternative arrangements for joint consultation on health and safety at work. But such arrangements cannot detract from the rights and obligations created by the Regulations. Recognised trade unions can at any time invoke the rights given by the Regulations and the obligations on the employer would then apply.

There are various 'model' agreements in existence, and many trade unions have examples, a recent one being that negotiated in 1992 between Bristol City Council and NALGO (now UNISON). The main points of this are as follows:

○ Safety representatives are to be fully informed and consulted on any proposed substantial changes to the workplace or equipment.

○ In the case of an accident, dangerous occurrence, near-miss or hazard, the safety representative will be informed immediately by the relevant manager and 'will be entitled to leave their work to inspect the situation. Until this

HEALTH AND SAFETY EXECUTIVE
Health and Safety at Work etc. Act 1974, Sections 21, 22, 23 and 24

Schedule

Serial No. I/Px 05/02/GJH/061294/02

To comply with this Notice you should comply with the Approved Code of Practice relating to Regulation 4 of the Management of Health and Safety at Work Regulations 1992 which is set out below.

This regulation in effect requires employers to have arrangements in place to cover health and safety. It should be integrated with the management system for all other purposes. the system in place will depend on the size and nature of the activities of the undertaking but generally will include the following elements which are typical of any other management function:

(a) Planning: Adopting a systematic approach which indentifies priorities and sets objectives. Wherever possible, risks are eliminated by the careful selection and design of facilities, equipment and processes or minimised by the use of physical control measures;

(b) Organisation: Putting in place the necessary structure with the aim of ensuring that there is progressive improvement in health and safety performance;

(c) Control: Ensuring that the decisions for ensuring and promoting health and safety are being implemented as planned;

(d) Monitoring and review: Like quality, progressive improvement in health and safety can only be achieved through the constant development of policies, approaches to implementation and techniques of risk control.

The Regulation also provides that undertakings with five or more employees should record their arrangements for health and safety. The arrangements recorded should include a list of those competent persons appointed under Regulation 6. As with the risk assessment, this record could form part of the same document containing the health and safety policy required under Section 2(3) of the Health and Safety at Work Act.

Note: The risk assessment covered by Regulation 3 of the Management of Health and Safety at Work Regulations 1992 is not subject to Improvement Notice action at this time.

FIGURE 2.12   Schedule to an Improvement Notice served by the HSE on the London Borough of Tower Hamlets, under the Management of Health and Safety at Work Regulations 1992, Regulation 4 on 6.12.1994 – to be completed by 1.2.1995

inspection has taken place nothing will be removed unless it constitutes a hazard.'

O 'Safety representatives will have the right to stop a dangerous working practice if they believe that there is a serious risk of injury (to her/himself, other employees or members of the public). No action will be taken against a safety rep exercising this right.'

O Appropriate mileage rates or bus fares will be provided by management for safety representatives representing members at more than one location.

O The safety representatives can request the assistance of 'an independent adviser appointed by the trade union or other trade union official. However … it is accepted that the involvement of external advisers will normally be by prior arrangement with management to whom copies of any findings will be supplied without delay.'

O Safety representatives will, 'where reasonably practicable', be informed immediately of an inspector on the premises and, at the discretion of an inspector, 'be entitled to tour her/his constituency with the inspector and communicate privately with the inspector.'

Commenting on this agreement, Peter Fryer, UNISON safety representative and chair of the joint union health and safety committee, said 'We are quite pleased with the new agreement. It improves the speed at which we can get things done. Senior directors now sit on the committee and, if nothing is done, you can go right to the top.'

Safety representatives and the environment

We have seen before (page 71) that the trade unions' involvement in environmental issues is far less than in health and safety. The SRSC 1977 give no rights on environmental issues. However, some unions, such as the TGWU, have a policy that all 'health and safety representatives' should be 'environmental representatives' as well. In a slowly increasing number of workplaces, more progressive managements are involving the unions in workplace environmental inspections and audits. Such arrangements could be incorporated into an agreement, such as that above. But we really wait for more specific regulations, rights and training before a trade union 'health and safety representative' will become a fully active and pollution-reducing, 'safety, health and environment representative'.

WORKPLACE HEALTH AND SAFETY REPRESENTATION WHERE THERE IS NO UNION

Until late 1996, in workplaces where there was no trade union, or where the employer refused to recognize a trade union (even if *all* the employees want a union, the employer is not obliged to recognize one), there was little that could be done. Of course, every employee, whether in a trade union or not, is protected by the 1974 Health and Safety at Work Act, and associated regulations. All employees have the right to call in an HSE or EHO inspector and complain about their working conditions, anonymously or otherwise.

In agriculture alone, where very few farmers recognize trade unions, the TGWU, with the aid of a small EU grant, has just run a pilot 'roving safety representative scheme'. Although praised by Tory ministers and even Frank Davies, chair of the Health and Safety Commission, with no real funding, no right of paid time off, very little back-up and no right of access to farms, not too much should be expected of such a scheme. The idea of 'roving safety representatives', that is ones who inspect workplaces other than their own, has worked very well in Sweden. Clearly, for the growing number of small and medium-sized enterprises and in the high-risk areas of agriculture and construction, they represent the best way forward, and the HSE-funded evaluation of the roving safety representative[44] must be used to carry out further, properly funded and supported, action in this important area.

However, in October 1996, the Conservative government was forced, by a European directive, to bring in *some* representation for employees with no trade union safety representative. The new regulations are known as the Health and Safety (Consultation with Employee) Regulations 1996, or HSCER 1996 for short. What follows is a brief summary of the main points of HSCER 1996. The HSC has produced a useful free leaflet[45] on these regulations, but for anyone really interested in these regulations the much more detailed HSE guidance[46] is invaluable.

There is a general feeling, among health and safety professionals (and trade unionists), that these regulations will make little impact on the improvement of workplace health and safety, for two main reasons:

1. The employer can either
    (a) 'consult directly with employees' (which she or he was always supposed to do under the 1974 Act anyway), or
    (b) arrange independent elections from the employees for the election of a 'delegate of employee safety'. Why should most employers want to do anything other than (a), which is what they have always done (or should have done)? Therefore, it is felt that nothing will really change in the majority of workplaces where there are no safety representatives.
2. Even if the employer *does* arrange for the election of a 'representative of employee safety', they will have much reduced powers, as compared with a trade union safety representative: no rights of workplace inspection; no rights to investigate accidents and incidents; a much reduced training; and, perhaps most important of all, no back-up from a national organization like a trade union.

We shall have to wait and see. The HSCER 1996 regulations require that an employer consult with employees and the HSE guidance to the regulations spells out what is meant by 'consultation':

> The difference between providing information to your employees and consulting with them, which the HSCER 1996 requires, is that consultation involves listening to their views and taking account of what they say before any decision is taken. (HSE Guidance, paragraph 7).

Regulation 3 of HSCER 1996 details what health and safety issues the employer should consult the employees or the 'representative of employee safety' on:

○ the introduction of any measure at the workplace which may substantially affect the health and safety of those employees
○ the arrangements for appointing or nominating a 'competent person' as required by the Management of Health and Safety Regulations 1993
○ any health and safety information the employer is required by law to provide to employees
○ the planning and organization of any health and safety training the employer is required to give by law
○ the health and safety consequences of any new technology the employer plans to bring into the workplace.

As with trade union safety representatives, and indeed any employees (page 97), there should be no victimization of any employee or 'delegate of employee safety':

> None of your employees must suffer any detriment because of anything reasonable they do, or propose to do, in connection with consultation on health and safety matters. If you penalise an employee (for example, by denying them promotion or opportunities for extra earnings) or dismiss them for such a reason, they could complain to a tribunal. (HSE Guidance, paragraph 30)

This protection applies to *all* employees, regardless of the length of time they have been with the company. Delegates of employee safety can also complain to an IT if they feel that their training is insufficient. All complaints to an IT should be made within three months of the incident complained of. The HSE or EHO enforces the HSCER 1996 regulations, and complaints, or enquiries about the regulations, should be made to them.

INVOLVING COMMUNITIES IN WORKPLACE SHE ISSUES

Over twenty years ago there was an explosion at a Laporte Chemical plant in East London, and one worker was killed. I investigated the explosion and wrote a brief news item on it for the *New Scientist* magazine. I can still remember attending a meeting one evening, in a large church hall, of the concerned residents who lived around the plant, the workers at the plant and the management, and enforcement (HSE/EHO) authorities and local politicians (councillors, MP and MEPs). An assortment of ragged and noisy children ran in and out of the hall. As usual, the people who worked inside and lived around the plant sat in the body of the hall, whilst the experts, managers and local politicians sat, raised above them on the platform. The local community was divided. Those who lived around the plant were frightened – those who worked in the plant were frightened too; they thought the plant might close down. No reasonable debate took place, no useful information was imparted and the experts, managers and politicians 'won' easily. This scenario is still quite common whenever a community raises reasonable questions about the safety, health or environmental hazards of a workplace. The workforce feel defensive. However, as the case study on cement kiln hazards (page 20) shows, change is in the air. Slowly, trade unions and employers are realizing that the communities around workplaces have a legitimate right to a say in the SHE hazards at that site.

Of course, around most hazardous sites there have been for many years 'community–factory liaison committees' and many of the better workplaces hold 'open days' and similar events to inform and reassure the local community. But, with the direct environmental action of the 1990s, backed up with the information rights of the 1990 Environmental Protection Act, many communities around hazardous workplaces are demanding more than bland reassurance and public relations exercises.

Communities Against Toxic Sites (CATS) have formed a UK network; they have a regular, and very informative, bulletin and hold seminars for themselves, with local authorities and with some of the world's experts on the problem industries. Having recently experienced the very knowledgeable critiques of the highly technical debate around burning toxic waste in cement kilns (see case study 4, page 20) I know that some of the communities of today are well informed. It is clear that the local community is an important 'stakeholder' (see page 47) if the SHE debate. One requirement of the joint trade union proposals on controlling the SHE issues associated with burning toxic waste in cement kilns was the need for effective and open 'local community liaison meetings', around each cement kiln community, with the local community, management, trade unions and enforcement authorities.

Of course, this is not limited to the UK. Communities, often as 'indigenous peoples', are waking up to their rights and responsibilities all over the world. Mitchell (1997) reviews the value of, 'local knowledge for resource and environmental management' worldwide.

It is not just the local communities around workplaces with potential SHE hazards that are organizing to fight and control SHE hazards. The last ten years or so have seen the rise of 'victim support groups' for those with SHE-related ill-health problems. People with an asbestos-related disease formed one of the first groups with Nancy Tait's SPAID – the Society for Prevention of Asbestosis and other

FIGURE 2.13   The Construction Safety Campaign have done more in the past ten years to draw attention to site safety and health hazards than any number of HSE committees and, sadly, the trade unions

Industrial Diseases – and this has been joined by the very active, and more militant, Clydeside Action on Asbestos and other asbestos victim support groups. The 1980s saw the growth of RSI support groups, with national associations and bulletins. Those exposed to pesticides have two main groups: the Pesticide Exposure Group of Sufferers (PEGS), and the Organophosphate Network. The terrible suffering, but amazing campaigning, of Ann Elvin (Elvin, 1995) led to the formation of the Relatives Support Group for those whose relatives, or friends, had been killed or seriously maimed at the workplace.

Most of these groups exist on a shoestring and with the voluntary effort of those whose lives have already been damaged. All need further financial support and help. There, are of course others – there are some smaller groups associated with 'hazards centres' and 'occupational health projects', for example – and there are overlaps with other support groups, for the victims of violent crime, including workplace crime, workplace bullying and so on. A local Citizen's Advice Bureau will usually know of any such group in your area, or nationally, and failing that, *Hazards* magazine[47] regularly updates its list of the active 'self-help' groups on workplace SHE issues.

NOTES

1. A. J. P. Dalton (1995) *Hazards*, **52**, 8–9.
2. Health and Safety Executive (1991) *Successful Health and Safety Management*, HSE, HMSO, HS(G)65 (p. 20–1) It is well summarized in the free HSE booklet, *Five Steps to Successful Health and Safety Management*, IND(G)123L.
3. Jenny Bacon (1977) Letter to the author, Ref DG/129/27, 11 June.
4. Ann Ridley and Louise Dunford (1977) Corporate killing – legislating for unlawful death? *Industrial Law Journal*, **26**, 99–113.
5. A. J. P. Dalton (1977) *Turn Left at Land's End – Walking, Talking and Thinking in Cornwall*, Red Boots Publications, 3 Montpelier Grove, London NW5 2XD.
6. Most of this case study is written up in the regular, and excellent, bulletins of Partizans, 41a Thornhill Square, London N1 1BE.
7. John Rimington (1995) *Valedictory Summary of Industrial Health and Safety since the 1974 Act*, London: The Electricity Association.
8. Jenny Bacon (1996) *Health and Safety Priorities*, NRPB Chilton Seminar, 28 June (available from HSE press office).
9. Health and Safety Executive (1997) *Health and Safety in Small Firms*, London: HSE Books.
10. John Locke (1981) The politics of health and safety, *Protection*, July, pp. 8–9.
11. Redgrave's (1976) *Health and Safety in Factories*, London: Butterworth.
12. John Hendy and Michael Ford (1993) *Redgrave, Fife and Machin Health and Safety*, London: Butterworths.
13. Roger Bate (ed.) (1997) *What Risk?*, London: Butterworth–Heinemann.
14. Anon. (1996) Risk: a suitable case for analysis? *Nature*, 7 March, 1, 10–14; Arrow, K. J. *et al.* (1996) Is there a role for benefit-cost analysis in environmental, health and safety regulation? *Science*, **272**, 221–2. J .D. Graham and J. K. Hartwell (1997) *The Greening of Industry: a Risk Management Approach*, London: Harvard University Press.
15. The Presidential/Congressional Commission on Risk Assessment and Risk Management (1997) *Risk Assessment and Risk Management in Regulatory Decision-Making*, 2 volumes, Washington, DC.
16. Ellen K. Silbergeld (1997) *The Limitations of Risk Assessment in Decision Making*, RoSPA Conference Reprints, Boreham Wood: Paramount Publishing Ltd, p. 1.
17. Department of the Environment (1997) The Wider Costs and Benefits of Environmental Policy – a discussion paper. Department of the Environment, February.
18. DoE rediscovers business benefits of environmental policy (1997) *ENDS Report* 266, 22–5.
19. Costs and Benefits of Occupational Safety and Health (1997) Conference: 28–30 May; Conference Secretariat, c/o Holland Organizing Centre, Eisenhowerlaan 77J, 2517 KK The Hague, Netherlands.
20. Ulrich Beck (1992) *Risk Society – Towards a New Modernity*, London: Sage; (1995) *Ecological Politics in an Age of Risk*, Cambridge: Polity Press. See also Mary Douglas (1992) *Risk and Blame – Essays in Cultural Theory*, London: Routledge.
21. Jane Franklin (ed.) (1998) *The Politics of Risk Society*, London: Polity Press.
22. (a) Health and Safety Executive (1996) *A Guide to Information, Instruction and Training*, HSE, IND(G)235L, (b) Health and Safety Executive (1996) *Five Steps to Information, Instruction and Training*, HSE, IND(G)213L.
23. Health and Safety Executive (1997) *Managing Contractors – a Guide for Employers*, HSE, C801.

24. The source for this case study is Throttled! – the asthma law the HSC decided was too good to be passed (1994) *Hazards*, **46**.

25. The Work of the Health and Safety Executive – minutes of evidence (1997) House of Commons Environment Committee, 25 April, p. 80.

26. A. J. P. Dalton (1995) Asbestos hazards: past, present and future. *Occupational Health Review*, September/October, 34–6.

27. Health and Safety in the Service Industries, Report for 1994–95. HSC Press Release, 24 June 1996.

28. Department of the Environment (1996) Annual Report, London: HMSO.

29. Susan Wolf and Anna White (1995) *Environmental Law*, London: Cavendish Publishing Ltd.

30. The Parliamentary Commissioner for Administration (1995) Report A9/1995.

31. A. J. P. Dalton (1995) VOC substitution in the printing industry, *Environmental Information Bulletin*, **44**, 10–13.

32. *Integrated Pollution Control – the First Three Years* (1994) London: Environmental Data Services, p. xvi.

33. Department of the Environment, Transport and the Regions (1997) UK Implementation of EC Directive 96/61 On Integrated Pollution and Prevention Control.

34. Environmental Impact of Cement Manufacture (1997) *3rd Report of the Environment Committee*, 5 March, The House of Commons, London: The Stationery Office.

35. A. Oates and D. Gregory (1993) *Industrial Relations and the Environment*, 2 volumes, Dublin: Dublin Foundation for the Improvement of Living and Working Conditions.

36. A. J. P. Dalton (1995) 21st Century safety rep, *Hazards*, **52**, 8–9.

37. Manufacturing, Science and Finance Union (1995) *Clean Production – from Industrial Dinosaur to Co-efficiency*. London: MSF.

38. A. J. P. Dalton (1995) *op. cit*, note 31.

39. Trade Unionists and Eco-Auditing (1996) and *Safety, Health and Environmental Issues and European Works Councils* (1997) Free from T&G Health and Safety Section, TGWU, 16 Palace Street, London, SW1E 5JD.

40. T&G (1997) T&G reps stand up for safety, *T&G Health and Safety Record 3*.

41. The Trade Union Congress (1997) *Hazards at Work*, London: TUC.

42. The 1977 Safety Representatives and Safety Committee Regulations (1996) London: HSE Books.

43. A. J. P. Dalton (1989) *Workplace Health – a Trade Unions' Guide* (1989) London: The Labour Research Department.

44. The HSE-funded evaluation, of the pilot EU-funded T&G 'roving safety rep' scheme in agriculture, has been carried out by Dr David Walters of South Bank University: David Walters (1997) *The Role of Regional Health and Safety Representatives in Agriculture: an evaluation of a trade union initiative on roving safety representatives in agriculture*, HSE Contract Research Report 157/1997, London: HSE Books.

45. Health and Safety Commission (1996) *Consulting Employees on Health and Safety*, HSC.

46. Health and Safety Executive (1996) A Guide to the Health and Safety (Consultation with Employees) Regulations 1996, HSE, L95.

47. For a free sample copy of *Hazards* magazine write to: *Hazards*, PO Box 199, Sheffield S1 1FQ.

3

SICK BUILDING SYNDROME (SBS), 'GREEN WORKPLACES' AND WORKPLACE INSPECTIONS

SICK BUILDING SYNDROME

A few years ago a central London council had its environmental health offices situated over a petrol station on a very busy road. Especially when there were deliveries of petrol, the offices were full of petrol fumes, although, the staff also complained at other times of vehicle fumes. An investigation showed that the air intake for the office air conditioning system was on the main road, just above the petrol station. Being environmental health officers, they served a notice on the petrol station to fill its tanks outside of working hours. They also moved the air intake away from the main road, and the incidence of headaches and complaints fell dramatically. This example illustrates how the siting of a building and the location of its air intake may be vital for staff health.

The Inland Revenue's St John's House, an 18-storey tower block in Liverpool, has been declared[1] 'Britain's sickest building'. Housing 2000 civil servants, this modern tower block was built in 1971, ironically to improve efficiency in the tax office, but it was not occupied until 1981. The complaints started at once, and included frequent colds, skin irritation, dry, itchy or watery eyes, blocked, stuffy and runny noses, dry throats, breathing difficulties, chest tightness and the vague symptoms of feeling sleepy, lethargic and groggy. Staff morale was low and at one time up to four out of ten (40 per cent) of the workforce were having to leave work early because of their symptoms.

Pressure from the union, the Inland Revenue Staff Federation (IRSF) led to a specialist survey by the UKs top sick building syndrome (SBS) experts, the Building Research Establishment (BRE). The BRE's detailed survey confirmed that there were many problems with the building: excess dust and dust mites (a major cause of allergic asthma); obstructions of the ducts providing air to the offices; high levels of bacteria in spray humidifiers supplying air to the offices; and high levels of sulphur dioxide from chimneys. To clean and renovate the building to

FIGURE 3.1   This office was suffering from sick building syndrome.

eliminate, or at least reduce, the SBS symptoms would have cost an estimated £55 million. To knock the building down and build a new one would cost an estimated £36 million. Therefore, the building is to be knocked down. David Rogan, the IRSF staff representative at St John's House said 'I think you could raise a lot of money by selling raffle tickets for the chance to press the demolition button.'

The World Health Organization (WHO) first recognized the existence of SBS in 1986. Since that time it has been studied extensively throughout the world. A 1988 Health and Safety Executive (HSE) estimate[2] was that almost one in three (30 per cent) of refurbished buildings and an unknown, but significant, number of new buildings may cause SBS. SBS symptoms are typically those listed in the Inland Revenue case study quoted above. They are common enough symptoms, with or without SBS, and any investigation of SBS is never easy.

A few years ago I was called in to help with a big SBS problem in a large town hall complex. The issue was further complicated, and made more frightening for staff, by a case of legionnaire's disease, which may or may not have been related to the SBS problems. The management did not help by putting up a notice, on the doors of the town hall, that read: 'A case of legionnaire's disease has occurred in this building. This building is therefore closed to the public. Staff are advised to use entrance C.' The heating and ventilation system was in a mess, had not been serviced well or cleaned and was worn out. Many offices were overcrowded and dirty and the staff had no control over their own temperature. But we were surprised that when we carried out a questionnaire survey of employees, to determine the full extent of the problem, and used local council, non-air-conditioned premises for a 'control' (i.e. hopefully with low complaints and no SBS), we found similar, high levels of typical SBS symptoms and sickness absence for the two groups. Further investigation revealed that staff in the 'control building', although in self-contained offices, with opening windows and fair temperature control, had much more stressful jobs (answering complaints about the lack, and care, of council housing) than the, mainly, professionals (architects, surveyors, environmental health officers (EHOs) managers) in the town hall with classic SBS. Both workplaces needed answers, although the solutions were different in each case.

No one single cause of SBS has been identified and a recent review[3] highlights some of the main causes, which include: temperature, humidity, ventilation, high dust levels, lighting levels and the lack of natural light, microbiological organisms, low levels of chemicals from furniture, walls, carpets etc., cigarette smoke and a poor human relations environment (especially lack of control over workplace/work content). The HSE has produced a very simple and easy-to-read guide on how to prevent or reduce SBS.[4]

GREEN ARCHITECTURE

In 1995 the famous architect Sir Richard Rogers, who designed the Pompidou Centre in Paris and the Lloyd's building in London, gave the prestigious 'Reith Lectures', where he linked the environment and architecture in a very forthright way:

> It is a shocking revelation – especially to me as an architect – that the world's environment crisis is being driven by our cities ... Our aim must be to search for a dynamic equilibrium between society, cities and nature. I believe that with vigilance and popular determination the concept of sustainability will grow in importance until it becomes the dominant philosophy of our age.[5]

But is there a link between an environmentally aware building and the prevention of SBS? In response to a review of a book on SBS, Martin Long of the world-famous architects, Ove Arup and Partners wrote recently: 'As a designer of air-conditioned buildings, I am fed up with friends asking me to work out why their particular office air-conditioning system is not working properly.'[6] He promised that 'Technology is now being used to give back control to the occupant.' However, the concerns are not just about air conditioning, as important as that may be, but about the wider fabric of the buildings and, indeed, the very location of the workplace (or home) itself.

A variety of publications give practical examples of 'green or ecological buildings', or even 'eco-industrial parks', based on the innovative American idea[7] of 'industrial ecology'. The basic idea of a 'zero-emission' industrial eco-park is just that: zero emissions of pollutants. This may seem fanciful, but there is great scope for organizing an industrial park so that the by-products of one company become the raw materials and feedstock of another. Possibly, with exceptional planning, the circle could be completed. Of course, this whole area is highly debated: even if it works – and that is a big 'if' – surely this reduces the incentive to cut down waste in the first place. But it is a fact that some 50 large corporations have now established a 'zero-emissions' division, and in the Danish town of Kalundberg, it actually seems to work in practice. The three core industries – Statoil refinery, Asnes power station and Novo Nordisk (enzymes and insulin) – feed off each other and supply other local companies with raw materials to produce heat for a fish farm, gypsum for plasterboard, light gad for oven heating and fertilizer for the local farmers' fields and so on (see also pp. 229–30).

To deal with the SBS problem and the wider issues, as outlined in Sir Richard Rogers' Reith Lectures, the idea of 'green architecture' has arisen. In America, the 45 million dollar a year ecological and environmental Audubon Society renovated an eight storey Manhattan office block to very high ecological and environmental standards, which it maintains are profitable, in 1992. It has written in great detail about the project,[8] and although John Berry of Ove Arup maintains that the 'result is uninspiring by European and Scandinavian standards',[9] the details are inspiring. Green architecture seems to have come of age, with the publication of several recent books on the subject.[10] In early 1997 it was announced that Edinburgh council is to build an innovative £8 million 'green estate', where no one owns cars, trees replace tarmac, water is recycled and heating and lighting are free.[11] The idea has interested councils up and down the country, and Camden Council, in London, is to vote whether to follow Edinburgh's example.

WORKPLACE SAFETY AND HEALTH INSPECTIONS

> I have not thought it beneath me to step into workshops of the meaner sort now and again and study the obscure operation of the mechanical arts.
>
> Bernardino Ramazzini, *Diseases of Workers*, 1713.

Amazingly, the art and science of workplace inspection – as fundamental as it surely is to safety, health and environmental improvements – has been little written about in the years since Ramazzini's seminal work quoted above. Yet there is no substitute for visiting a workplace and experiencing the reality. When you visit a workplace you get a real feel for the management style, employee interest, the hazards at the workplace, how they are dealt (or not dealt) with and the priority of issues. Real-life workplace hazards cannot be learnt from any number of telephone interviews, letters, Internet contacts, academic papers and books and 'virtual reality' images, as useful as all of these are. As any good journalist knows there is no substitute for the 'site visit', whether a 'walkthrough survey'[12] or an 'in-depth' survey.[13]

Elsewhere (page 249) I have dealt in more detail with the 'environmental audit', but it is more convenient at this time to deal with health and safety workplace inspections separately. This will not be the case in the not-too-distant future, as the management systems required to deal with safety and health and environmental issues are rapidly being brought closer together. Indeed, I have already been part of extension courses to convert management and trade union 'safety and health' risk assessors into 'safety, health and environment' (SHE) risk assessors.

Traditional safety and health inspections, although quite definite in their aims ('The objective of any inspection of any workplace or work-process is to detect hazards to health and safety'[14]), almost always concentrate on the hardware of safety and health: the hazardous material or processes. Under such a philosophy, the three key questions were:

1. Where work is performed.
2. What is used at work.
3. How work is performed.

Linked to these basic questions were two other related questions: what is wrong? and why is it wrong? It is still true that many enforcement inspectors and health and safety officers work to this basic pattern. Done properly, it can still get results with specific hazardous operations or situations, especially if linked with the question: how can be make it safer or healthier?

But with the cut-back in enforcement officers and the downsizing of workplaces (involving the reduction of professional health and safety staff) and the rise of 'risk assessments', often performed by (hopefully) trained managers and supervisors, there has risen a more modern, and comprehensive, approach to workplace inspection.[15] It looks in more detail at the *management systems* for dealing with health and safety issues. This approach sees health and safety inspections, or audits, firmly linked to other management systems, such as total quality management and environmental management systems.[16]

Adopting this approach, a draft checklist for workplace inspections would look something like the following:

1. *Background notes on*: the known hazards of the workplace (literature search, contacts in similar workplaces, contacts with enforcement officers, trade unions, trade associations etc.). Get as much technical information (e.g. risk assessments, process data, hazard data sheets, occupational hygiene reports, accident and injury reports, insurance assessor reports, fire surveyor reports) from the workplace as possible. In the US and Canada the idea of 'risk mapping' – getting employees to mark the hazards on a workplace map – has recently gained favour and seems to have been successful in encouraging employees to identify hazards from their knowledge and experiences.[17]
2. *Background notes on*: the general attitudes of management in that industrial sector, and particular workplace if possible, towards safety, health (and environmental?) issues. Get as much management system background

information about the workplace as possible (e.g. safety policy, SHE training policy, enforcement letters/action, safety representative inspection/complaints reports, safety committee minutes for the past year, independent audits, insurance assessors' views of the management system).

3. *Site visit for 'walk-through' or preparation for 'in-depth' survey.* Where is the workplace located, what other sites exist? What is the standard at these sites? Arrive early and walk around the workplace before entering. What impression do you get? Is it clean and efficient in appearance, and well cared for? Or is it run-down and scruffy? Meet with management, workforce representatives and SHE professionals (e.g. nurse, doctor, occupational hygienist, environmental or safety engineer, fire officer, safety officer, first aiders, insurance surveyor), apart from and together with management. What does the safety policy say? What are the risk assessments like? What are the accident, injury, near-miss and disease data like? Are the trade union safety representatives (if they exist) active? What training have they and supervisors had? Has its value been assessed? How? What auditing has been carried out? Do you need to speak to enforcement officer(s)?

4. *Specific site inspections*, in large workplaces with new processes, if done properly can be very tiring. You can only take so much in at one time. Do not be afraid to stop and revisit. Take copious notes, tape recordings, photographs, and videotape if appropriate (especially for ergonomic problems), draw diagrams and maps of key areas/processes, and, most importantly, speak to the people actually doing the work (preferably without management, union or professionals present).

5. *Write up your observations* and conclusions soon after your visit; memory soon fades. Also, if it is a repeat visit or inspection, try and take someone new along, as familiarity does, indeed, breed contempt; or at least complacency. Having visited, you may well need to ask questions of the people you spoke to before (item 4) and revisit the literature (item 1).

6. *Make recommendations for improvements.* Who will they go to (management and union, as a minimum)? If you have observed serious situations/exposures, do you need to inform enforcement agencies and/or national trade unions or head office, if a large company? To end where we began: the point of inspections is to improve safety and health (and environmental) conditions; if this is not done they are pointless and, indeed, may do damage, as the people may feel that inspections alone improve the situation. You must be part of the solution, not part of the problem.

7. *Audit your recommendations* and any subsequent action if at all possible. Were your conclusions and recommendations right? Did they work? If not, why not? Could they be improved upon?

8. Remember, workplace inspections alone do not improve the working environment; only positive management (or other) action can do that.

NOTES

1. Ceri Jackson (1995) Is this Britain's sickest building? *The Daily Mail*, 21 February.
2. J. M. Sykes (1988) *Sick Building Syndrome: A Review*, Health and Safety Executive, Specialist Inspector Reports No. 10.
3. Jack Rostron (ed.) (1997) *Sick Building Syndrome – Concepts, Issues and Practice*, London: E & F Spon. A very useful and wide-ranging book with a good checklist of what to look for and what to do.
4. Health and Safety Executive (1995) *How to deal with Sick Building Syndrome – Guidance for Employers, Building Owners and Building Managers*, HSE Books, HS(G)132.
5. Richard Rogers (1997) *Cities for a Small Planet*, London: Faber & Faber. Some great ideas on the future of cities and buildings for people.
6. Martin Long (1997) Alienated by sick buildings, *The Independent*, 10 April.
7. Karen Schmidt (1996) The zero option, *New Scientist*, 1 June.
8. National Audubon Society (1994) *Audubon House – Building the Environmentally Responsible, Energy-efficient Office*, Chichester: John Wiley.
9. John Berry (1994) A home fit for eco-warriors, *New Scientist*, 30 July.
10. (a) Brenda Vale and Robert Vale (1991) *Green Architecture – Design for a Sustainable Future*, London: Thames and Hudson; (b) Randall Thomas, Max Fordham and Partners (eds) (1996) *Environmental Design*, London: E & FN Spon; (c) Stewart Brand (1994) *How Buildings Learn – What Happens After They're Built*, London: Orion.
11. John Arlidge (1997) All-green homes for people who promise not to buy a car, *The Observer*, 12 April.
12. J. P. Kornberg (1992) *The Workplace Walk-Through*, London: Lewis Publishers.
13. P. L. Perkins (1997) *Modern Industrial Hygiene*, London: Chapman and Hall.
14. F. A. Alcock (1982) *Safety Inspections – the Detection of Hazards at Work*, London: H. K. Lewis, p. 18.
15. European Foundation for the Improvement of Living and Working Conditions (1996) *Assessing Working Conditions*, Dublin.
16. Alan Waring (1996) *Safety Management Systems*, London: Chapman and Hall.
17. (1997) Mapping our workplace hazards, *Hazards*, **60**, 8–9.

4

SOME KEY WORKPLACE SAFETY ISSUES

ACCIDENTS AT WORK: REPORTING AND INVESTIGATION

BLAME THE WORKERS?

> The report ... affords strong grounds for thinking that ... the bulk of the accidents occur to a limited number of individuals who have a special susceptibility to accidents, and suggests that the explanation of this susceptibility is to be found in the personality of the individual. (The incidence of industrial accidents upon individuals with special reference to multiple accidents, Industrial Fatigue Research Board, Report number 4, 1919)

We have seen elsewhere (page 34) how most accidents at work could have been prevented by positive management action. That is, they were not true 'accidents' – as defined as an unforeseen event – at all. For many years – and it is still seen today as its new version, 'human-centred safety' – there has been a theory of accidents being 'the fault of the worker'. This theory of 'accident proneness' started with the researchers of the Industrial Health Research Board, set up to study fatigue during the First World War, as quoted above. It was helped along by comments such as those by Jung in 1928, who thought that most accidents had a 'psychological origin' (Hunter, 1955). The prevalent view was that roughly three-quarters of all accidents happened to one-quarter of those exposed, and the probable number of these 'accident-prone' individuals was 10–25 per cent of the total employees.

In fact, the explanation for most of this research and theory can be found in the simple statistical distribution of events among a group ('poisson theory'). Thus, in a factory employing 200 people and having 100 accidents a year, on average:

- ○ 121 people will have no accidents
- ○ 61 people will have only one accident
- ○ 15 people will have two or more accidents
- ○ 3 people will have three or more accidents

It is easy to pick out those three and find that they are 'accident prone'.

A 'victim-blaming' culture in workplace accidents started that continues until this day. Accident prevention courses are still sometimes advertised under such headings as 'More than 80 per cent of accidents are caused by human error.' This is only true in as much as most managers are human. Even the Health and Safety Executive (HSE) has succumbed, to some extent, to this approach, with its 1989 publication, *Human Factors in Industrial Safety*, which states that:

> It is now widely accepted that the majority of accidents in industry generally are in some measure attributable to human as well as technical factors in the sense that actions by people initiated or contributed to the accidents, or people might have acted better to avert them. (Para. 6, p. 1)

In fact, in practice, this publication looks largely at the management organization and workplace environmental factors that lead to accidents (and contains a very good checklist on these issues); but the title alone gives comfort to those who want to blame the worker.

Of course, it is very easy and convenient for a corporation and company, and even a government, to blame 'human error', when the bow doors of a ferry are not shut, when the points of a railway are not wired correctly, when a train or coach crashes and so on. Many commercial accidents are caused by drivers falling asleep, and in one sense this is the driver's fault. But when we look beyond blame to why the driver fell asleep, it is more complicated: very long hours of driving, hard work loading, too little sleep at home (or in the cab), difficult and inhuman shiftwork patterns and so on.

In fact, for many years, since the famous work of Heinrich in the 1930s, it has been known that accidents are multi-factorial and Heinrich developed his 'domino' theory to account for many accidents and to suggest how to prevent them (remove the easiest of the dominoes, or factors in the accident; 'the unsafe act or mechanical hazard'). Of course, the application of this 'theory' of accident proneness amongst workers has not led to any reduction in workplace accidents. One of the most significant UK studies in this area was the 1972 study of 2000 accidents by the National Institute of Industrial Psychology, who concluded:

> It may be surprising to some that we failed to discover conclusively any personal factors which characterised people who had accidents. We think that the lack of positive results is due to the far greater influence of accidents on exposure to task risk, i.e. the type of work and amount of work done. (Para. 620, p. 165)

Of course, anybody who has worked for any length of time has come across the odd worker who is very clumsy and seems to have more accidents than other employees, but they are very rare. The workplace should not be a battlefield or minefield where the slightest 'accident' or loss of concentration means that our lives are in danger. Professor Nichols, of Bristol University, in his recent book (Nichols, 1997) has reviewed in more depth the background and theory of 'accident proneness'.

It is very important that the investigation of accidents is approached with the right frame of mind: to find the real cause of the accident and eliminate or reduce it, *not* to blame the victim.

THE REPORTING OF INJURIES, DISEASES AND DANGEROUS OCCURRENCES REGULATIONS 1995 (RIDDOR)

We have seen elsewhere (page 4) that any system that relies on the employer to report accidents and dangerous occurrences to the enforcement authorities will always result in a gross underestimate of the real number of workplace injuries (but not deaths – it is not so easy to cover up a death in the UK). The HSE convictions under RIDDOR for 1995–96 totalled 56, with an average fine of £694.

Of course, the larger and more responsible employers do have good systems for collecting and collating accidents and injuries (and sometimes near-misses) and do report under RIDDOR. On the other hand, many small and medium-sized enterprises do not, and nor do construction sites and farms, where under-reporting is acknowledged by the HSE to exceed 50 per cent. That is not to say that the current RIDDOR reporting system, which has just been changed to make it more user-friendly (and extended to cover 'violence at work', but not the accidents to those whose job involves driving for a living), does not serve a very useful purpose in recording trends in industries and identifying some 'hot spots'. Of course, all managers and safety representatives should ensure that all their relevant accidents, diseases and near-misses are reported.

There is plenty of good HSE guidance on RIDDOR, with books of the required forms and so on.[1]

FIGURE 4.1   A motorcycle courier has an accident: not reportable as a 'workplace accident' under RIDDOR.

Who is covered?

Every one at work is covered: employees, self-employed, trainees, students, visitors, customers to the workplace.

What should you report and to whom?

In essence, all major and serious accidents and injuries (where the person is in hospital for more than 24 hours) and/or specified serious 'dangerous occurrences' (e.g. collapse of scaffolding more than five metres high, collapse of hoist or crane) should be reported to the enforcement authority (HSE or environmental health officer (EHO)) 'by the quickest practicable means', normally by telephone or fax, followed within seven days by a completed relevant form. If in doubt, it is better to report than not. The list of occupational diseases to be reported is the same as that on the Prescribed Diseases List.

Recording of accidents

RIDDOR requires the employer to record the following details of any accidents, dangerous occurrences and diseases:

○ date and time of accident and dangerous occurrence
○ full name of the person affected
○ occupation of the person affected
○ nature of injury or condition
○ place where the accident or dangerous occurrence happened
○ a brief description of the circumstances

For diseases, the following information is required:

○ date and diagnosis of diseases
○ occupation of the person affected
○ name or nature of the disease

The records should be kept for a minimum of three years and the accident book should be readily available to the injured person or their representatives (e.g. safety representative). Since the common 'accident triangle' shows that the average company or organization will have a large number of 'near-misses' for each actual accident, every attempt should be made to record and act upon near-miss information and not just accidents.

INVESTIGATING ACCIDENTS, NEAR-MISSES AND DISEASES

The quick and accurate investigation of accidents, near-misses and diseases is central to ensure that they are not repeated and, where appropriate, the injured person obtains the appropriate compensation. The following is the general approach, but it may need to be modified, depending on the particular accident and workplace. The investigation of diseases is somewhat different (unless they are fairly immediate, like legionnaire's disease, dermatitis etc.) but follows the same general plan. Past medical problems, workplace exposure history, drug habits (e.g. smoking or drinking), outside hobbies, medical treatment and workplace exposure levels may also be important when investigating the cause and prevention of workplace diseases. However, it is important not to infringe on people's normal freedom (e.g. is smoking relevant to a non-fire or non-health related problem?). Employers are legally bound to pay trade union safety representatives for the time taken to investigate accidents (including visiting injured/ill workers at home if necessary).

○ Get to the accident as soon as possible. Ensure that injured people receive first aid (page 128), the emergency services are called (if appropriate) and, if necessary, someone known to the injured person accompanies them to hospital and a near-relative and/or friend is informed.

○ Ensure that nothing is disturbed at the scene of the accident. Take photographs and make sketches and detailed notes of the working environment: state of machine/floor; lighting, temperature, machine guarding etc.

○ If possible, interview the accident victim and any witnesses as soon as possible. If serious, a recording may be better. Establish the build-up to the accident, the circumstances of the accident and what happened after the accident. Be sure to get the names, addresses, phone numbers and date and time of the witness statements. Take into account such things as: the length of time the injured person had been working; their age and experience; their training and information given; any personal protective equipment (PPE) they were wearing (or not wearing); any legal standards; any previous accidents or near-misses; the maintenance of the workplace or equipment; and so on. Check on any similar accidents in other companies or organizations and/or the literature.

○ Write a report of the accident as soon as possible, whilst events are fresh in your mind, even if it is just a first draft. The conclusions should seek to prevent an occurrence of the accident and not to apportion blame in general.

○ Communicate the results of your investigations to those in management who can act on your recommendations, other members of staff who may be affected by the accident, and last, but not least, the person(s) injured in the accident.

○ Review to ensure that any recommendations are acted upon. It may be appropriate to send a copy of your report and conclusions to the enforcement authority; you should also give a copy to the trade union safety representative and/or delegate of employee safety, if there is one.

RISK ASSESSMENT

> ... assessing risks is full of uncertainties; that the science underlying most risk assessment assumptions is often inconclusive and untestable. In short risk assessment in its present form can only be used to inform a decision. It should not be used blindly to dictate it.[2]

There is really nothing new about carrying out a risk assessment at the workplace. We have seen elsewhere (page 45) the political implications of 'risk assessment', and how, in the USA at least and especially in the environmental area, there is some disillusionment with risk assessments. But a simple 'risk assessment' is simply common sense in many ways: what are you using or doing, what are the hazards and risks and are the controls adequate to control the risks?

○ 'Hazard' means anything that can cause harm, e.g. a chemical, electricity, working from ladder.

○ 'Risk' is the chance, great or small, that someone will be harmed by the hazard.

A busy road is a danger, so when you cross it you carry out a quick mental 'risk assessment'. If it is very busy, you most probably walk up to the crossing (if there is one quite near). If it is quiet with little traffic, you cross; even if there is a crossing nearby. If you have a young child with you, or are ill yourself, you use the crossing on most occasions. If the weather is bad and the visibility poor, you are more likely to use the crossing, and so on.

It is useful to make a practical distinction between the large macro risk assessments – should we build this power station or not – and the smaller, more manageable risk assessments carried out at the workplace. In many ways, an environmental 'life cycle analysis' is the most advanced form of environmental risk assessment carried out at the workplace, and this is discussed elsewhere (page 229). This section will therefore concentrate on safety and health risk assessments, as carried out under the 1974 Health and Safety at Work Act and associated regulations. It was the Management of Health and Safety at Work Regulations 1992 that really put risk assessment on the safety and health 'map'. But, as a recent[3] HSE publication points out, the concept of 'risk assessments' had existed before 1992, in the 1980 lead regulations, the 1987 asbestos regulations, the 1988 Control of Substances Hazardous to Health (COSHH) Regulations, and the 1989 noise at work regulations. In 1992, in addition to the management regulations, the manual handling, display screen equipment and PPE regulations all required risk assessments. Thus *eight* major pieces of common safety and health law require risk assessments, in addition to more specialized regulations on ionizing radiation, genetic manipulation etc. The HSE guide[3] compares and contrasts the risk assessments required under each of these eight sets of regulations.

Many trade associations and trade unions have produced excellent guides to risk assessment. Although there are many, often expensive, commercial guides to carrying out 'risk assessments' (some of which, for specific hazards or workplaces, are very useful), the HSE has produced an excellent, basic, free guide to carrying out a simple risk assessment on a process or task.[4] For most purposes this guide is more than enough.

According to the HSE, the key five elements of most risk assessments are:

1. Look for the hazards.
2. Decide who might be harmed and how.
3. Evaluate the risks and adequacy of current precautions.
4. Record your findings (if you employ more than five people).
5. Review, and revise if required, your assessment from time to time.

The HSE leaflet provides more detail about each of these five elements, such as: identifying workers particularly at risk (e.g. young people, pregnant women, the elderly, those with disabilities); whether the hazard and risk can actually be eliminated altogether or just controlled; how to identify whether health surveillance is required; detailed procedures for immediate hazards and dangers; the arrangements for shared premises and shared hazards and risks; the appointment and training of 'competent persons' to carry out the risk assessments and the need to involve trade union safety representatives and/or representatives of employee safety in both the appointment and training of competent persons and the risk assessments (although it is management's responsibility to carry out the risk assessment); and the arrangements for and frequency of the review or audit of the risk assessments (e.g. when the process or task undergoes a change, when new employees carry out that task, when new information on the hazard or risk becomes available, after a set time period).

In addition to the general guidance on risk assessment, the HSE has produced an excellent guide on 'health risk management' for small and medium-sized enterprises that gives examples of risk reduction in practice. This guide ends with a very useful checklist for managers, the main points of which are as follows:

○ Do directors and senior managers know what they want to achieve in relation to work-related health risks?
○ What priorities have been set?
○ Are those responsible for work-related health risks aware of their responsibilities?
○ Is the role of in-house and external sources of expertise clear?
○ How are responsible directors, managers etc. accountable?
○ Are employees, trade union safety representatives, representatives of employee safety, health and safety committee members, in-house and external health and safety experts etc. involved in making risk assessments and deciding on methods of control?
○ Is everyone who needs to being told about risks to their health at work (e.g. cleaners, part-time staff, trainees, students)?

○ Are employees properly trained to:
  - avoid risks to their health at work;
  - make proper use of control measures;
  - make proper use of PPE;
  - report accidents, ill-health and near-misses?
○ Has a competent adviser been appointed?
○ Are there any arrangements for monitoring exposure?
○ Is there a plan to make progressive improvements?
○ Are checks carried out on whether plans are being implemented and priorities being tackled?
○ Is there a proper system for recording and analysing cases of work-related ill-health and sickness absence?
○ Are cases of ill-health and sickness absence investigated so that lessons can be learnt and steps taken to prevent a similar problem arising again?

The HSE guide[5] to risk assessment for health hazards provides very useful guidance for managers and safety reps in small and medium-sized enterprises (SMEs).

FIRST AID

The provision of first aid at work has been a basic service provided by the employer, especially in the more dangerous industries, for many years. After all, it is in the employer's interests that employees are treated quickly and return to work. In offices and smaller workplaces 'first aid' is often just a first aid box that, when opened, has a few mouldy sticking plasters and an empty aspirin bottle in it. Yet first aid, even in a so-called low-risk situation, can be vital if someone falls ill at work or has an accident. First aiders are trained what *not* to do as much as *what* to do. Doing nothing – apart from ensuring that someone is breathing, not bleeding to death and is generally comfortable (e.g. warm) and safe – whilst the emergency services are called takes confidence, especially if other people are panicking.

Training helps in a situation like this. Unfortunately, recent HSE-funded research has shown that many trained first aiders have lost much of their useful knowledge of first aid after six months. This raises doubts about the traditional four-day first aid course and one-day refresher required after three years. Considering the amount of money that employers spend on training and retaining first aiders, there has been little research into their effectiveness. Some years ago I found some Canadian research that suggested first aider training could be improved to make them more preventative as well as treatment orientated.

Although the first aid regulations date from 1982, the approved code of practice was last revised in 1997.[6] In general, in recent years, there has been less emphasis on the *numbers of first aiders required per employee* and more on the *actual risks* present at the workplace. There is a distinction between a 'first aider' and an 'appointed person':

O A 'first aider' has approved first aid training and holds a current first aid certificate (valid for three years).

O An 'appointed person' is someone appointed by the employer to know how to call the emergency services and to keep the first aid container complete. The HSE recommends a four-hour minimum 'emergency training course' that covers: what to do in an emergency, cardiopulmonary resuscitation, first aid for the unconscious casualty and first aid for the wounded or bleeding.

The minimum requirements[7] for first aid for *any* workplace are:

O a suitably stocked first aid container
O a person appointed to take charge of first aid arrangements
O information for employees on first aid arrangements

In general, the first aid regulations requirements for numbers of first aiders/appointed persons are as follows:

O For low-risk premises (e.g. an office or a library) at least one first aider for every 50–200 people employed. If fewer than 50 people are employed then an appointed person is sufficient.

O For a medium-risk organization (e.g. light engineering or food processing), there must be at least one first-aider to every 20–100 people. Below 20 people an appointed person is sufficient.

O For high-risk industries (e.g. heavy industry, dangerous machinery, a chemical works), there must be at least one first-aider to every 5–50 people. Below five people an appointed person is sufficient.

Much more detailed guidance, is available.[7] Of course, these are minimum figures and many employers have many more first aiders, and appointed persons, than the law requires. In 1982, when the first aid regulations first became law, I surveyed around 500 well-unionized workplaces and found conditions much better than the law required.[8] A subsequent survey found that conditions had improved further.[9]

When the recent first aid regulations were revised in 1996, some commentators (e.g. the trade unions and first aid training bodies) wanted *all* the people on the premises to be counted for the purposes of providing first aiders. For example, in a school, college, shop and library there are many more students or users than staff, and it could be argued that the visitors are more at risk than the staff, since they are unfamiliar with the premises. Why not base the number on the average number of occupants at any one time?

There are sometimes problems with first aiders when they are off sick or on holiday, or shiftwork or overtime is worked. For all of these reasons it makes sense for the employer to have far more than the minimum number of first aiders.

Employers often say that they cannot get employees to come forward as first aiders, but it is a responsibility and a legal requirement on management. Whilst some, indeed many, people are prepared to do the job voluntarily because they think it is worthwhile, others will only do it if they are paid to do it. Fifteen years ago the payments ranged from nothing to almost £10 a week;[8] and I would have thought something near the latter is appropriate today. Organizations with payments nearer the higher end of the scale had no problem recruiting first aiders.

There is guidance given on the contents of first aid containers, and they should contain *no* medication (e.g. aspirins) of any kind. It is also suggested,[7] that first aiders and appointed persons are given a book to record incidences which they attend. The information kept is suggested to be:

○   date, time and place of incident
○   name and job of the injured person
○   details of injury/illness and what first aid was given
○   what happened to the person immediately afterwards (for example, went home, went back to work and went to hospital)
○   name and signature of the first aider or person dealing with the accident

The HSE suggests that this information may be useful for spotting accident trends; however, a first aider's training is not preventative, so where appropriate the management safety officer or engineer and the trade union safety representative should always be consulted; indeed, the latter have legal rights to be consulted on the number of first aiders and competent persons, the level of risk and hazard at the workplace and their training etc.

First aid rooms are only required where 'the assessment of first-aid needs identifies this as necessary'. In general, this is in high-risk industries (e.g. shipbuilding, chemical companies and large construction sites) and at larger premises at a distance from medical services. A designated person should be responsible for the room, and the code of practice[7] details what should be in the room.

Employees must be informed about the first aid arrangements and who the first aiders or competent persons are, with at least one notice in each workplace. Where other languages are commonly used in the workplaces there should be the appropriate translation (this would be true for all key SHE regulations and guidance, of course).

THE WORKING ENVIRONMENT

The Workplace (Health, Safety and Welfare) Regulations 1992 lay down the bare minimum standards for most workplaces. The HSE has produced a very useful and free guide[10] to these crucial regulations. It is important to note that they only provide for *minimum* standards, and in many cases professional advice, negotiated standards and personal needs will dictate higher standards being applied. Whilst these regulations cover most ordinary workplaces, others (e.g. construction, agriculture, forestry, temporary and mobile sites, transport) are not fully covered by these regulations and sometimes (e.g. construction) have regulations of their own. The following is a quick summary of these important regulations.

○ *Regulation 4: responsibility of employers* – must take into account all who work or visit their premises (e.g. contractors, self-employed). Where premises are shared, there is joint management responsibility.

○ *Regulation 5: maintenance* – all workplace equipment and devices should be well maintained. This means a regular system of inspection, maintenance and the keeping of records.

○ *Regulation 6: ventilation* – this summarizes the need for efficient (but not draughty!) and clean-air ventilated workplaces. There is much professional guidance available on ventilation, which is a major cause of many workplace problems (e.g. sick building syndrome; see page 113).

○ *Regulation 7: temperature* – a reasonable temperature must be maintained inside buildings and sufficient thermometers must be provided. The 'reasonable temperature' is at least 16°C for most types of work and at least 13°C for work involving 'severe physical effort'. Both extremes of cold and heat can, and do, cause many problems,[11] and it should be noted that there is no maximum temperature; only a minimum. This is a big weakness and during the 'sticky' summer of 1997 the Trades Union Congress (TUC) campaigned for a maximum temperature of 27°C (which many thought too high). Of course, humidity and ventilation rates are important too. The issue of sunburn and skin cancer is also becoming a problem for outside workers, with the destruction of the protective ozone layer.

○ *Regulation 8: lighting* – it must be sufficient and suitable and natural, 'so far as is reasonably practicable'. Emergency lighting must be supplied where lighting failure would cause danger. Bad lighting causes many problems and there is HSE guidance in this area.[12] The siting and use of visual display units (VDUs) can cause a lot of problems, especially with regard to glare, and the HSE has produced a good general guide on this issue.[13]

○ *Regulation 9: cleanliness* – workplaces and furnishing must be kept sufficiently clean. Waste materials must not accumulate, unless in suitable waste bins. This is a very important regulation, especially for the prevention and control of sick building syndrome (page 113) and other respiratory problems (e.g. asthma).

○ *Regulation 10: space* – work rooms must have sufficient floor area, height and unoccupied space. The guidance given per person is a minimum of 11 cubic metres per person, not counting any height above three metres. Fixtures, fittings and furniture must be taken into account, so this legal minimum will not be met if a room is crowded with furniture.

○ *Regulation 11: workstations and seats* – they must be suitable for the worker and the work being done and a seat must be supplied where necessary. It is now known that poor seating can lead to many health problems (backache etc.) and that standing is also hazardous to health.

○ *Regulation 12: floors* – must be suitable and not slippery or uneven and kept free from obstructions. Handrails must be provided on staircases. There should be secure fencing where there is a risk of falling from two metres or more. Slips, trips and falls are the cause of many accidents and the HSE has provided specific guidance in this area for especially dangerous industries (e.g. in the food industry).

○ *Regulation 13: falls* – suitable and sufficient measures should be taken to prevent people falling and/or people being struck by falling objects. Tanks and holes should be securely covered and fenced where there is a risk of a person falling into a dangerous substance.

○ *Regulations 14–16: windows and moving walkways* – clear doors should be marked to prevent people knocking into them. Windows must be safe to operate. Escalators and moving walkways must be safe to use and operate. The HSE has produced guidance in this area.[14]

○ *Regulation 17: traffic* – workplaces must be organized to allow safe circulation of pedestrians and vehicles. Each year about 70 people die and more than 1000 are seriously injured because of accidents involving workplace vehicles. The HSE has produced a very good free booklet, and a more detailed guide, in this very important area.[15]

○ *Regulation 18: doors* – doors and gates must be safely constructed and meet certain specifications.

○ *Regulation 19: escalators* – must function safely and be equipped with emergency stop controls.

○ *Regulation 20: toilets* – must be clean, well maintained, and well lit, have toilet paper, provision for coats, access for disabled, separate for females and males and, for women, must contain means for the safe disposal of sanitary dressings. More detailed guidance is given for the number of toilets according to the numbers of employees (e.g. one to five, one water closet; six to 25, two; lower standards for men only apply where urinals are taken into account).

○ *Regulation 21: washing facilities* – must be suitable and sufficient at convenient places. They are suitable if near toilets and contain hot and cold (or warm) water, soap and a means of drying (hot air or towel). They must be kept clean, ventilated and well lit. If there is more than one person using the facilities, there should be separate facilities for females and males. Recommendations are given for numbers (e.g. one for every five employees; one extra for every 25, etc.). Certain dirty or dangerous trades (e.g. asbestos removal) have specific regulations that require the provision of showers etc.

○ *Regulation 22: water* – an adequate supply of clean water and cups must be provided.

○ *Regulations 23 and 24: clothing* – suitable and sufficient accommodation for clothing must be provided as well as changing facilities where special clothing is worn.

○ *Regulation 25: restrooms* – suitable and sufficient rest facilities must be provided at readily accessible places. These rooms should make provision for the protection of non-smokers from discomfort. Suitable provision must be made for pregnant or nursing workers. Provision must be made for workers to eat their meals. Guidance is given on chairs, tables and the means to prepare a hot drink and warm food. The issue of smoking at the workplace is one of growing concern, not just in restrooms, and the HSE has provided guidance.[16] The issue is discussed elsewhere (page 212).

NOTES

1. (a) *Everyone's Guide to the Reporting of Injuries, Diseases and Dangerous Occurrences Regulations 1995*. HSE 31. (b) *A Guide to RIDDOR 95*, HSE 73. The HSE also produces guidance on accident recording and prevention in specific industries and general guides to accident recording and cost evaluation in publications such as *The Costs of Accidents at Work*, HSE, HS(G)96, 1993.
2. *Use of Risk Assessment Within Government Departments* (1996), Report of the interdepartmental liaison group on risk assessment, HSE Ref. MISC038, January.
3. Health and Safety Executive (1996) A guide to risk assessment requirements, HSE, IND(G)218(L).
4. Health and Safety Executive (1995) Five steps to risk assessment, HSE, IND(G)163L.
5. Health and Safety Executive (1995) *Health Risk Management – A Practical Guide for Managers in Small and Medium-Sized Enterprises*, HSE, HS(G)137.
6. Health and Safety Executive (1997) *Basic Advice on First Aid at Work*, HSE, IND(G)215L.
7. Health and Safety Commission (1977) *First Aid at Work – Approved Code of Practice and Guidance*, HSC. The key guidance in this area.
8. First Aid at Work (1982) *Bargaining Report Survey*, London: The Labour Research Department.
9. First Aid at Work (1993) *Bargaining Report Survey*, London: The Labour Research Department.
10. Health and Safety Executive (1997) *An HSE Guide to the Workplace (Health, Safety and Welfare) Regulations 1992*, HSE.
11. (a) Rory O'Neill (1995), Work in winter, *Occupational Health Review*, 10–13. (b) Jackie Le Poidevin (1996), The cold war, *Occupational Health Review*, 21–4. (c) Cold weather, *HSE Construction Industry Advisory Committee Sheet 2*, 1985.
12. Health and Safety Executive (1987) *Lighting at Work*, HSE, HS(G)38.
13. Health and Safety Executive (1994) *VDUs an Easy Guide to the Regulations*, HSE.
14. (a) Health and Safety Executive (1984) *Escalators: Periodic Thorough Examinations,*

HSE, PM45. (b) Health and Safety Executive (1991) *Prevention of Falls to Window Cleaners*, HSE.

15. (a) Health and Safety Executive (1995) *Managing Vehicle Safety at the Workplace – Leaflet for Employers*, HSE, IND(G)1999(L). (b) Health and Safety Executive (1995) *Workplace Transport Safety*, HSE, HS(G)136.

16. Health and Safety Executive (1993) *Passive Smoking at Work*, HSE, IND(G)63(L).

5

SOME KEY WORKPLACE HEALTH ISSUES

STRESS AT WORK

[Negative stress occurs] When the demands made on the individual do not match the resources available (in the person or provided by the organisation) or do not meet the invididual's needs and motivation.[1]

Just living can sometimes be stressful and, indeed, the only stress-free state is death. There are many surveys showing that stress in the UK really has been increasing in the last 20 years. In the words of Alan Thomas, manufacturing manager at the giant pharmaceutical company Zeneca's Yalding site, 'We're all doing more with less.' Recent stress surveys have shown the following:

○ Over half (53 per cent) of 699 managers questioned said that their organization had experienced an increase in stress levels during the past three years.
○ Stress is bad and getting worse. It was a problem for almost nine out of ten managers of 1100 surveyed in a 1996 Institute of Management survey.
○ The 1996 Trades Union Congress (TUC) survey of some 7000 trade union safety representatives found that stress was the principal workplace hazard of concern to their trade union members.
○ The Health and Safety Executive (HSE) supplement to the 1990 Labour Force Survey (page 4) found that an estimated 183,000 workers believed they had suffered from work-related stress, depression or anxiety in the preceding year, and 105,000 of these believed that the condition was caused, and not just made worse, by work.

THE SYMPTOMS

The key symptoms of stress are increased absence and staff turnover, irritability, permanent fatigue, emotional behaviour and mistakes. Below is a longer list of commonly accepted symptoms. One of the problems with identifying stress is that the symptoms are not specific to stress, there could be other work-related, or non-work-related and medical, causes of these symptoms. And, of course, all of us will have some of these symptoms, some of the time, and not be especially stressed (or be stressed in the short term and not suffer unduly). However, the more symptoms there are and the longer they last, the greater the indication of a stressed work environment and the greater the chance of long-term stress health problems.

Physical

○ Over-eating or loss of appetite
○ Frequent indigestion or heartburn
○ Insomnia (sleeplessness)
○ Constant tiredness
○ High blood pressure
○ Frequent crying or desire to cry
○ Nervous twitches
○ Breathlessness or panic attacks
○ Inability to sit still without fidgeting
○ Muscle tension/headaches
○ Tingling in arms and legs

Mental

○ Constant irritability
○ Apathy
○ Difficulty in making decisions
○ Loss of sense of humour
○ Poor concentration
○ Excessive concern about physical health
○ Withdrawal and daydreams
○ Excessive and rapid mood swings
○ Anxiety
○ Inability to feel sympathy for other people
○ Suppressed anger

RESULTS OF STRESS

Stress can make people ill. Stress is implicated in the incidence and development of:

○ coronary heart disease
○ mental illness
○ certain types of cancer

○ poor health behaviours such as smoking, dietary problems, lack of exercise, excessive alcohol consumption and substance abuse
○ life and job dissatisfaction
○ accident and unsafe behaviours at work
○ a whole range of minor ailments, including migraine, stomach ulcers, hay fever, asthma, skin rashes, impotence and menstrual problems
○ marital and family problems

THE COSTS OF STRESS

From the above it can clearly be seen that the costs to the individual in suffering and pain are immense. But the costs of stress to the organization and society are immense too. For example:

○ Six million people suffer from mental illness each year. Mental illness is as common as heart disease and three times as common as cancer. Each year suicide accounts for as many deaths as road accidents. For every ten employees, two or three each year will suffer some form of mental health problem.
○ Mental illness is responsible for 80 million lost working days each year at an estimated cost to the UK industry alone of £3.7 billion.
○ In 1997, based on a survey of 327 companies and organizations, The Industrial Society estimated[2] that work absence cost the economy a minimum of £13 billion a year. Stress-related problems were considered to be a major cause of sickness absence.
○ Thirty-five million working days are lost annually through coronary heart disease and strokes, at an estimated annual cost to the average UK organization of 10,000 employees at £2.5 million.
○ Eight million working days are lost through alcohol-related disease at an estimated cost of over £1.3 billion.
○ The Confederation of British Industry (CBI) estimates that 30 days are lost to stress for every single day lost through industrial action.
○ Overall, an estimated 360 million working days are lost annually through sickness, at a cost of £8 billion. At least half of those lost days relate to stress-related absence.

SICKNESS ABSENCE

In 1894, Mather and Platt's engineering works in Manchester reduced the working week from 53 to 48 hours.[3] Despite a 9.4 per cent fall in working time, production levels remained the same and absenteeism fell from 2.46 per cent to 0.46 per cent. According to the 1995 Industrial Society survey, 'Our survey indicates that stress is much more widespread than is reported, and may be the second most common cause of absence, after colds/flu'.[2] It is now recognized that sickness absence, which has been rising in industrialized countries in recent years, is a complex phenomenon. Many employers respond to an apparently high sickness rate by increasing the penalties for being off sick: tightening up the sick pay scheme and/ or using the discipline system to try and reduce sickness. A recent review of absence from work noted that: 'Disciplinary systems are widely used, yet there is little evidence about their effectiveness. There is, however, evidence that reward systems such as attendance bonus schemes can reduce absence rates.'[4] The carrot seems better than the stick. A review of the sickness absence rates in over 9000 civil servants – the so-called 'Whitehall study' – found greater rates of sickness in lower grades than in higher grades.[5] The review concluded that more effective 'monitoring' of employees' sickness rates was 'reactive rather than proactive' and recommended that the causes of sickness absence be looked at; these included 'poor working conditions and a stressful working environment'. They noted that, 'favourable conditions at work might be expected to lower rates of short spells of absence'.

THE CAUSES OF STRESS

Over the years, many scientific medical studies have shown that stress at work is mainly caused by: rapid change, uncertainty, lack of control and high workload. All of these events have become much more common during the 1980s and 1990s. Of course, events outside of work (such as relationship problems, house change) influence and interact with work-related stress. Professor Cary Cooper and colleagues detail several main sources of stress,[6] summarized below. Of course, there are many overlaps between these categories and many people suffer from more than one of these causes of stress.

○ Factors intrinsic to the job: poor physical working conditions (and lighting, noise, heat, high/low humidity); working alone and/or unsocial hours and shiftwork; work overload or underload; repetitive and unstimulating tasks; poorly designed equipment and machines; physical danger; chemical and biological hazards; person–job mismatch.

○ Role in the organization: role ambiguity; role conflict; too much/too little responsibility.

○ Relationships at work: relationships with superiors, colleagues and subordinates.

○ Career development: linked to job insecurity; short-term contracts; over-promotion; job relocation and early retirement; lack of retraining.

○ Organization structure and culture: no participation in the decision-making process, lack of effective communication, restrictions on behaviour and new management techniques (e.g. quality circles, total quality management team working) were identified as a major cause of stress by almost half (48 per cent) of the TUC's 1996 survey of 7000 safety representatives.

○   Home-work interface: this is especially important for female workers, who also bear the brunt of looking after the children, caring for elderly relatives, cooking, cleaning, shopping etc. Long hours, for both females and males, mean less family life and stress on relationships with partners, children and family, and friends.

LONG HOURS AND SHIFTWORK

The Ten Hours Bill was not only a great practical success; it was the victory of a principle; it was the first time that in broad daylight the political economy of the middle class succumbed to the political economy of the working class.

Karl Marx, *Das Kapital*, 1864.

It is obvious to most people that working longer hours can add to stress and fatigue. In 1996 in the UK there were 3.9 million people working more than 48 hours per week. This compares with just 2.7 million in 1984 when the figures were first collected. By 1990 the UK had about twice as many employees than any other EU country working more than 48 hours in a normal working week. In addition, nearly 2.5 million workers (12 per cent of the workforce) get no paid holidays at all, and one in five employees (4.1 million) receive less than three weeks' paid holiday per year. The previous Conservative government strongly resisted the EU Working Time Directive. However, in November 1996 it lost its case against this Directive in the European Court of Justice. Even so, in March 1997 it said that if it won the general election of May 1997, it would demand a change of treaty law, retrospectively stopping the use of health and safety provisions to enact, what the Conservatives - but not other European Countries - saw as employment law.

FIGURE 5.1   Some disputes are over long hours of work.

It is ironic that a Conservative government that used the long history of UK 'Factory Acts' to influence EU law with regard to 'reasonably practicable' and 'risk assessment' (page 45), should try and argue that long hours of work are *not* a health and safety issue. Have they forgotten their history? The first effective – in that it was enforced by the first ever four factory inspectors – UK Factory Act was that of 1833. It was largely concerned with obtaining a maximum 12-hour day for young persons in cotton, woollen and linen mills. In the event, the appeal to EU Court of Justice, by the then Conservative government, led to a widening of the definition of Article 118a of the EU Treaty of Rome to that of the World Health Organization: 'Health is a state of complete physical, mental and social well-being and that does not consist only of the absence of illness or infirmity.'[7]

Health effects of long hours/shiftwork

Last year, I had the experience of listening to a keynote lecture[8] on health, shiftwork and long hours from Dr Anne Spurgeon of The Institute of Occupational Health at Birmingham University, where three key papers cited were from 1884 (Mather, engineering), 1901 (Abbia, optical instruments) and 1918 (Vernon, munitions workers).

Both Professor J. M. Harrington, of the Institute of Occupational Health at Birmingham University and Professor Simon Folkard, of the Medical Research Council's Body Rhythms and Shiftwork Centre at the University of Swansea, reviewed the medical evidence for the European Commission. Harrington's work is in the public arena. Harrington (1994) concludes that: the link between shiftwork and heart disease is 'strong enough', although there is not yet a clear link with long hours; the case for gastrointestinal disorders (especially peptic ulcer) is 'quite good but by no means overwhelming', 'on balance, night shift work carries a poorer performance and safety record than other shifts', and 'overall, the effect of shift work has been likened to a long distance traveller working in San Francisco and returning to London for rest days.' He comments that:

> ... evidence has accrued that suggests that shift work and long hours of work do increase the workers' stress rating and, yet again, the night shift emerges as the greatest stressor. The freedom to choose one's own shift schedule appears to be an important factor in determining stress levels.

Anecdotally he notes that many major catastrophes, such as Three Mile Island, Chernobyl and Exxon Valdes, all happened in the early hours of the morning, through people who had been on duty for long hours making errors. This correlation has been noted by others concerned with the health and safety effects of a '24-hour society'.[9]

On a medical basis of health, and especially circadian rhythm principles (humans work on a 25-hour circadian rhythm), Harrington (1994) concludes:

○ Limit night work wherever possible.

○ If limiting night work is not possible, rapid rotating shifts are the best possible option, as permanent nights are rarely an acceptable solution.

○ Compressed working weeks (e.g. 12-hour days) carry increased fatigue per shift, but an extended rest break of several days appears to mitigate most of this extra fatigue and is usually acceptable to the workforce.

○ Avoid a 0600 hour start to the morning shift (but this is difficult without changing the length of some other shifts).

○ Allow at least one rest day, preferably two, between shift changes and ensure that, wherever possible, some of these rest days coincide with weekends.

THE EU WORKING TIME DIRECTIVE

The EU Working Time Directive gives employees new legal rights to:

○ a maximum 48-hour week, including overtime, *averaged* over a four-month reference period

○ an *average* eight-hour night shift in any 24 hours measured over a reference period specified in collective agreements or national legislation

○ a rest break when the working day is longer than six hours which is defined either in collective agreements or in national legislation

○ a daily rest period of 11 consecutive hours in every 24 hours and a rest period every seven days of 24 hours plus the 11 hours daily rest (i.e. 35 hours in total)

○ a minimum of four weeks' annual paid leave.

Much of the detail is open to collective bargaining agreements between the employer and trade unions.[10] Many groups of workers are excluded (e.g. air, sea, road, inland waterways, fishing, doctors in training) but public employees have been covered by the Directive since 23 November 1996. Although draft UK government proposals were issued by the Department of Trade and Industry before the general election of May 1997, it was agreed that such an important issue would wait until after the election, as there was a considerable disagreement between the two main political parties over controlling working time. The (now) Prime Minister, Tony Blair, said before the election, 'A vote for the Tories is a vote for no holidays!'

One contentious issue is whether the working time regulations should be enforced via industrial tribunals, as the Conservatives proposed, or by HSE inspectors through the courts. History and the possibility of effective enforcement suggests that it should be the HSE that enforces the working hours regulations,[11] as they are health and safety based in any case.

STRESS PREVENTION

The 1995 Industrial Society survey[2] of 699 managers found that whilst one-third of organizations had taken measures to help employees cope with stress, only one in five had done anything to prevent workplace stress. This is commonly the case: even when stress is recognized at the workplace, only the symptoms are dealt with, not the cause.

CASE STUDY 12: NOT ONLY STRESS COUNSELLING

In 1996–97, in conjunction with Professor Cary Cooper and Kate Sparks of the University of Manchester Institute of Science and Technology (UMIST), I surveyed Transport and General Workers Union (TGWU) safety representatives who had said that stress was a problem at their workplace to an earlier, more general survey, at 245 workplaces. The most common causes of stress were: pressure and deadlines (60 per cent), work overload (54 per cent), the threat of job losses (52 per cent), lack of consultation and communication (51 per cent), understaffing (46 per cent), long working hours (41 per cent), low rates of pay (41 per cent) and feeling undervalued (43 per cent). Two out of three (67 per cent) TGWU safety representatives said that their management had taken no action to reduce workplace stress. Where some action was taken, the most common management action was stress management/lifestyle programmes (30 per cent), counselling (28 per cent), or health promotion such as health screening, healthy food or exercise (27 per cent). Cooper and Sparks commented on the results: 'What is needed is not only stress management training and counselling but also stress audits and risk assessments of underlying structural problems at work.'[12]

Of course, there is nothing wrong with treating the symptoms of stress, if there is a stressed workforce. As for any other workplace ill-health problem, good and effective treatment should be freely available (it rarely is). But there can be problems with this approach. Some employees might reasonably ask, 'Why should I give up my valuable lunch hour freetime to go to exercise/relaxation to reduce workplace stress classes when it was caused by the company in the first place?' In another recent case, of a medium-sized organization with a large stress problem, I heard that some members of staff were driving from Norwich to London for their 'stress counselling', and then carrying on with a day's work. The answer is, of course, to deal with the *causes* as well as the *symptoms*, and this approach is supported by the 1974 Health and Safety at Work Act and some recent HSE guidance on stress.

THE LAW ON STRESS

The driving force for stress awareness and action has come, unusually in the area of workplace health and safety, more from common law claims than HSE guidance, although this may now be slowly changing. The first stress-related compensation claims were for post-traumatic stress disorder (PTSD), the modern term for the old-fashioned sounding 'nervous shock'.[6] These claims first came about as a result of large public disasters, such as those at Hillsborough and Zeebrugge. However, violence at the workplace appears to have grown in recent years and claims for PTSD are now being won on an individual basis (see page 149).

Common law claims

Without doubt, the key stress at work common law case has been that of social worker John Walker in 1996.[13] Mr Walker became a social worker in 1965. In 1974 he was appointed area manager responsible for the Blyth Valley division of Northumberland County Council. Over the next 13 years the population of that division rose from 65,000 to 80,000, leading to a six-fold increased case load. For example, the number of children on the abuse register jumped from 15 to 88. He repeatedly sought extra staff and administrative back-up, but his verbal and written requests were refused.

Because of the stress, in November 1986 he suffered from a nervous breakdown, returning to work in March 1987. The authority did nothing to ease his workload or the stress and by September 1987 he was diagnosed as having a state of stress-related anxiety and was advised to go on sick leave. He suffered a second nervous breakdown and was retired on medical grounds in May 1988.

After several court appearances, in April 1996 he was offered an out-of-court settlement of £175,000, which he accepted. John Walker (who is 59 years old, and a father of four) says that although he has largely recovered from the depression and anxiety, he can no longer hold down a stressful job and is now a painter and decorator, earning less than half of the £28,000 a year that he would have been earning. Roger Poole, Assistant General Secretary of UNISON, John Walker's union, who took his case to court, said:

> It is sad that it has taken John nearly eight years to receive just compensation for the enormous damage to his health. It is sad that an excellent social worker, a man of normally robust personality who had so much to give, was forced out of his job. Employers everywhere should take note that you can't gamble with the health of your workforce. (UNISON press-release, 26 April 1996).

As usual, the lawyers are divided over the significance of the John Walker case. The general feeling is that, because the grounds were so specific, there will not be a flood of stress cases (and there has not been in the past two years). In the somewhat cautious words of John Walker's UNISON solicitor John Usher: 'As we have proved in this case, the law is very slow in these matters. We have cut a path through the jungle, but it will be many years before there is a three-lane highway.'

Yet shortly after the John Walker case, UNISON was successful in a common law stress (anxiety and depression) claim yet again.[14] In this case Janet Ballantyne had been bullied by a senior manager and was awarded, in an out-of-court settlement, £66,000.

HSE STRESS GUIDANCE

For some years the trade unions have been pushing the HSE for legal guidance on the control and prevention of workplace stress,[15] although this was not the case some ten years ago, when I reviewed the trade union approach to stress.[16] Then there was still a feeling among some trade unionists that stress was not really a trade union issue; it was too 'soft'. Yet ironically, at the same time I identified various academic studies that had revealed the stress of being a trade union shop steward, safety representative, branch secretary or full-time officer. This situation is even worse today with the 'downsizing' of trade unions. Without doubt, the leading trade unions on stress have been the teachers' unions. Various scientific surveys throughout the 1980s, produced for the main teaching trade unions, identified stress as the principal issue for school teachers.

The most recent, a 1991 UMIST survey for the NASUWT, found that:

○ one of five teachers suffer levels of anxiety, depression and psychosomatic symptoms at or above the level of psychoneurotics
○ two out of three (66 per cent) teachers had considered leaving teaching in the preceding two years
○ one in four (28 per cent) teachers were currently looking for alternative employment
○ over one in ten (13 per cent) teachers were seeking early retirement

In fact, the number of teachers currently seeking early retirement has swamped the scheme and the government tried to curtail such retirement in early 1997. A legal challenge by the teachers' unions forced the government to back down. Yet the teachers' pension fund does not have enough money. This would seem to be a waste of valuable, trained teachers, and may damage the future of our children. For many years the HSE refused to recognize that stress was an occupational disease. Then in 1990, under great pressure from the teachers' unions, the HSE at last produced stress guidance for teachers.[17] This HSE guidance, according to teachers active in the area of stress reduction, has been 'very useful' in raising the issue with school management and local authorities.

In 1993 the HSE published the results of a literature search and recommendations by stress expert Professor Tom Cox[18] and this research lead directly to the first ever general HSE guidance on stress, published on 30 May 1995, *Stress at Work – a Guide for Employers*.[19] Introducing the HSE guidance, Dr Paul Davies of the HSE said, 'Surveys undertaken by the HSE and others suggest that the problem is now seen as a major contributor to work-related illness and sickness absence.' However, although the HSE guidance is very general and offers less than is discussed above, its importance lies in that *it is the first general recognition of the problem of stress at work by the HSE.*

The guidance reminds employers that they have a legal duty to control stress at work under the 1974 Health and Safety at Work Act and The Management of

Health and Safety at Work Regulations 1992. The guidance notes that:

> Not enough is known to set detailed standards or requirements ... Employers should bear stress in mind when assessing possible health hazards in their workplaces, keeping an eye out for developing problems and being prepared to act if harm to health seems likely.

In other words, stress should be treated like any other health hazard.

Is the HSE stress guidance effective?

Using the government's Code of Practice on Freedom of Information during 1996, I was able to get the four-page guidance to HSE inspectors on enforcing this stress guidance. The guidance, now available to anyone from local HSE offices, states that enforcement action should, 'only be considered in the most exceptional circumstances'. It adds:

> In all cases it is important not to raise expectations or give the impression that enforcement action will be taken. Attention can be drawn to the difficulty of setting and enforcing specific standards in this area ... there is no basis for setting specific standards nor, except in exceptional circumstances, in taking formal enforcement action.

However, the HSE guidance to inspectors does state: 'If it is clear that:

○ There is a risk to health caused by work;
○ Reasonable practicable action is possible to help prevent it; and
○ The employer has been made aware of her/his legal responsibilities but still refuses to take action, then the first stages of enforcement action need to be considered – probably an improvement notice requiring an organisation to assess the risks from stress.'

In March 1997 I tried to find out from the 21 HSE area offices whether they had taken any enforcement action over stress and to obtain copies of any stress improvement notices issued. The reply back came not from the area officers, but from Ms Jenny Bacon, director general of the HSE. She made it quite clear that there had been little, if any, HSE enforcement action over workplace stress.

Her reply has received backing from the results of the survey I carried out with Professor Cary Cooper and Kate Sparks of UMIST.[12] The survey from TGWU safety representatives in 245 workplaces found that:

○ only one in five (22 per cent) of the TGWU safety representatives had seen the HSE guidance on stress
○ just over one in ten (12 per cent) said their management had seen it
○ almost half (45 per cent) did not know whether their management had seen it or not
○ more than nine out of ten (93 per cent) said that no action had been taken to reduce stress as a result of the HSE guidance

A full copy of these results was sent to Ms Jenny Bacon, but she just gave me a general 'We are concerned' reply. What is clear is that there has been little or no enforcement – letters, notices served or prosecutions – on workplace stress issues by the HSE. There is clearly a need for specific legislation, backed up by an approved code of practice, on controlling and reducing workplace stress. This was a key demand by the TUC during 1997.

A SWEDISH STRESS LAW

In 1991 the Swedish Work Environment Act was amended to include stress as an issue. The amendment required that:

○ working conditions are to be adapted to people's physical and psychological conditions
○ employers are to be given opportunities of participating in the arrangements of their own work situation
○ work should be organized to prevent employee exposure to physical or mental loads that may lead to ill-health or accidents.
○ forms of remuneration and work schedules that involve an appreciable risk of ill-health and accidents are not to be used
○ strictly controlled or tied work is to be avoided or restricted
○ work should afford opportunity for variety, social contacts, co-operation and connection between individual tasks
○ working conditions should provide for opportunities for personal and occupational development as well as for self-determination and professional responsibility.

A STRESS POLICY

Employee questionnaires are a good, and relatively easy, way of determining whether a workforce is stressed, the causes of stress and some of the possible solutions. It is well known that surveys by trade unions, not just on stress, usually reveal more problems than those by management. There is a fear – rightly or wrongly – from already stressed employees that if they admit to being stressed they may be further victimized or 'medically retired'. Therefore, if management carries out the survey, confidentiality is very important to obtain meaningful results.

In fact, many union surveys are also confidential. There may be no need to make it confidential – it depends on the employees – and, of course, such questionnaires should be modified to local circumstances and workplaces. It is important to try and get a good response (at least 90 per cent) to the survey, so that it is truly representative of all the workforce.

Having identified the problem, one way forward is to draw up a stress policy, based on the above principles. UNISON has issued a draft one for consideration, the main points of which are as follows:

○ The parties to this agreement recognize that stress is a problem under the 1974 Health and Safety at Work Act and employers are required to carry out a risk assessment on health and safety, including stress, under the Management of Health and Safety at Work Regulations 1992.
○ This agreement will apply to all employees.
○ Stress is a health problem and there will be no discrimination against individual employees suffering from stress.
○ The HSE guide, *Stress at Work*, will be used to determine the causes of stress and to control them.
○ The organization and agreements for dealing with stress at work will form part of the employer's health and safety policy.
○ Priority will be given to assessing the causes of stress at work and heads of departments (or equivalent) will be responsible for those assessments, in consultation with the union. Specific training will be given for people carrying out stress assessments.
○ Confidential counselling will be offered by trained counsellors.
○ Employees suffering from stress-related illnesses will be offered paid time off for counselling. Counselling should be made available outside of working hours also and the names and how to contact such counsellors drawn to the attention of all staff.
○ Stress information and training will be given to all staff, including a copy of this agreement.
○ Employees unable to carry out their normal duties because of stress will be offered suitable alternative posts, with relocation as last resort (unless requested by the employee).
○ This effectiveness of this stress policy will be reviewed jointly by management and unions on a regular basis; after the first six months and then annually.

BULLYING AT WORK

Janet Ballantyne worked in Strathclyde's Social Work Department from 1979 to 1992, and was appointed to be deputy officer-in-charge of Strathclyde Regional Home for the Elderly. In 1991 a new officer-in-charge was appointed to the home who was outspoken and abrasive and who ignored and humiliated colleagues.

Despite continuous complaints to senior management, no action was taken, and eventually Mrs Ballantyne was driven off work suffering from panic attacks and stress in November 1992. She eventually took early retirement due to illness in 1993. In July 1996 she accepted an out-of-court settlement from South Lanarkshire Council (who inherited Strathclyde's liabilities) of £66,000.[14]

In October 1997 trainee solicitor Andrea Harrison received £50,000 in an out-of-court settlement from a Manchester law firm, Lawrence Murphy and Co. She had been subjected to relentless sexual harassment by a legal executive at the firm, which had resulted in her suffering extreme stress and leaving the firm. The solicitors' senior partner had witnessed much of the conduct, but had failed to take action even when asked. (See Frances Gibb (1997) Law firm pays out £50,000 for bullying, *The Times*, 28 October.)

The increased pressure on managers and staff has seen a rise in the number of cases of workplace bullying, like that of Janet Ballantyne quoted above. Many trade unions (e.g. MSF, UNISON, BIFU, CPSA, NASUWT) have been researching, producing guidance and raising the issue of bullying at work, after the 1994 publication of a key book on the subject by Andrea Adams.[20] The MSF union found that more than half of Britain's top 100 companies have no policy to combat workplace bullying. The unison quotes a BBC survey of 1137 workers which found that more than half complained of being bullied and 78 per cent had actually witnessed workplace bullying. (See Barry Clement (1994) Workplace bullying attacked, *Independent*, 7 November.)

In the first week of December 1997 the TUC set up a helpline for those who felt they had been bullied at work. In one week they received almost 5000 responses (see Barry Clement (1997) Bullying bosses make working life a living hell, *Independent*, 22 December). The key features were:

O 4 out of 10 calls to the hotline were from people who felt they were being bullied, and nearly half of them were men
O More than one in four calls came from managers complaining about authoritarian and unreasonable bosses
O One in three calls were from white-collar workers
O Three in four callers worked in medium-sized firms, with fewer than 1000 employees
O One in four callers complained of low pay (some earned as little as £1 an hour, while nearly half earned less than £2.50 an hour)

The issue of workplace bullying is taken much more seriously in the Scandinavian countries (where it is known as 'mobbing'). In Norway for example, the law actually recognizes it as an occupational health problem. (See Helge Hoel (1997) Bullying at work: a Scandinavian perspective, *Journal of the Institution of Occupational Safety and Health*, **1**, 51–9.)

UNISON has recently produced an excellent guide on bullying[21] that advises that employers must:

O recognize the seriousness of the issue and the detrimental effects on the staff and the organization
O prepare a public statement that bullying is unacceptable behaviour
O develop procedures for recording, reporting and dealing with incidents

○ provide access to trained counsellors, with confidentiality respected
○ provide training for managers and supervisors
○ undertake an investigation into:
  –   management style
  –   morale levels
  –   sickness absence levels
  –   sickness presence levels (the 'working wounded')
  –   any unexpected changes of behaviour, staff turnover etc.

There is a case for considering bullying and workplace violence, and perhaps stress, as a single issue, and a recent, useful and up-to-date booklet by the Labour Research Department does just this.[22]

VIOLENCE AT WORK

A nurse was violently attacked by a patient at work. She was permanently traumatized and years after the attack still has to live in sheltered accommodation. She is generally anxious and cannot work. She is afraid of being left alone, and finds it difficult to answer the door or go to the shops alone. On the grounds of ill-health, she was sacked by her employer 15 months after the attack. With the help of her union, UNISON, she was awarded £88,000 compensation for her post-traumatic stress disorder from the government's Criminal Injuries Compensation Scheme. But David Stothard, UNISON solicitor dealing with her case, said, 'All the money in the world will never be able to cure her.'

In 1996–97, for the first time, HSE figures became available (HSE, 1997) for the level of violence reported at work to the authorities: 2 people were killed, 697 received major injuries (such as fractures) and 3980 received injuries which made them stay away from their normal work for over three days.

According to the British Retail Consortium 1995–96 annual survey, published in 1997:

○ 9000 shop staff were subjected to physical violence
○ 47,000 were subjected to threats of violence
○ 120,000 were subjected to verbal abuse.

This translates to one member of shop staff being assaulted or intimidated every minute in a typical shopping day. The data indicate that there has been a 5 per cent increase in the number of victims of physical violence in the last year.

A 1996 survey by the trade union UNISON of its NHS members found that:

○ 40 per cent of health staff reported suffering from violence at work during the previous year
○ 62 percent were worried about the violence at work

FIGURE 5.2   There have been disputes over workplace violence going back some years.

○   67 per cent were more worried about workplace violence than they had been a year ago

In response, the HSC published in December 1997 a new report that showed healthcare workers were three times more at risk from work-related violence than the general population (see *Violence and Aggression to Staff in Health Services*). The guidance also gave a framework for action based on policies and procedures, such as working patterns and practices, staffing levels and competence, training and means to deal with any incidents which do occur. Launching the report, HSC chair Frank Davies said:

> Whilst these measures do have minor cost implications, this needs to be offset by the high costs of failing to act. A high level of violence to staff affects not only the staff exposed to the risks. Employers face costs in terms of reduced efficiency, sickness absence and a bad 'image'. In relation to these costs, the expense of effective prevention measures is small. (Press notice C51/97, 10 December 1997)

Trade union concern over the growth in workplace violence has resulted in the HSE commissioning the London Tavistock Institute (1997) to review workplace-related violence. The review identifies the major problem areas and risk factors, and suggests further work and strategies for prevention. Experience from the US, where workplace violence has been recognized by the government as a major workplace health and safety hazard – each week 20 workers are murdered and 18,000 are assaulted while at work – suggests the most effective workplace programmes for reducing violence were based on the following actions:

O pre-screening of prospective employees (in consideration of the fact that most of the job harassment comes from colleagues)
O training (short sessions, videos and publications) and information pro- grammes (newsletters)
O task forces focusing on violence and other forms of employee support (hotlines, regional intervention teams)
O zero-tolerance policy and related communication campaigns

In December 1997 the rail union, RMT, released a summary of a survey of violence on the London Underground by independent consultants, Trident Consultants Ltd. They found that in any one year, nearly half (44 out of every 100) the ticket collectors had been assaulted. Supervisors had a one in ten risk of being assaulted and some train crew faced a 1 in 20 risk. The report made recommendations to reduce the level of violence, including a better service, training and improved information for passengers.

The HSE guidance on workplace violence[23] states:

Employees whose job requires them to deal with the public can be at risk from violence. Most at risk are those involved in: giving a service, caring, education, cash transactions, delivery/collection, controlling and representing authority. (p. 1)

The HSE definition of work-related violence is 'any incident in which a person is abused, threatened or assaulted in circumstances relating to their work', such as those:

O requiring medical assistance (major injury)
O requiring only first aid (minor injury)
O involving a threat with a weapon/object but causing no physical harm or injury
O involving verbal abuse

The HSE suggested ways of preventing or reducing workplace violence are:

O to list all jobs where workers come into contact with the public and to identify those where there is a risk of violence
O to ensure that all incidents are reported, analysed and acted upon
O to develop a preventative strategy, through a working party chaired by a senior member of management (with union or employee involvement)
O to consider a range of preventative measures for each problem area, in conjunction with the employees in that area
O to ensure that preventative measures are implemented and regularly monitored

○   to ensure that any employee who is the subject of a violent attack receives the appropriate support and counselling and compensation.

There is specific guidance on reducing violence in the bus[24] and retail[25] industries. There is a case for considering bullying and workplace violence (and perhaps stress) as a single issue, which is what the Labour Research Department (1997) *Stress, Bullying and Violence – A Trade Union Action Guide* does.

HAZARDOUS CHEMICALS

Comprehensive exposure data are only held world-wide for around 400 of the 100,000 odd chemicals in the marketplace.
Jenny Bacon, director general of the Health and Safety Executive,
Lane Lecture, University of Manchester, 1995.

Employee exposure to a wide range of chemicals, often at low doses, has been a problem of increasing concern at the workplace. A brief discussion of three key problem areas will illustrate the current concern: the problem of multiple chemical sensitivity (MCS); the reproductive hazards of chemicals, and the problems of respiratory sensitizers causing asthma at work.

MULTIPLE CHEMICAL SENSITIVITY

Gillian McCarthy, a former biochemist, is now so sensitive to most chemicals – perfumes, petrol fume and even tap water – that she has been forced to live far away from 'civilization' in a tent 300 yards from the sea, off the Dorset coast.[26] She is a sufferer from multiple chemical sensitivity (MCS). For many years, doctors in America have recognized that there is a growing group of people in the population – possibly up to one in seven (15 per cent) – who are sensitized by low-level exposures to many commonly used chemicals: solvents, detergents, pesticides (including wood preservatives), metals, formaldehyde etc.[27]

A UK report published in May 1997 (see Schools swept by ME plague, *Guardian*, 22 May) – surveying 1000 schools in six local education authorities – found that myalgic encephalomyelitis (or ME) was responsible for long-term sickness absence in around half (51 per cent) of pupils. there is clearly an overlap between MCS and ME. ME is known as chronic fatigue syndrome by the medical profession, and remains to be fully explored.

Many people who suffer from MCS are especially sensitive to a wide range of other common chemicals: perfumes, new paints and varnishes, cigarette smoke, hair and body shampoo, cooking odours, car exhausts, nail polish, new furniture and so on. The symptoms of MCS are very wide: headaches, runny nose, itchy eyes and skin, fatigue, depression, anxiety, anger, flu-like symptoms, sore throats, tight chest, dizziness, memory loss, joint pain, stomach upset and so on. Clearly, with such a wide range of symptoms, MCS can, and often is, misdiagnosed or just not diagnosed at all. Some people, like Gillian McCarthy, are so sensitized to very low levels of chemicals that they can hardly live in a modern industrial society and are forced to adhere to a very strict pollution-free regime, wear a face mask in public places, undergo periodic 'cleansing' of their systems at (expensive) private clinics and, in some cases, cut themselves off from normal society all together.

MCS has now been examined within the EU,[28] and only very recently the Department of Health and the HSE awarded the Institute of Occupational Medicine, in Edinburgh, a contract to research what is known about MCS in the UK; the outcome of this research is awaited with great interest.

Over many years I have come across many people with MCS and, at first, I did not recognize it. One of the first times I can remember was around 1982, when I was involved in many cases of 'formaldehyde poisoning' from ureaformaldehyde foam then being used to insulate the cavity walls of many schools, elderly persons' homes and other buildings. In more recent years I have helped many people with the symptoms of MCS from exposure to solvents and pesticides (especially as used in home and work – wood treatments for dampness and infestation). I can testify that their lives were ruined by the fact that they often could hardly go anywhere without the symptoms being brought on: by a recently painted room; a tin of lacquer left open in a room; being stuck in a traffic jam and exposed to exhaust fumes; and so on.

CASE STUDY 13: OPERA SINGER'S HEALTH RUINED

Bettina Jonic-Calder has been a successful opera singer for many years and she often performs in small soireés at the Royal Albert Hall. In January 1989 some contractors came to treat the dry rot and woodworm in her flat in South Kensington, London. They arrived unannounced, told her not to worry, put up a bit of inadequate plastic sheeting, sprayed the stuff all around and left. Thus was to begin a nightmare that has continued to this very day. Her flat had been sprayed with a then common formulation for this type of treatment: Lindane, tributyl tin oxide (TBTO) and pentachlorophenol (PCP). Almost immediately after the spraying she started to suffer from inflammation of the sinuses, streaming of the eyes and headaches. Her au pair suffered ill-health too. It was not until she took her cat to the vet and he diagnosed liver damage that she thought the treatment might have caused her ill-health. She still suffers from fatigue and has to watch her exposure to common chemicals that might trigger another attack. She has had several courses where her body has been 'cleaned out' in a clinic to help her immune system.

I met her about a year after her exposure, by which time she had written hundreds of letters to try and get some compensation and justice for her exposure, and helped her with her two ombudsman complaints. Eventually, in 1993 she won a successful Parliamentary ombudsman complaint against the

HSE. Then in 1994 she won a successful local ombudsman complaint against the EHO and local council. She was awarded £1000 compensation from Westminster Council for her anxiety and ill-health, and it was ordered to pay for a complete decontamination of her flat (about £25,000). As Bettina says, 'I never intended a long drawn out period of conflict. I simply needed help and neither the HSE nor the EHO responded to my distress. Two different ombudsman – to whom I am grateful – upheld my complaints. I think it is deplorable that I had to go to such lengths to remind them of their statutory duties.'[29]

In late 1997 she received £25,000 compensation in an out-of-court settlement, and her au pair received £5000. Bettina wanted to go to court, but by that time she was too ill with breast cancer. 'Could this be related to my pesticide exposure?', she asked me.

REPRODUCTIVE HAZARDS

The year 1997 opened with the media and press headlines such as 'Men are producing 50 per cent less sperm.' The cause was a new study by Finnish doctors, reported in the *British Medical Journal*, suggesting that men of age 53 had on average half the amount (26.9 per cent) of normal sperm of men ten years previously (56.4 per cent). In other words, only one in four of the men was making normal sperm. This is just the latest of many medical papers, starting in 1992, that have traced the decline in sperm count and quality in recent years. Traditionally, the emphasis on work causing reproductive damage has been on the woman: when pregnant, and when exposed to ionizing radiation, lead and certain chemicals known to harm the foetus. In the USA, women have even had themselves sterilized to work in lead plants. In the UK, women may not work in relatively high lead level areas if they are of 'reproductive capacity'. Many years ago, a woman driver was 'fairly' dismissed from driving loads of dimethyl formamide (DMF) because of possible reproductive effects on her. But it is often forgotten, that the male is involved in the reproductive act, if only briefly.

For many years it has been known that a wide range of chemicals can have effects on the reproductive systems of both females and males. In 1982, a key book in this area documented such effects for 50 commonly used chemicals, noting the lack of hard information, and real research, in this area.[30] In 1985 the Manufacturing, Science and Finance (MSF) trade union, with the help of a grant from the Equal Opportunities Commission, were able to commission Dr Tony Fletcher to review the literature on substances and other agents that were reproductive hazards at the workplace.[31] In 1996 the US government's National Institute for Occupational Safety and Health (NIOSH) produced guidance that listed 17 common workplace agents (from various chemicals, to heat, radar and welding) that caused one or all of the following: lowered sperm count; abnormal sperm shape, altered sperm transfer and altered hormones/sexual performance.[32]

However, the real bombshell in this area came in 1996 with the publication of the controversial American book, *Our Stolen Future*.[33] In a wide-ranging, detailed and compelling analysis, the authors demonstrated that many commonly used chemicals – pesticides, plasticizers, hormones – were affecting the fertility of both humans and animals. In a preface to the book, US Vice-President Al Gore likened this book to Rachael Carson's 40-year-old classic, which started the world concern about pesticide hazards, *Silent Spring*. It is impossible to ignore the public and employee concerns about the reproductive effects of many chemicals today.

RESPIRATORY SENSITIZERS (ASTHMA-CAUSING AGENTS)

The late twentieth century has seen an amazing growth in asthma, both inside and outside of the workplace. Some surveys suggest that around one in ten of our children may have asthma, and this is a frightening fact. How much of this rise is due to diagnosis, better treatment, environmental factors etc. is still the subject of much public and scientific debate. Whilst there is still doubt about the role of the pollution from exhaust fumes in causing asthma, there is little argument that such fumes exacerbate asthma once you have it. Anyone who knows an asthmatic will know the effects that pollution can have on them, in congested traffic, and at certain times of the year.

Whilst there are some doubts about the environmental role of pollution in causing asthma, there is no such doubt about the fact that exposure to many substances at work can, and does, cause occupational asthma. Over 200 substances used at work are known to cause asthma. The HSE (1997) gives the following information on occupational asthma, which is admitted to be rising:

○   In the 1990 Labour Force Survey, 68,000 people reported that they had asthma caused or made worse by work; 20,000 thought that it had been caused by work.
○   Occupational chest consultants saw 851 new cases of asthma during 1995.
○   During 1995 there were 514 new cases of DSS disablement benefit awarded.

In 1995 the TUC launched a major publication, in conjunction with the Sheffield Occupational Health Project, on the incidence, causes and prevention of workplace asthma.[34] They estimated that some 400,000 people – or almost one in five of adult asthma sufferers – are affected by asthma because of their work. This is now a generally accepted figure by the medical profession. We have seen elsewhere (page 53) how the HSE, under pressure from industry, downgraded a legally binding approved code of practice to ineffective guidance in this important area.[35]

FIGURE 5.3   Violette Hutchins (Photo: PJ Arkell)

CASE STUDY 14: ASTHMA, 'A LONG-TERM DEATH SENTENCE'

In 1989, 46-year-old mother of four, Violette Hutchins, was very glad to get a job at a local electronics factory as a cable solderer. It meant that she did not have to work weekends and late nights, could see more of her children and six grandchildren and carry out more of her leisure activities, like karate, fishing and camping. The only drawback was that when she came home her children would tell her to take a bath as she stank of the soldering fumes. As she told me, 'The fumes used to fill the workshop. We worked through our tea breaks and eat our lunch in the workroom. You were never away from the fumes.'

But within three months of starting work she found she had a persistent cough, sore throat and runny eyes. She thought she had a cold and her GP gave her a hay fever pump. She went back to work, but within another three months she was hospitalized with an asthma attack. She was given a ventolin pump and went back to work. But by June 1991 she was back in hospital again and this time her consultant asked her what she worked with. The firm was informed by her doctor that her asthma was work-related. It did put her on office work, but she frequently had to visit the fumy workshop, and so continued to have asthma attacks and have to take time off work. Then, in February 1992, with no consultation, the firm sacked her.

Angry at being made ill by the company, and then being sacked, she fought back – with the aid of her union, the TGWU, as she says, 'I could not have done it without the union' – for *some* compensation. After five years, and a long and sometimes frustrating struggle, she was awarded £500,000 in January 1997. But by then she could not walk unaided, needed constant oxygen, could not sleep well at night, was on six types of drugs (some, steroids, made her gain four stone), and was incontinent; also, the constant coughing had damaged her back. As she says, 'I am existing, not living. I would give every penny back for my lungs. The money just gives me a better standard of misery.'

For 20 years it has been known that the soldering fumes can cause asthma and the company should have provided good extraction. It supplied none and did not even report her accident to the HSE, as is required by law. The last words should go to Violette: 'If my case prevents just one person getting asthma like me it will have been worthwhile. I would not wish this on my worst enemy. I would say to people, do not be afraid to speak up and ask about the hazards. It is better to lose your job, rather than your health. Asthma is a long-term death sentence.'

THE CONTROL OF SUBSTANCES HAZARDOUS TO HEALTH REGULATIONS (COSHH) 1994

The key to the control of substances likely to cause asthma at the workplace – and any other chemical or biological hazard – is the Control of Substances Hazardous to Health Regulations 1994 or COSHH for short. These regulations were first introduced in 1989 and the HSE evaluated[36] their effectiveness in 536 workplaces during 1992.

In summary, the HSE found that:

○ Three out of five (60 per cent) of employers had completed their COSHH assessments.
○ In almost nine out of ten (87 per cent) the control measures were assessed to be more than adequate or satisfactory. However, in more than one in four workplaces visited, exposure limits were thought to be above allowed levels for more than one activity.
○ Four out of five (80 per cent) employers had given their employees adequate information, action in emergencies, routine precautions and the use of protective equipment for the hazards of the substances they were using.
○ Less than one in three employers were informing, instructing and training their employees to an adequate level.
○ Four out of five employers carried out monitoring as recommended.
○ Fewer than half the workplaces that should have been carrying out health surveillance were actually doing so.

In the 536 workplaces surveyed, one in five employers had recorded 1111 cases of ill-health resulting from workplace exposure to hazardous substances in two years. *It was estimated that the correct application of COSHH would have prevented two out of five, or 444, cases of ill-health.* The general conclusion was that COSHH had been successful.

However, a more recent survey[37] of the effectiveness of COSHH, looking at a very vulnerable group – those exposed to workplace sensitizers – found a somewhat different picture from the above HSE survey. Dr Sherwood Burge investigated a group of 61 workers with occupational asthma and found that:

○ almost half (48 per cent) were exposed to a known major cause of occupational asthma
○ three out of five (60 per cent) had not seen a hazards data sheet
○ almost nine out of ten (85 per cent) had been given no information on their risks of developing asthma
○ almost three out of five (54 per cent) had received no regular health surveillance
○ 50 per cent had used protective masks and equipment, but only one in three had been given any instruction on the equipment and less than one in five had been trained in its use.

In August 1997 the HSE released the somewhat surprising results of an extensive survey of 1000 companies and 150 trade unions' safety representatives' knowledge of COSHH and safety standards ('occupational exposure limits').[38] The results were surprising in that trade union safety representatives knew more than the company safety officers or managers. Thus:

○ Ninety per cent of union safety representatives could give a 'reasonable, unprompted response when asked what they understood to be the principles of COSHH' compared with 75 per cent of heavy users of chemicals and only two-thirds of lower-use firms.
○ One in three (35 per cent) of heavy users of chemicals were not aware of occupational exposure limits, compared with just one in five (21 per cent) of union safety representatives.

Of course, the selection of employers was more random than that of the safety representatives (who may, therefore, have been more active), but even so it shows the very real value of trade union safety representatives. But the most depressing part of the survey was the conclusion that:

> Most users are opting for protection rather than prevention. They are using masks, ventilations systems and staff training to reduce the risks to staff, rather than tackling the problem at source by eliminating the hazardous airborne substance or by substituting with a less hazardous one.

Thus three in four (76 per cent) users issued masks; two in three (66 per cent) installed ventilation systems; and less than half (42 per cent) said that 'steps were taken to eliminate the harmful substance'.

In 1996–97 the HSE (HSE, 1997) issued 1183 improvement and prohibition notices concerned with COSHH. There were 20 successful prosecutions, but the average fine was just £1686. This is no deterrent to the criminal employer exposing its workforce to hazardous chemicals or biological materials. If the COSHH regulations were enforced firmly, there is no doubt that the incidence of illness at work would decrease considerably. This is an area where the HSE has excelled itself in producing very useful general guidance[39] and sometimes specific industry guidance.[40] Many trade associations and trade unions have produced their own guides on HSE/COSHH as well. The following, brief notes on COSHH are largely taken from the very useful, recently revised COSHH guide for employers.

In essence, the COSHH regulations contain six key elements:

1. Assess the risks to health arising from the substances/organisms and work methods used.
2. Decide what precautions are needed to control the hazards presented by the use of these substances/organisms. What are the risks?
3. Prevent or control the exposure to these risks.
4. Ensure that the control measures are used and maintained.
5. Monitor the exposure of workers to hazardous chemicals or organisms and, where appropriate, carry out medical health surveillance.
6. Ensure that employees are properly informed, trained and supervised.

THE HAZARD DATA SHEET

A key to assessing the risks to health is the hazard data sheet. It is most commonly – and legally – used for a chemical or product containing chemicals, but there is no reason why it should not be for a biologically active substance as well. There are still some very poor hazard data sheets around, but new HSE guidance should improve the situation.[41] According to the HSE, a good, and legal, hazard data sheet should contain the following information:

○ Identification of the substance/preparation and company.
○ Composition/information on ingredients.
○ Hazards identification.
○ First aid measures.
○ Fire-fighting measures.
○ Accidental release measures.
○ Handling and storage.
○ Exposure controls/personal protection.
○ Physical and chemical properties.
○ Stability and reactivity.
○ Toxicological information.
○ Ecological information.
○ Disposal considerations.
○ Transport information.
○ Regulatory information.
○ Other information.
○ It should be dated and if revised this should be so marked.

Further guidance is available[41] on what each of these headings mean, and if you are unsure you should always seek guidance from the suppliers of the hazard data

TABLE 5.1 Example of poor data sheet

Data sheet

PRODUCT NAME:	Machine Wash
CHEMICAL CLASSIFICATION:	A blend of chlorinated petroleum solvents and by-products.
FLAMMABILITY:	No flash point – No fire point.
THRESHOLD LIMIT VALUE:	340ppm.
HANDLING:	Prolonged contact with skin to be avoided. Could irritate sensitive skin. Wear neoprene gloves, if necessary.
FIRST AID:	If taken internally do not induce vomiting. Keep at rest. Call a doctor. If splashed into eyes, irrigate with copious amounts of clean water. Call a doctor. If skin is exposed remove soaked clothing, irrigate skin thoroughly, dry clothing before wearing.
FIRE FIGHTING:	
STORAGE:	Keep container closed.
DISPOSAL:	Dispose of in accordance with local regulations.
FURTHER COMMENTS:	Contains no TDI, benzene, carbon tetrachloride or tolvene.

sheet. If you are still unsure, seek further guidance from enforcement authorities, trade associations, trade unions, advice agencies (page 255), etc.

The most important deficiencies are:

○ Product composition is not adequately defined.
○ Little information given on physical or chemical properties (volatility etc).
○ Quoted threshold limit value is numerically impossible (not listed in Guidance Note EH40) and cannot be interpreted without details on composition. Advice on handling precautions is unhelpful.

TABLE 5.2 Example of an effective summary data sheet

HAZARD DATA SHEET

Triethylamine
$(C_2H_5)_3N$

Other names
—

Description
Colourless liquid with a strong ammonia-like odour.

Threshold Limit Value
25ppm

Flash point
−17°C (1°F)

Boiling point
90°C (194°F)

Lower explosive limit
1.21

Hazards
1   Highly flammable vapour.
2   Contact with eyes and skin causes burns.

Precautions
1   No smoking, naked flames, hot elements or other ignition sources.
2   If flammable concentrations are likely, use flameproof electrical fittings.
3   Ensure adequate earthing.
4   Avoid exposure to vapour at levels above the Threshold Limit Value.
5   Use gloves, eye protection and protective clothing at all times when handling this material.

Storage
1   Store in steel drums, tightly sealed and clearly labelled.
2   Drums should be stored in a flammable liquids store, which should be a cool, dry, well-ventilated place, protected from direct sunlight, heat and frost.
3   No smoking, naked flames, hot elements or other ignition sources.

Fire fighting procedure
Extinguish with foam, carbon dioxide or dry powder.

First aid measures

Inhalation
Remove to fresh air.
In severe cases, or if exposure has been great, obtain medical attention.

Skin contact
Wash with plenty of water.
Remove grossly contaminated clothing and wash before re-use.
In severe cases obtain medical attention.

Eye contact
Irrigate with plenty of water.
Obtain medical attention.

Ingestion
Obtain immediate medical attention.

Spillage
1   Eliminate all possible sources of ignition.
2   Wear goggles or face shield, gloves and protective clothing.
3   Use breathing apparatus in handling anything other than a small spillage.
4   Absorb on sand, earth or proprietary absorbent material and dispose of as chemical waste.
5   Wash site of spillage thoroughly with water.

EEC warning phrases
Highly flammable.
Irritating to eyes.
Irritating to respiratory system.
Keep away from sources of ignition — no smoking.
In case of contact with eyes, rinse immediately with plenty of water and seek medical advice.
Do not empty into drains.

Relevant legislation includes:
1   Disposal of Poisonous Wastes Act 1974.
2   Control of Pollution Act 1974.
3   Highly Flammable Liquids and Liquefied Petroleum Gases Regulations 1972.

Note: this single page format has been prepared by a user based on information supplied by various manufacturers and from other sources.

RISK ASSESSMENT

A collection of hazard data sheets, however good, is not a COSHH risk assessment. yet, all too often, when I ask a company safety officer, doctor or occupational hygienist – or a trade union safety representative – for a copy of the COSHH risk assessment for a chemical or biological hazard and/or process they hand me a bunch of hazard data sheets stapled together. This is the start, of course. We have discussed the politics and practice of general risk assessments elsewhere and those general points are valid for COSHH.

Basically:

○ Are the hazard data sheets relevant (i.e. are there mixtures of substances/organisms being used when the data sheets are for single substances)?
○ Under what conditions are the substances/organisms being used (e.g. a chemical which is 'safe' at room temperature, when exposed to a high temperature may decompose to more harmful products, an organism 'safe' at 0°C may multiply rapidly and be very dangerous at 20°C)?

SAMPLING FOR CHEMICALS, DUST AND BIOLOGICAL HAZARDS

This is a very specialist skill,[42] and an occupational hygienist, as they usually are, needs specialist and up-to-date training. The employees need to be involved and talk to the people doing the sampling. Are they sampling in the 'worst-case' situation? Are they using personal samplers (i.e. on the person doing the job)? What are they sampling for? What standards are they using when assessing the risk assessment/efficiency of protective measures, etc. Will the full report be available to the employees? If in any doubt, seek expert advice in this area (page 255). This is one area where apparently 'good' COSHH assessments fall down; sampling is not control. Just like the 'COSHH assessment' that is just a pile of data sheets stapled together. I have seen many thick COSHH assessments that are nothing more than (often inadequate) sampling data stapled together to fool the busy manager or safety representative that 'we have sampled' and everything is OK.

CONTROL

Has the COSHH recommended hierarchy of control measures been examined, followed and implemented? That is:

○ Changing the process to eliminate or reduce the hazard.
○ Replacing the hazard with safer alternative (e.g. water-based for solvent-based paints).
○ Using the product in a safer form (e.g. pellets, not powder).
○ Can the process be totally enclosed?
○ Is partial enclosure or 'local exhaust ventilation' possible?

○   Has general ventilation been considered (not suitable for toxic substances).

○   Can the work methods be improved to reduce exposure (e.g. water and surfactant wetting of dry asbestos before removal)?

○   Can the number of employees exposed, or their exposure time, be reduced by job rotation?

○   Personal protective equipment (PPE) is the last, and most dangerous, means of controlling substances hazardous to health.

SUBSTITUTION

The HSE guidance on substitution[39] gives some good case studies that can be modified to many other process. It is sometimes possible to 'jump out of the frying pan into the fire' with substitution and it is always best to take a broad – or even 'life cycle' or 'clean technology' (page 229) – look at substitution, in case one hazard is substituted for another.

CASE STUDY 15: THE PERILS OF SUBSTITUTION

It has been long known that solvent-based paints, adhesives, glues and other substances are harmful to the nervous system and, especially in the Scandinavian countries, there is concern over possible brain damage by such solvents. Hence the concern of many parents, social workers and doctors about 'glue sniffing' among young people. For many years workers have been 'glue sniffing' at work when exposed to organic solvents, and, indeed, some workers have even become addicted to the solvent effects. Since the late 1980s, the advent of COSHH, there has been a great pressure to replace these organic solvents with safer water-based paints, adhesives and glues.

At Camden Council, London, considerable union pressure, plus an HSE improvement notice in 1990, resulted in the council promising 'in principle' to phase out solvent-based paints, where possible, in September 1990. The council dragged its feet and the HSE had to warn, 'If the (COSHH) assessments have not been completed by 30 November, then the council will be in breach of their legal requirements, and legal proceedings may be taken against individual officers.'

In June 1991 Liam Teague, a Camden Council carpenter, turned up to carry out a small job that involved sticking some plastic skirting to a wall using adhesive. It was hot and dry and he was working in a small room with no ventilation. After about one and half days at the job he staggered out of the room, as he told me, 'like I was drunk'. Thus began his nightmare, where he suffered from: headaches, drowsiness, breathlessness, sickness, blurred vision, disturbed balance and soreness in the eyes and throat. He suffered from temporary blindness, hallucinations, depression and extreme mood changes, and he thought he was going to die. In 1996 a court found that he was suffering from post-traumatic stress disorder and awarded him substantial compensation. However, Camden Council has appealed to the Court of Appeal and this may take another 18 months.

A detailed 16-page investigation by Camden Council's safety officer found that: the adhesive used should have been a much safer water-based product; no hazard data sheets were provided; there had been no COSHH assessment; there was inadequate supervision; Liam had received no health and safety training; no one in management would take responsibility, and the council bonus scheme did not encourage health and safety. As Camden Council safety officer, Mathew McNeal said, 'He had been, in effect, slowly sniffing glue for a day and a half. Had he continued, he could well have died.'

In May 1992 Camden Council was fined a total of £3500 plus £750 under COSHH for this breaking of the law:

O   Failure to prevent or control a substance hazardous to health (Regulation 7(1); £1000 fine).

O   Failure to provide information, instructions and training sufficient for an employee to know the risks and precautions that were needed (Regulation 12(1); £1000 fine).

O   Failure to make a suitable and sufficient risk assessment (Regulation 6(1); £1500 fine).

The key point is that Liam should have used a safer, water-based product, and some complacency set in when this was not available and a more dangerous solvent-based adhesive was used instead. *Substitution must be enforced and monitored.* The last words should go to Liam, whose health has been permanently ruined (not least by Camden's failure to admit guilt and pay just compensation): 'They poisoned me and got away lightly. OK, I might get some compensation in the end. But what have the council learnt? Who do the HSE protect? The fine was pathetic after what they did to me.'[43]

LOCAL EXHAUST VENTILATION (LEV)

Although a very common answer to dust and fume reduction, and in use since the HSE ('Factory Inspectorate') was first formed, the real-life application of LEV still causes a multitude of health hazards.[44] The basic principles of LEV were laid down in the 1930s, and seem little changed since then; the subject does not seem fashionable enough for any real research on design, operation and limitations in practice. This has left the field wide open for any 'metal basher' who can put some other form of fume hood, ducting and extraction fan in place to call themselves 'heating and ventilation engineers'. Like many practising health and safety people, I regularly see: fans wired up to blow and not extract; ducting that is all split and not balanced (i.e. the suction not being where it is supposed to be, if it exists at all); totally ineffective fume hoods and waste bags stuffed full of dust and debris; and the by-pass in operation (sometimes recycling back into the plant).

Some basic questions to ask about LEV are as follows:

○ Is is really needed? Can the process be substituted or modified to remove the need for LEV?

○ What levels of chemical/dust/biological hazard in the air is the LEV designed to reduce the breathing zone down to? Or, alternatively, what pressure should the LEV system work at?

○ Is there an automatic alarm (best) or indicator/pressure–flow gauge (second best) to show when the system is falling below specification?

○ When was the LEV system last serviced and what were the results? How do they compare with the original specification? Regulation 9(2) and Schedule 3 of COSHH specify the minimum requirements for a 'thorough examination' of LEV equipment, which are, in general, at least once every 14 months and for the following specified processes:

  – blasting or cleaning metal castings and jute cloth manufacture – every month.

  – any dry grinding, abrading or polishing of metals (other than gold, platinum or iridium) that is carried out for more than 12 hours each week or any process giving off dust or fume from non-ferrous metal castings – every 6 months.

○ Is the captor hood as near the source of fume/dust as possible? Could it be better designed to capture more fumes or dust? Is the air velocity at the face of the hood that recommended by the designer of the system or in HSE guidance?

○ Does the fan extracting the dust come on immediately the extractor is switched on? Does it extract and not blow (this, amazingly, is not that uncommon)? Does it have all of its blades?

○ Check the ducting for any obvious dust/chemicals, any leaks, loose bolts, worn gaskets/flanges, poor connections, open outlets not in use, etc.

○ What are the procedures for emptying the carbon filter/dust bag, etc. How often should the filters be changed? How do you know when they are full? Is the procedure for changing them safe?

○ Where does the exhaust from LEV go? If internally exhausted (not a good idea, but often used to save money) what are the exhaust levels of contaminants? Is it safe or polluting the environment.

FIGURE 5.4   Local Exhaust Ventilation to a car exhaust pipe. Protects the employees, but what do the neighbours think?

PERSONAL PROTECTIVE EQUIPMENT (PPE)

> Unless and until the employer has done everything – and everything means a good deal – the workman can do next to nothing to protect himself.
>   Sir Thomas Legge (1863–1932), the first Medical Inspector of Factories in the UK.

The COSHH regulations[39] are quite clear that the provision of personal protective equipment should be used *only as the last resort* as a control measure:

So far as is reasonably practicable, the prevention or adequate control of exposure to employees of a substance hazardous to health, except to a carcinogen (i.e. causes cancer) or a biological agent, shall be secured by measures other than the provision of personal protective equipment. (Regulation 7(2)).

Ten years ago, in what, unfortunately, remains a unique guide, I surveyed the use of PPE from a user's point of view in 245 workplaces, employing some 43,000 people.[45] The results were not encouraging: although the equipment was provided, it was often not maintained and was uncomfortable; over 50 per cent were not even trained in its use. Since that time we have had the new 1992 PPE regulations,[46] and hopefully they will improve the situation for PPE wearers. In 1996–97 (HSE, 1997) 68 improvement and prohibition notices were issued by the HSE under these regulations and just six prosecutions were successful (out of eight taken), with an average fine of only £1350.

We will see later on (page 217) that even the 'top of the range' asbestos masks do not fully protect, and can leak in certain circumstances. Much PPE is tested in the laboratory and not in real-life situations. Therefore, it is vital that if you have to wear PPE, the law[46] is followed (see also page 219) and that:

○   it is provided
○   it is comfortable to wear
○   it offers adequate protection for its intended use (this may mean chemical, biological, fume or dust measurement to ensure that the 'protection factor' provided by the PPE is adequate)
○   you are trained in its use
○   it is properly cleaned and maintained and there is an effective system for reporting defects
○   it is returned to its proper accommodation after use
○   you are medically examined on a regular basis to ensure that (a) it is protecting your health against the hazards and (b) that the PPE is not damaging your health (especially your heart in hot and cramped conditions of strenuous work).

BIOLOGICAL HAZARDS

A biological agent is any microorganism, cell culture or human endoparasite, including any which may have been genetically modified, which may cause an infection, allergy, toxicity or otherwise create a hazard to human health.
                    The EU/UK (COSHH) definition of a harmful biological agent.

Almost each week, a new 'super bug' scare appears in the press and media. The recent scandal over mad cow disease or BSE (bovine spongiform encephalopathy), which it is thought may lead to Creutzfeld–Jakob disease (CJD) in humans, is only the latest. AIDS (acquired immune deficiency syndrome) and legionnaire's disease (from infected cooling towers) are additions to older biological hazards, such as anthrax (from wool sorting) and leptospirosis (from rats' urine). It is hardly surprising that working people are more frightened of biological workplace hazards than previously. The film and the book *The Hot Zone* – about the Ebola and Marburg viruses – only add to the general fear and worry.[47]

However, there is evidence[48] that there is a *real* increase in biological hazards, and thus more emerging infections appearing throughout the world. Worryingly, they are becoming more dangerous, as they mutate and become resistant to our commonly available antibiotics. One of the more recent in the UK is the new 'super bug', methicillin-resistant *Staphylococcus Aureus*, or MRSA, that is infecting increasing numbers of patients, and causing some concern among employees in workplaces like nursing homes.

It is in recognition of the growing hazards that biologically active organisms present that the EU produced its 'Biological Agents' Directive, and this has been incorporated into new-style 1994 COSHH regulations[49] that have much more emphasis on biological, as well as chemical, hazards. The Advisory Committee on Dangerous Pathogens has recently produced an 'interim report' on microbiological risk assessment. The report noted that, whilst there were many features common to *all* risk assessments, the ability of microorganisms to replicate, spread from person to person and to mutate were not shared by chemical and physical agents. In addition, intervention strategies with antibiotics and vaccines were not a feature of other risk assessments. The report also noted: 'Uncertainty is, however, a common crucial factor, as is the frequent lack of sufficient data to complete a microbiological risk assessment.'

HOW JUSTIFIED IS THE CONCERN?

The HSE admits in its annual statistics (HSE, 1997) that 'There are few useful sources of information on occupational infections.' Most occupational infections have the same symptoms and outcome as non-occupational infections (e.g. caught from family and friends) and thus most people and their doctors do not relate the infection to the workplace, unless you work in a hospital (and not always then). Some occupational diseases caused by biological agents are reportable under the government's reporting of accidents and diseases scheme, RIDDOR (page 123).

RIDDOR reported 225 cases of work-related infections in 1996–97. The HSE notes that 'this figure probably vastly underestimates the true incidence of occupational infections'. In 1996 there were an estimated 136 cases of work-related infectious diseases, seen by chest and occupational physicians – this was more than earlier years. The number of work-related infections in Britain from the 1995 self-reported survey was 27,000. The HSE considers that the underlying trend in recent years, from all the sources of data, suggests little change in the numbers of occupational infections.

The Surveillance of Work-related and Occupational Respiratory Disease (SWORD) system, which collects information from chest consultants, estimated that in 1992–95 there were 20 cases of allergic alveolitis (down from 115 in 1993) and 31 cases of 'infectious diseases' (down from over 50 per year in each of the three previous years).

Other data come from the Communicable Diseases Surveillance Centre (CDSC), which has confirmed under-reporting at least for 'zoonosis' infections (i.e. infections transmitted from animals to humans). They give the estimates shown in Table 5.3 for cases reported to the CDSC during 1975–94.

TABLE 5.3 Common infectious diseases and their occupational origin

Disease	Cases to CDSC	% occupational
Anthrax	27	70
Brucellosis	424	65
Leptospirosis	714	62
Chlamydiosis	6800	3
Streptoccoccus Suis infection	40	80
Q fever	2056	7

Some exposures to potentially infectious biological material are obvious and others less so. It may be fairly obvious that compacting hospital waste, to make for more efficient incineration, is an infection risk[50] but less so that construction workers are exposed to the opportunistic fungus *Aspergillus Fumigatus*[51] and that the formation of microbiological growth on respiratory filters as worn when working in cow barns and in water-treatment plants may present 'a considerable health risk'.[52]

ROUTES OF TRANSMISSION

Airborne

Some infective agents (e.g. legionnaire's disease, Q fever) can travel long distances (e.g. over 50 metres), whilst many travel less than 50 metres (e.g. measles, chickenpox, flu) and some only need contact of less than five metres (e.g. diphtheria, TB, anthrax, plague).

Direct skin contact

Some infective agents can pass direct through damaged skin (e.g. leptospirosis, hookworms, herpes, scabies).

Oral and faecal–oral transmission

Poor hand and general hygiene encourages this type of transmission (e.g. viral hepatitis, listerosis, CJD and possibly BSE).

Blood and body fluid transmission

Hepatitis B, C and D and HIV (AIDS) are commonly transmitted in this way.

In addition to direct animal-to-human transmission (zoonosis: anthrax, Newcastle disease, rabies, ringworm, Lyme disease etc.) a wide range of arthropods (e.g. lice, fleas, ticks, bugs, flies, mosquitoes) consume the blood of an infected animal or human and pass the infection on by biting another human or animal.

Of course, an infection may take place by more than one of the above routes.

CLASSIFICATION OF BIOLOGICAL HAZARDS

Clearly, as with chemical hazards, not all biological hazards present the same risk and hazard. Simply put, an infection by the herpes virus, which is treatable, is very different from a rabies virus infection. More commonly, *Legionella* pneumonia – which can kill up to one in ten infected people – is treatable if caught early. On the other hand, Lassa fever and Marburg virus have no known cure.

This has led to a four-type classification of pathogens – where a larger number means an increasing hazard – by the EU and HSE, under schedule 9 of COSHH:

O *Group 1*: unlikely to cause human disease.
O *Group 2*: can cause human disease, may be a hazard to employees, unlikely to spread to the community and there is usually effective pro-phylaxis (vaccination etc. to prevent or reduce ill-health) or treatment available.
O *Group 3*: can cause severe human disease and may be a hazard to employees; it is likely to spread to the community and there is usually no effective prophylaxis or treatment available.
O *Group 4*: causes severe human disease and is a serious hazard to employees; it is likely to spread to the community and there is usually no effective prophylaxis or treatment available.

Some examples of the various classifications are:

O *Group 2*: *Listeria* pneumonia, influenza viruses A, B and C, *Streptococcus* suis, *Legionella*, herpes virus.
O *Group 3*: anthrax virus, brucellosis virus, hepatitis B virus, *Salmonella typhi*.
O *Group 4*: Lassa fever virus, Marburg virus and the smallpox virus.

ASSESSING THE RISK

COSHH requires the employer to assess and control the risk of exposure to biological hazards. The risk assessment should at least consider:

○ the hazard group of the biological agent concerned
○ the possible routes of infection and ease of transmission
○ the concentration and total amount of biologically active material to be handled
○ the structural and procedural measures required to prevent or control exposure

The principles of control generally follow those for chemical exposure (page 161), and are as follows:

○ Try and substitute the biological hazard with an organism of no or less hazard or a different process, etc.
○ Keep as low as possible the number of people exposed to the biological agent.
○ Design work processes and methods to reduce exposure or minimize release of biological agent.
○ Display warning bio-hazard signs.
○ Draw up plans to deal with accidents.
○ Specify appropriate decontamination and disinfection procedures.
○ Arrange for safe collection, storage and disposal of biologically active materials.
○ Specify safe procedures for taking, handling and processing samples that may contain biological agents.
○ Where exposure cannot be controlled by other means, ensure the appropriate supply of protective clothing, etc.
○ Where appropriate, ensure that there are available effective vaccines for those who are not already immune to the biological agent.
○ Provide adequate hygiene control and monitoring measures, including appropriate washing and toilet arrangements and the prohibition of eating, drinking and smoking and the application of cosmetics where there is a risk of contamination by biological agents.

The HSE guidance gives much more detail for laboratories, animal rooms and industrial processes, including working with genetically modified organisms,[53] the use of which has to be notified to the authorities.

NOTIFICATION, INFORMATION FOR EMPLOYEES ETC.

Any employer, or organization (e.g. college) wishing to use or store, for the first time, biological agents in groups 2, 3 or 4 above *must* inform the HSE of their intention to do so at least 30 days before they use or store such products. There are specified details that must be included under the COSHH regulations and the notification must include a COSHH assessment of the hazards and risks.

All employees should be informed of the hazards and risks and procedure to take in case of accident. The employer should also inform the safety representatives of any accident or incident which resulted in the release of any biological materials.

The employer should keep a list of all employees exposed to group 3 or 4 biological agents (type of work done, agents used, records of exposure, accidents, incidents, etc.) for at least ten years since last exposure, or, where the exposure could have led to an infection, for at least 40 years. Every employee should have access to their own information on the list. In addition, an HSE doctor and any employees with specific responsibility for the safety of exposed employees (e.g. trade union safety representatives) should have access to the list.

MONITORING AND HEALTH SURVEILLANCE

The standards and sampling methods for assessing the risk of biological hazards are not nearly so advanced as those for chemical hazards, although the general principles of occupational hygiene and sampling still apply (page 162). In specific cases, such as the sampling for *Legionella* in water cooling towers, the methods and protocol are well established (even if the real significance of the results is not always that clear). However, even in the absence of set standards, good-quality sampling can be used to assess and control the hazard, as the rat case study (page 173) clearly shows.

FIGURE 5.5   Sampling for biological hazards can be more difficult than for chemicals.

CASE STUDY 16: REDUCING RAT ALLERGY

There are around 1000 people licensed to conduct experiments on animals in the UK. In 1986 there were 860,000 experiments involving rats. Medical studies have shown that about one in three people (30 per cent) exposed to laboratory animals have allergic symptoms (e.g. runny nose, cough, headaches) and up to one in ten have full-blown asthma. Urine is the major source of rat allergen.

Under the pressure of COSHH, The National Heart and Lung Institute in London examined various methods – involving 'simple and practical changes to animal husbandry' – to reduce the airborne concentrations of rat allergen in the animal houses: using filter top instead of open cages (reduction of 75 per cent); using non-absorbent bedding; and reducing the number of rats kept in each cage.

Significantly, they found that personal sampling (e.g. on the lapels of the employee) when working directly with animals gave three to ten times the measured levels of static or background room samples, highlighting, yet again, the vital importance of personal sampling. As the authors conclude, 'The reduction of airborne rat urine protein concentrations in animal houses will almost certainly be associated with a decrease in the incidence of disease.[54]

Health surveillance is an important addition to biological sampling, especially when there is no known safety standard – as is often the case – and/or the sampling method is poorly developed or inaccurate. There is often a demand from employees for vaccines, where they are available. These have their own risks, and the risks and benefits must be assessed. For example, the smallpox vaccine is occasionally offered to builders, architects and laboratory workers. But it is an infectious agent in its own right, can cause important side-effects and is extremely dangerous in pregnant and immunosuppressed people.

Although the assessment and control of workplace biological hazards is not so advanced as for chemical hazards, the experience shows that relatively simple, basic hygiene practice can control most workplace biological hazards. For example, with regard to the newly emerged MRSA infections, the Department of Health recommends the following:[55]

O Good hand hygiene practice by staff and patients/residents.
O Disposable gloves and aprons should be worn when attending to dressings and dealing with blood or body fluids.
O Cuts, sores and wounds in staff and patients/residents should be covered with impermeable dressings.
O Blood and body fluid spills should be cleaned up at once.
O Sharps should be disposed of safely.
O Equipment, such as commodes, should be cleaned well with detergent and hot water after use.

○   Clothes and bedding should be machine washed.
○   Cutlery, crockery and clinical waste should be dealt with in the usual way.

Although the awareness is increasing, the recent history of the five-year campaign for an American government bloodborne pathogens standards – to protect employees against hepatitis B and AIDS – shows the vital importance of trade unions and public health agencies in fighting for the control of workplace infection hazards.[56]

AIDS AT THE WORKPLACE

Acquired immune deficiency syndrome (AIDS) is caused by the human immunodeficiency virus (HIV). The virus can affect the body's normal immune system and make the infected person more susceptible to a host of other diseases. A person can be HIV-positive for many years and not develop full-blown AIDS. Drug treatment has improved considerably in recent years – so much so that some hospitals are shutting AIDS wards – but it is still true to say that there is no cure for HIV infection or AIDS.

Overall, the current rate of HIV infection in Britain is not rising quickly (although this is not true worldwide, especially in some developing countries). In 1995 there were 2041 new HIV infections, as compared with 189 in 1986. Whilst most of these are gay men (1995, 1402; 1985, 1555), the number of new heterosexual cases rose from 95 in 1986 to 798 in 1995.

The important fact, from a workplace perspective, is that the HIV virus is not easily transmitted, as hepatitis B is, for example. HIV is transmitted:

○   by sexual intercourse with an infected person
○   from an infected mother to her baby
○   by inoculation with blood or body fluids infected with the virus

Because HIV/AIDS is not very infectious by normal occupational transmission routes, very few people have been infected by HIV at the workplace. The risk is greater – but still very small – to staff who are nursing people with HIV and/or AIDS on a day-to-day basis. Studies of health care workers worldwide, who have nursed more than 22,000 AIDS-infected patients, have failed to show any HIV infection among nursing staff. In the UK there have been six medical studies, involving about 4500 AIDS patients, and none of those tested were found to be infected. Accident and emergency (A&E) staff in hospitals do appear to be at an increased risk, however. Recent surveys have revealed that up to one in 50 patients at A&E departments may be HIV-positive, and the incidence appears to be rising.[57]

This is, of course, no reason to be complacent and not to enforce hospital infection control policies fully. A couple of years ago, a student of mine, who was nursing to pay her way through college, pricked her finger on a needle in an over-full sharps box. There was a good chance that the dirty needle was from an HIV-infected patient. Then started a nightmare six months for her: she lost her job ('best to be careful'), many of her friends and some of her family avoided her, and she had the thought that she might be HIV-positive herself, for it took six months to know if she was safe. Luckily, she was not infected, but her life was in tatters! Recent research has shown that whilst all hospitals had 'infection control policies', half the staff were ignorant of them.[58] One in ten patients, about 100,000 people, a year get a hospital-acquired infection, and in some areas, like intensive care, almost one in five patients get infected in hospital. American research has shown that one-third of hospital-acquired infections could be prevented with better controls.

Washing your hands is a simple, but very important, hygiene measure, but the study, in 19 hospitals over a three-year period, showed that hospital staff tended to wash their hands after intimate contact with patients and not before. There was a 20-fold difference in infection rates between the best and worst hospitals studied, showing that there is considerable room for improvement. In addition to training about correct hand washing, there is an urgent need to develop and enforce a safe sharps disposal policy. As Professor Peter Borriello, head of The Central Public Health Laboratory, said, 'Infection control guidelines were useless if not enforced. They have to be policed. People only adhere to them if they are monitored.'

GUIDELINES

There are very good free government workplace guidelines available on AIDS and HIV at the workplace, with an example of 'model HIV workplace policy' included.[59] A recent review of HIV/AIDS policies and procedures in over 400 workplaces gives very good practical guidance on how to deal sensibly with HIV/AIDS at the workplace and, equally importantly, how to avoid discrimination and/or victimization of someone with HIV/AIDS.[60] Even as I write this section, the so-called responsible press still has headlines such as, 'Three get HIV from blood donation' (*The Independent*, 19 April 1997) and 'HIV doctor put 1700 patients at risk' (*The Independent*, 8 March 1997) which are bound to cause worry and concern among many people coming into contact with HIV-infected people, whether at work or at home. Yet there are also positive signs of changes of attitude towards people infected with HIV. In late 1996, after an exhausting two-year battle, ear consultant Professor George Browning – who contracted AIDS through gay sex – was allowed to return to work and to carry on with four out of five non-invasive operations.[61] Normal hygiene procedures cope well with the HIV virus and there is no danger to anyone just working with someone who has HIV/AIDS. Indeed, it is illegal, and inhumane, to discriminate against someone who has the HIV virus or full-blown AIDS.

DUSTS

> Dusts are very dry and the constant dust enters the blood and lungs producing difficulty in breathing that the Greeks call asthma. When the dust is corrosive it ulcerates the lungs and produces consumption (TB); hence it is that in the Carpathian Mountains there were women who have married seven husbands all of whom this dreadful disease has brought to an early grave.
>
> Georgius Agricola, *De Re Metallica*, 1556.

As the above quote indicates, it has long been known that many, if not all, dusts irritate and damage the lungs. Indeed, most chest physicians will say that *no* dust is good for the lungs. To absorb oxygen from the air the lungs have a massive surface area and this makes the lungs vulnerable to attack by dust and fumes. Of course, the lungs have a variety of defence mechanisms, and it is true that a large amount of any dust that is inhaled is either exhaled, excreted (e.g. via the stomach) or, if it is soluble in lung fluids, dissolved. An added problem, in the past 50 years or so, is the prevalence of smoking. It is a well-established fact that smoking destroys, or reduces the capacity of, some of the lungs' defence mechanisms as well as damaging the lung in its own right. Thus the effect of smoking and dust are additive. In the case of asbestos they are multiplicative; that is, together they cause much more ill-health (e.g. lung cancer) than either would alone.

There are many medical textbooks devoted to the lung diseases.[62] Asbestosis (from asbestos), silicosis (from silica), coal worker's pneumoconiosis, byssinosis (from cotton), asthma, farm worker's lung and mushroom worker's lung have all become part of a common language. The medical textbooks list many more lung diseases related to exposure to various dusts: minerals, organic fibres, metals, animals, chemical and biological agents, and other substances. A general term for lung damage by dust is 'pneumoconiosis' which originally meant any lung disease caused by dust. Since 1946, however, it has come to mean only lung fibrosis – or scarring – caused by silica ('silicosis'), asbestos ('asbestosis'), cotton ('byssinosis') and other dusts.

There are so many dust diseases that all I can do here is pick a couple of common dusts – asbestos and mineral fibres – to illustrate some of the problems with dusts in general.

THE DUST YOU CANNOT SEE IS DANGEROUS

A major problem with most dust exposure is that it is the dust you cannot see with the naked eye (except sometimes when a ray of sunlight shines into a darkened room) that gets deep into the lungs – into the alveoli – where the real lung damage is done. Therefore, you cannot trust your eyes to tell you whether or not you are working in a dust-free environment. The dust lamp[63] – using the principle of a bright light against a dark background – is very useful for showing the presence of dust and highlighting where dust leaks (e.g. from exhaust equipment) may be occurring.

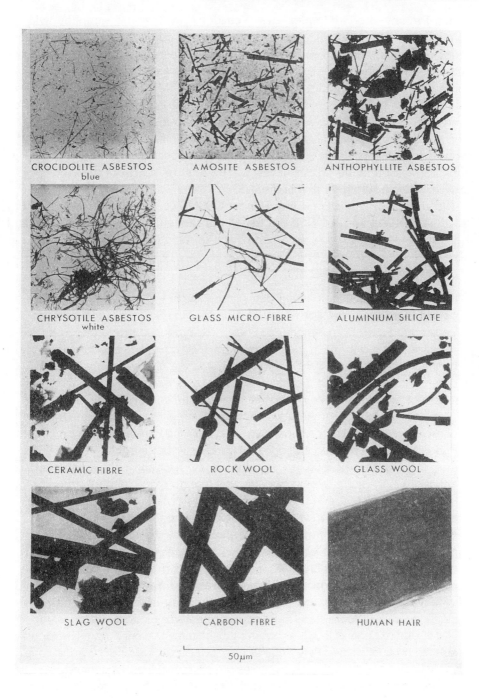

CROCIDOLITE ASBESTOS
blue

AMOSITE ASBESTOS

ANTHOPHYLLITE ASBESTOS

CHRYSOTILE ASBESTOS
white

GLASS MICRO-FIBRE

ALUMINIUM SILICATE

CERAMIC FIBRE

ROCK WOOL

GLASS WOOL

SLAG WOOL

CARBON FIBRE

HUMAN HAIR

50μm

FIGURE 5.6   Many common hazardous dusts and fibres cannot be seen by the human eye, and are much thinner than a human hair.

But for any more complex dust situation, professional sampling will be required. It is essential that such sampling is carried out in the worker's breathing zone – so-called 'personal sampling' – when carrying out normal working tasks. The dust levels measured are then compared with a so-called legal safe standard, under COSHH, and if the levels are anywhere near this standard (e.g. more than half the allowed dust level), then the dust levels must be reduced, preferably by control at source, by enclosure and/or extraction, but, if this cannot be done, by means of personal protection (see page 217). Even if the dust levels are below the allowed level, every effort should be made to reduce the dust levels as low as possible. Measurements of dust levels will be required to check the efficiency of any extraction equipment that is installed.

The general principles of control under COSHH (page 157) can be applied to any dust problem and the HSE has issued detailed guidance on the control and medical monitoring of most commonly used dusts in industry.

CASE STUDY 17: 'EVIL' ASBESTOS

In 1898 the Annual Report of the Factory Inspectorate to Parliament contained a detailed section on the 'evil' effects of asbestos dust. Now, 100 years later, the Health and Safety Commission (HSC) has finally produced proposals to ban *all* asbestos import and use in the UK (some other EU countries have already banned asbestos, but it is still widely used elsewhere and especially in the so-called Third World). But, in the intervening 100 years, there have been millions of tonnes of asbestos put into our homes, schools, hospitals and workplaces.

In 1995 Professor Julian Peto, who has constantly underestimated the hazards of asbestos, dropped a bombshell with some HSE-funded research. He, and most researchers, had assumed that asbestos diseases would level off in the 1990s, as most of the asbestos exposure was assumed to have been in the past, when conditions in the industry were bad. His new research revealed that, instead of levelling off to 'only' 3500 asbestos-related deaths a year (mainly from cancer), these deaths would go on rising for the next 30 years to between 5000–10,000 deaths a year by 2025. This is a public health disaster that could have been prevented. I have written about this elsewhere extensively,[64] and the asbestos companies, the government (HSE) and many academics and doctors have all played their part in the asbestos cover-up. We now have teachers dying from asbestos-related diseases, people who just played as children around asbestos plants, a police officer whose 'asbestos exposure' was as a 'scenes of crime officer' and so on. And, if all the asbestos that is currently in our buildings is ripped out with no control, then Peto's figures may well be a gross underestimate, and we will have another asbestos public health disaster in the 21st century!

What is now needed is: an immediate asbestos ban; a legal requirement to identify and control asbestos exposure in all buildings; an effective licensing scheme for asbestos removal firms; imprisonment for negligently exposing people to asbestos; and a fair compensation scheme for the many thousands of asbestos victims. The May 1997 election of a Labour government seems to have made these sensible demands a reality, although there is to be no immediate ban (as in France), but one in the next year (or two) after 'consultation'.

MINERAL FIBRES

Asbestos use is nearly finished in the industrialized world, but so useful has the fibre[65] been technically, that industry has replaced it with mimic fibres: 'synthetic mineral fibres' such as: glassfibre, rock wool, slag wool, superfine fibre, ceramic fibre, refractory fibre, carbon/graphite fibres, polyamide 'aramid' fibres (e.g. 'Nomex', 'Kevlar' and 'Twaron'), polyolefin fibres and so on.[66] Of course, as these fibres were designed to mimic the very useful properties of asbestos, there has been a very real concern that they may mimic the health hazards too.

It is sometimes salutary to re-read something you wrote on a subject many years before, and I have just re-read the chapter on 'substitutes for asbestos' in my 1979 book, *Asbestos Killer Dust*. There is not much I would have to change today, as, despite hundreds of medical and scientific papers in the past 20 years on asbestos substitutes, and glass fibres in particular, the real health questions have still not been resolved.

DO GLASS FIBRES CAUSE CANCER?

An authoritative review[67] in the 1994 *American Journal of Industrial Medicine* concluded that 'On a fibre-per-fibre basis, glass fibres may be as potent or even more potent than asbestos.' The more cautious 1990 HSE guidance note[68] on mineral fibres quotes from the 1987 Department of Health's Committee on Carcinogenicity (COC): 'It would be prudent to act on the basis that sufficient exposure to any form of mineral fibre in the production industry (or in the user industries) may increase the risk of lung cancer among the workforce.'

There are discussions currently going on in the EU about the labelling and categorization of glass and other 'vitreous (silicate) fibres'. In essence, the EU arguments about what mineral (they prefer the term 'vitreous/silicate') fibres can cause cancer, or not, revolve around two progressive principles:

○   That all fibres should be manufactured so that in both production and use they do not produce respirable fibres that can go deep into the lung, where the major biological damage is done.
○   That all fibres should be biosoluble, so that if they do get into the lung they are cleared quickly by the lung's defence mechanisms.

In the USA since 1993 and despite company opposition, glass fibre has had to be labelled: 'Fibreglass may be reasonably anticipated to cause cancer.' It appears that we shall not get this type of warning in the EU, although I do not see why not if there is evidence to that effect (which there is). Such a label, on the appropriate products, would certainly encourage mineral fibre producers to fulfil the above two criteria. The proposals[69] for the labelling of mineral fibre products – from the industry body, the European Ceramic Fibres Association (ECFIA) – is the following: 'Possible risk of irreversible effects, harmful by inhalation, may be irritating to skin, eyes and respiratory system.'

As I have mentioned before, using the government's Code of Practice on the Freedom of Information, it is now possible to obtain the instructions given to workplace inspectors (HSE or EHO). That for EHOs on mineral fibres[69] is very interesting, in that it mentions the trade union concerns about the standards. The current standards for mineral fibres are: 5mg/cubic metre of air (m^3) and 2 fibres/ml of air. The EHO guidance notes that the TUC wanted 1 fibre/ml for superfine fibres, where it was 'reasonably practicable', and adds, 'Inspectors should be aware of this commitment given to the TUC.'

MEDIUM-DENSITY FIBRE BOARD (MDF)

MDF is a composite material, made of various wood fibres glued together with carbamide resin glue, which contains formaldehyde. It is very popular with both professional carpenters and DIY people since it is cheap, easy to work, versatile and stains well. What happens to the chemicals in the glues and adhesives at the high temperature of the cutting saw is not clear, but history teaches us to be careful. It is often said that 'You do not see an old welder', and welding is a high-temperature reaction. Further, a few years back there was an outbreak of 'meat wrapper's asthma'. The fumes from the heat sealing of the film around meat was causing asthma in the 'meat wrappers'.

To my knowledge there have only been very limited medical and scientific studies[70] of the hazards of MDF. They confirm that it is more irritant to the eyes, nose and skin than conventional wood, that the sense of smell was poorer and that there was more nasal obstruction but concluded:

> Thus far, no proof is available that MDF is more hostile to the nasal or pulmonary tissues after long-term exposure, even though the nasal symptoms are more pronounced after short-term exposure than they are after exposure to wood dust or traditional fibre board (page 413).

But these are early days, and I was very glad to see that my carpenter used a good-quality face mask when machining MDF.

SAFETY MEASURES

Of course, any use of any dust is subject to COSHH and therefore a risk assessment, control of dust (where possible without a face mask), health surveillance etc. is required. The HSE has produced much guidance in this area, often for specific dusts.

WORK-RELATED UPPER LIMB DISORDERS (REPETITIVE STRAIN INJURY OR RSI)

> ... RSI is in reality meaningless in that it has no pathology ... RSI has no place in the medical books.
> Judge John Prosser, giving judgement against a claim for RSI by journalist Rafiq Mughal, caused by his work for Reuters News Agency, 1993.

Fortunately, the one bad judgement quoted above did not appear to influence the courts, and in 1996 the Court of Appeal upheld the case of Ann Pickford.[71] She worked as a secretary for ICI Pharmaceuticals, Macclesfield. In 1984 she started to develop repetitive stain injury (RSI) symptoms (severe pains and tightness in both hands and stiff fingers) from her extensive typing and VDU work. From 1987/88 onwards her typing load increased, and so did her RSI, and she was medically retired in 1990. In 1996 the Court of Appeal found that her RSI was caused by her keyboard work, and ICI's failure to warn her of the need for rest breaks, and she will be awarded substantial damages in due course. It is sometimes forgotten that, up until recently, the vast majority of successful RSI common law claims were by manual workers, such as 42-year-old Muriel Simpson, who suffered from severe pains in the arm when working a machine making toilet paper during 1987–1990 at Bowater Scott's in Barrow in Furness. She retired through ill-health and will never do manual work again. In January 1997 she was awarded £186,000 damages.

Work related upper limb disorders (WRULDs) are: aches and pains, swelling or stiffness in the neck, shoulders, arms, elbows, wrists, hands and fingers. However, many people, especially the victims, prefer the less medically and scientifically accurate term, repetitive strain injury (RSI). In fact, even the medical profession seem to prefer RSI, as a recent and very useful, review[72] had this title in a leading medical journal, *The Lancet*. Historically, RSI was known as 'tenosynovitis' ('teno') in the UK, and there are many different names for RSI all over the world.

For example, the Americans favour the term 'cumulative trauma disorder' (CTD). A recent book (Dembe, 1996) has looked in detail at the historical development of CTD (and RSI) and how doctors, in many different countries over many years, have often refused to diagnose the condition – sometimes saying that the patient has a 'neurosis' (whatever that is) – and he makes a plea that:

> My hope is that those investigating the chronic hand disorders of the future will examine the history of how similar disorders have been recognized and treated in the past, and that all those involved in occupational health – whether physicians, ergonomists, managers or workers – adopt a common objective and co-ordinated strategy for preventing and treating these maladies. (p. 101)

VDUS ARE A PROBLEM

At least in recent years the HSE has fully recognized the existence of RSI and produced some very good free[73] and priced[74] publications in this area. Indeed, in November 1993, just a month after Judge Prosser's infamous remark, quoted above, speaking at the launch of the HSC's Annual Report, chair of the HSC, the UK's top health and safety government agency, Sir John Cullen, said, 'He was not speaking with any medical expertise or experience in the field ... We have no doubt it (RSI) exists and we believe there are things employers can do to minimise the outbreak of the condition.'[75]

A TUC survey showed quite clearly that one of the major causes of RSI was working on display screen equipment (DSEs) or visual display units (VDUs).[76] Their survey of 7000 trade union safety representatives found that over four out of ten (43 per cent) said that DSE work was a problem. In industries using DSEs more intensively the problem was greater: 83 per cent in banking and finance; 72 per cent in the voluntary sector; 69 per cent in central government. Yet this is one area where there are specific regulations to control or reduce RSI: the Display Screen Equipment Regulations 1992.

A recent evaluation[77] of the DSE regulations, in many workplaces, for the HSE found that:

O   an estimated 2.8 million people use DSEs in Britain and are covered by the DSE risk assessment regulations
O   one in four of the companies surveyed said that they were not aware of the DSE regulations (rising to over half in small companies)
O   only four out of ten (39 per cent) of companies surveyed had carried out a risk assessment
O   two-thirds of employers had not provided eye sight tests
O   pressure from the HSE or EHOs was the least motivating factor of all to comply with the regulations

In 1995–96 there was one prosecution under these regulations, with a fine of £2000. There is no record of any improvement or prohibition notice being served in connection with these regulations. Good guidance is all very well, but some enforcement might help prevent RSI. There is, however, very good guidance on the prevention of RSI from VDU work available.[78]

RSI – HOW COMMON?

The HSE states (HSE, 1997) that 'Musculoskeletal disorders (including backache) are the largest form of work-related ill health in Britain'. The estimated prevalence of all musculoskeletal disorders rose from 964,000 in 1990 to 1,227,000 in 1995. In 1992:

O   50 per cent (299,000) were back disorders
O   19 per cent (110,000) were upper-limb disorders (neck, shoulder, elbow, wrists and hand complaints) – the RSI diseases

FIGURE 5.7   Typist, and Banking Insurance and Finance Union (BIFU) member Pauline Barnard was one of the first people to get some decent compensation for her RSI that lost her the job, caused her much pain and suffering, and even stopped her fully enjoying playing with her young child.

○ 10 per cent (58,000) were lower-limb disorders (hip, thigh, knee, ankle and foot complaints)
○ 21 per cent (126,000) were other or unspecified sites

The HSE ascribes the increase in these symptoms to different methodology, increased awareness (and hence more reporting), new regulations, HSE campaigns, etc. There also may be, of course, a very real increase in symptoms due to the increased pressure of work in the 1990s.

The TUC, based on its survey of 7000 safety representatives, has estimated that, every year, 200,000 people suffer from some form of RSI.[76] It identified, through the trade unions, cases where compensation had been paid to 2000 sufferers through legal action. As Owen Tudor, the TUC's health and safety, officer said, 'RSI is not just a product of new technology. It is the disease of old management.' The TUC survey found that RSI is a major problem in one in three British workplaces and was most common among the following occupations:

○ packers (especially those working in cold conditions, such as meat packers)
○ electronic component assembly line workers
○ supermarket checkout operators
○ typists and data entry process workers (especially in the finance sector)
○ journalists and designers (who use VDUs a lot)

However, it appears that RSI can occur in almost any occupation, given the right (or wrong) circumstances. A recent survey of the health of musicians in 56 orchestras worldwide found that more than half the musicians reported feeling pain in the neck, back, shoulder, elbows, thumb or fingers during or after playing. Most experts agree that pain should not occur when playing a musical instrument correctly. But the RSI is caused by a combination of faulty posture, poor technique and emotional stress. It is thought that when women are nervous their muscular tension is often greater than men's, so female orchestral players are more likely than males to suffer pain during or after playing. They are also more likely to have the stress of family responsibility whilst working the antisocial hours that most orchestral work requires.

PREVENTING RSI

The free HSE guide[73] gives a good checklist to identity whether or not there could be an RSI problem in your workplace. It asks the following questions:

○ Does the job or task being assessed involve a lot of frequent or forceful or awkward:
  – gripping (e.g. a tool or workpiece)?
  – squeezing (e.g. tool handles)?
  – twisting?
  – reaching?
  – moving things (pushing, pulling, lifting)?
  – finger/hand movement (e.g. keyboard work)?
○ Are there any warning signs of upper limb disorders (ULDs), such as:
  – actual cases of upper limb disorders in this or similar work?
  – complaints by workers, e.g. aches and pains in hands, wrists or arms? Ask employees if they have any of these symptoms.
  – home-made, improvised changes to workstations or tools (e.g. handles cushioned or made longer)?

The HSE guidance suggests that if the answer is no to any of the above questions, then 'you are unlikely to have any ULD problems caused by work'. If, however, you have any ticks, then they recommend that a full risk assessment of the task is carried out and give a suggested eight-page survey of how to do just that. Having identified the problem, there is considerable HSE guidance[73] and case studies, although in more complicated cases the help of an independent expert from the Ergonomic Society[76] may be required.

CASE STUDY 18: THE BISCUIT PACKERS

In one year, 29 packers on a production line in a biscuit factory suffered from: 59 cases of RSI, 88 cases of dizziness and 65 complaints of nausea. In addition there was a high accident rate, and labour turnover. Management required an increase in production and, with the help of ergonomic experts, decided to examine the problems and redesign production.

A complete ergonomic risk assessment identified many problem areas, and new designs, in consultation with the workers, were drawn up using ergonomic principles. In addition to key production line modifications, seats and anti-fatigue matting was introduced, the speed line was reduced by one-third and the number of workers increased by 25 per cent. All the ill-health symptoms declined, as did the turnover of staff. Productivity increased from 900 to 1200 tins of biscuits per hour.[79]

TREATMENT

The best form of treatment for RSI is prevention. As the comprehensive *Lancet* review concludes:

> Sufficient information exists to confirm that RSI is an important clinical problem. Moreover, a large amount of information has accumulated on the feasibility and effectiveness of prevention. Physicians have a central role in early recognition and management, and in particular in stimulating workplace ergonomic interventions.[72]

Clearly, however, many people will still require treatment, and herein lies a big problem. There is no single form of treatment for every RSI sufferer: rest, physiotherapy, osteopathy, hydrotherapy, ice packs, counselling, Alexander technique, massage, relaxation, aromatherapy, acupuncture, homeopathic medicines and, in the last resort, surgical operations have all been reported to have some successes and failures.[72]

However, American studies have shown that some forms of physiotherapy can actually make the RSI worse, so great care is required for individuals in selecting the right treatment, and it is wise to join an RSI self-help group to compare notes on different types of treatment and for social support.[80] The pain of RSI for many sufferers is accompanied by the pain caused by their working colleagues and, sometimes, family and friends, who like Judge Prosser just do not believe that RSI exists. There is also a trend among employers to penalize anyone who has RSI and to 'medically retire' them.

The fact that employers are penalizing employees for having RSI can, and does, have a big impact on people reporting RSI. The National Union of Journalists (NUJ) has many members with RSI. The NUJ has found, in many workplace surveys of RSI amongst its members that it has carried out, a far higher incidence of RSI than shown in management surveys, sometimes double the incidence. Journalists are just too frightened to be identified as 'RSI sufferers', as their current job may be in jeopardy – especially as many of them are on short-term contracts – and their future employment may be jeopardized as well.

CASE STUDY 19: TURKEY PLUCKERS WIN AND SUFFER

In 1993 six Turkey process workers at Bernard Mathews farms won a famous compensation case for RSI. With the help of their union, the TGWU, they won awards of between £644 and £5949, to total £21,000. However, three cases were dismissed and during 1994 another 100 cases were settled out of court. As 47-year-old Joy Mounteney, who received £5949 for her damaged wrists said, 'Working on the line is bad. It is a revolting job. Two-thirds of the workers had problems with their wrists … It is cold, wet and noisy, and it stinks like hell.'

Reviewing the situation in 1995, the main improvements appeared to have been: workstation redesign, including some automation, more frequent work breaks, more job rotation and the better reporting of symptoms to the company nurse. The staff are required to read, and sign in the presence of a witness, a statement that, in part, warns them that:

> Despite the precautions the company takes, the risk that you will develop upper limb disorders remains. Treatment may require you to stop work for a period of time. If the condition happens again the company may have to dismiss you on medical grounds but you must still report your symptoms or you will be liable to disciplinary action.

Not suprisingly, the TGWU union official Peter Medhurst said, 'Many people are reluctant to report problems, because they are afraid of the consequences it will have on their employment prospects.[79]

MANUAL HANDLING (BACKACHE)

In 1996, two in five adults said they had suffered from low back pain in the previous year, according to a 1997 government survey (Back pain plagues Britons, Government Statistical Office). There was a small increase, from 37 per cent to 40 per cent, in the proportion of adults saying they had low back pain in the three years since the previous 1993 survey. More worrying is that almost one in three

(30 per cent) of those aged 16 to 24 reported back pain in 1996, as compared with one in four (24 per cent) in 1993.

Backache in the UK has increased dramatically in recent years.[81] Over 80 million days a year are lost due to registered disability, but the real incidence is probably in the order of 150 million days. This is four times the figure of 20 years ago. The 1990 Labour Force Survey (HSE, 1997) found that 299,000 people thought that their backache had been caused by work. Coal miners have four times the average backache and nurses three times. This is a worldwide phenomenon,[82] with – for social reasons it seems – the exception of Japan. It is a very common condition, second only to arthritis in those aged 45–65. A 1993 Department of Health survey found that one in three (37 per cent) people said that they had suffered backache in the past year that lasted more than one day. One in four (25 per cent) people thought that their backache related to the type of work they did, and one in seven (14 per cent) cited an accident or injury at work. Of course, far fewer seek medical treatment or lose time off work; between one in 50 and one in 20 a year. The costs of back pain are huge, currently about £6 billion a year. Prevention, control and treatment would thus bring great emotional and financial savings to the individual, company and state.

Backache can affect people of all ages, although it is most common in the 45–60-year age group, and there is little difference between men and women. Most people return to work within a month. However, around one in ten (10 per cent) will be off work for six months. The longer you are off work with backache, the less chance of your returning to work: only one in four of those off work for more than a year return to work, and only one in ten of those off work for more than two years return to work.

There is no pre-screening medical test that is of any value (lumbar radiographs are not helpful) and the only general risk factor for back-pain is past backache, especially if it was recent and severe enough to cause absence from work. Hence the 'backache' question on many pre-employment medical questionnaires.

Some other risk factors have been identified, such as doing heavy manual work, exposure to whole body vibration (e.g. drivers, page 209), smoking, being working class, being overweight, being tall and being stressed at work or not enjoying your job. Workers at a Boeing aircraft factory who did not enjoy their jobs had a greatly increased risk of reporting back injury.

The treatment of backache varies considerably, but all agree that treatment should begin as soon as possible. With so-called simple backache the emphasis is now on the relief of pain with paracetamol or something similar, gentle physical activity (possibly aided by manipulation, etc), and returning to work as soon as possible. Rest is recommended only if essential, and generally only for one to three days. More complicated backache, including nerve root pain, requires more specialist assessment and treatment. Many people will turn to various forms of alternative medicine for such help rather than conventional medicine and, especially, back operations.

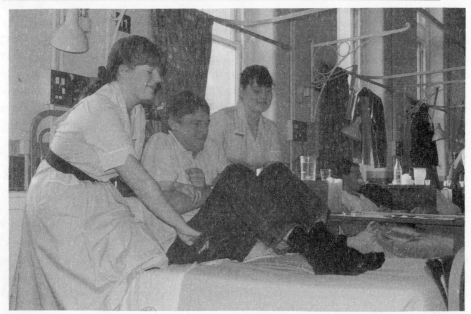

FIGURE 5.8   Up to one in seven nurses suffer from severe backache. Simple devices, like the one shown for sliding a patient along the bed, can reduce this pain and suffering.

PREVENTION

The fact that at least one in four cases of backache are caused by heavy or awkward lifting at the workplace, or vibration and bad posture in seating, shows the potential for considerable preventative measures at the workplace, although, surprisingly, there is a lack of in-depth studies showing the human and financial benefits of reducing manual handling tasks at the workplace.[82] Those that have been carried out (in nursing homes, telecommunications, local councils, hospitals, woodworking industries and police vehicles) show both an improvement in health (up to 40 per cent reduction in backache) and considerable cost savings.

In the UK the 1992 Manual Handling Regulations provide the basic guide for the prevention of workplace backache. The HSE has produced a very good, free, guide to these regulations.[83] In essence the regulations require the employer to:

○   avoid hazardous manual handling operations as far as is reasonably possible – lifting aids may be appropriate
○   make an appropriate 'risk assessment' of any manual handling task that cannot be eliminated
○   reduce the risks from these operations, 'as far as is reasonably practicable'.

The principles of a manual handling 'risk assessment' depend upon four key, often interrelated factors: the tasks, the loads, the working environment, and individual capability.

The task

- ○ Is the load held or manipulated at a distance from the trunk (roughly, holding a load at arm's length imposes a stress about five times that of the same load held close to the body)?
- ○ Does the task involve twisting?
- ○ Does the task involve stooping?
- ○ Combinations of the above are worse.
- ○ Is there excessive lifting or lowering (not from floor level and, if possible, not above waist height)?
- ○ Is there excessive carrying over long distances (more than 10 metres)?
- ○ Is there the risk of sudden movement of the load?
- ○ Is there prolonged and frequent effort?
- ○ Are there sufficient rest/recovery periods?
- ○ Is the work rate imposed by the process?
- ○ Are the loads handled whilst seated?
- ○ Team handling (two people, two-thirds; three people, half the sum of individual).

The load

- ○ Is it heavy (only one factor!)?
- ○ Is it bulky (more than 75 cm in any direction)?
- ○ Does it cause sight problems?
- ○ Is the centre of gravity off-centre?
- ○ Is it difficult to grasp?
- ○ Is it unstable or likely to shift?
- ○ Does it contain people or animals?
- ○ Is it sharp or hot?

The working environment

- ○ Are there space constraints (especially restricted headroom)?
- ○ Are the floors uneven, slippery or unstable?
- ○ Are there variations of floor level?
- ○ Are there extremes of temperature or humidity?
- ○ Are there problems of ventilation or wind gusts?
- ○ Is there poor lighting or glare?

Individual capability

○   Is unusual strength or height required?
○   In general women can lift less than men (about two-thirds of weight).
○   People can lift less in their teens and when over 50 years.
○   Are the lifters experienced?
○   Is the person pregnant (especially after three months)?
○   Are there any other health problems?

Other factors

Is personal protective equipment to be worn?

IS IT POSSIBLE TO 'LIFT SAFELY'?

The essential approach of the above regulations is to remove or make safer the workplace for manual handling. Over the years another, much less effective, but popular approach has been to try and change the worker and not the workplace. The most common use of this method has been the selling of 'the right lifting technique', 'isokinetic lifting' or most commonly, 'keep your back straight, and bend your knees' when lifting. There have been many courses, usually accompanied by a skeleton, using this approach over the years and, in fact, little evaluation of the effectiveness of this training. When, from the 1970s onwards, insurance companies and others evaluated the value of all 'lifting training', they found as much backache in companies and organizations (e.g. hospitals) with a 'lift safely' or 'mind your back' training programme as in those without.[82]

In a similar way, the well-advertised backbelts[84] have been shown to have little value in reducing back injury during heavy lifting. That is not to say that training and other approaches are not useful and, indeed, essential, but only in conjunction with a manual handling task reduction programme, and not as a substitute for one.

The HSE has produced two excellent publications, full of practical case studies, on how to reduce or eliminate manual handling problems at the workplace.[85]

CASE STUDY 20: PRIVATE INVESTIGATORS GET CRITICIZED

Mr Lindsay worked as a lorry driver for eight years for TNT Express Ltd. In November 1991 he was required to deliver a boxed TV set with no wheel barrow. He had to 'walk like a monkey' with the TV on his knees. He felt a twinge in his back at the time, which turned into a sharp and extensive pain, and he has not been able to work since. TNT employed a private investigator to spy on him and even to lie and gain access to his home. In November 1996 Judge Lord Johnson deplored the investigator's methods and dismissed his evidence as 'worse than useless'. He awarded Mr Lindsay £120,000 damages for his back injury against TNT.[86]

NOISE

Apart from two years national service (where it was quiet!) since 1941, I have worked as a fettler – someone who chips or grinds off the excess metal from foundry castings – in a Sheffield foundry. It has always been a very noisy job. Around 1970 I first noticed my hearing problems: I could not hear people well on the telephone. Now I do not hear a lot of what people say, even amongst my own sons and grandchildren, and especially in company. I can still hold a reasonable conversation, one to one, face to face (where I lip read), but I'm lost in groups and it's socially isolating. It causes ill-feeling and arguments among my friends and family.

Foreman fettler Edward Boldock was awarded £5750 compensation for his deafness in 1980; Dalton, 1982.

According to the HSE (1997), 1,700,000 workers are thought to be exposed to noise above levels considered safe. In 1995, 183,000 people reported deafness, tinnitus or other ear conditions caused or made worse by work. In April 1995, a total of 14,200 (99 per cent male) were receiving some DSS payment for occupational deafness. There were 531 new cases that qualified for disablement benefit in 1996. The criteria to gain some government compensation are very strict (when disability is 50 dB loss of hearing), and at this level of deafness the handicap is so substantial that one would have to lip read. There is evidence that people do not apply for compensation because they know the conditions are so stringent.

If you have to speak up to be heard at work, the noise levels are most probably damaging your hearing. People who are exposed to loud noise at work often suffer from 'temporary deafness' at the end of a working day, a warning sign that their hearing is at risk.[87] At first the ears, and hence the hearing, recover overnight. But in time permanent, irrevocable, hearing loss develops. Also, some people who are exposed to loud noise suffer from 'ringing in the ear', or tinnitus. This can be very uncomfortable and disabling. In addition to causing deafness, loud noise at work can affect pulse rates, raise blood pressure, and lead to disturbed sleep/increases in accidents.[88] There is evidence that two hazards together – such as noise exposure and solvent exposure, noise and vibration, noise and heat – may be more harmful. Noise also causes fatigue and stress and increased sickness absence. In offices, studies have shown losses of productivity of up to 40 per cent, with data entry errors rising to 27 per cent in an excessively noisy environment. Exposures to heavy metals (such as lead, arsenic and mercury) and solvents can also cause hearing loss.

People do not readily admit that they are hard of hearing or even deaf. I once did some lead and noise surveys in an old printing works that still used lead type, where the noise levels were very high. But when I went with the trade union safety representative to the manager and I told him of the noise results he replied, 'I find the noise levels are no problem.' I was astonished, until the safety representative pulled me aside and told me that he was deaf. A few years later I measured very high levels at the ear of a man on a brick-cutting machine. Again,

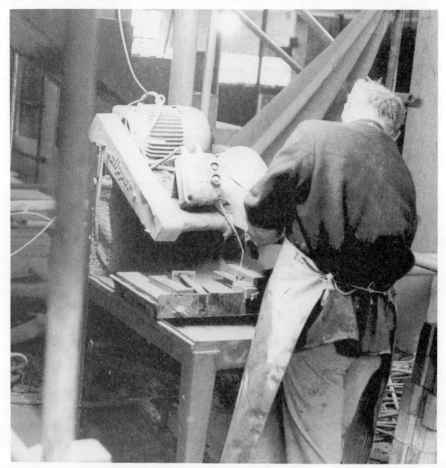

FIGURE 5.9   The noise (106 decibels) from this brick-cutter had already deafened the operator before I had time to recommend closure.

he was not bothered and the other workers told me, 'We put old Bill on that job. It doesn't worry him as he's deaf.'

The discovery that noise causes deafness is not new. In 1886, Dr Thomas Barr in Glasgow demonstrated quite clearly the harmful effects of noise on hearing. He examined 100 boilermakers by holding a ticking watch, along a ruler, nearer and nearer to their ear until they heard the tick of the watch. In fact, for many years occupational deafness was known as 'boilermakers' deafness' because it was so common amongst this occupation (Hunter, 1955). The 1908 Annual Report of HM Inspector of Factories to Parliament noted that when workers were exposed to loud noise, 'Their sense of hearing is seriously impaired, if not entirely destroyed in the course of time.' In the 1930s portable equipment became commercially available to test hearing levels ('audiometry') and portable noise meters, to measure sound levels, became fairly common in the 1950s.

NOISE REGULATIONS INEFFECTIVE

It was not until 1972 that an HSE code of practice to reduce noise at work was produced. It was comprehensively ignored by employers for at least 13 years, as a 1985 HSE survey of 500 companies showed. The employers resisted the introduction of noise regulations throughout the 1980s and it was only the EU Noise at Work Directive of 1986 that led to the UK Noise at Work Regulations 1989.

Two recent HSE survey have evaluated the effects (or lack of them) of these 1989 noise regulations. The first,[89] in 1994, found that most (over 90 per cent) of the 400 firms surveyed knew about the noise law. But, whilst the law emphasizes control at source, and personal protection as a last resort, the preferred way of dealing with the noise hazard – by four out of five employers – was by the use of personal hearing protection (ear muffs or plugs). Even so, the crucial training in the use of hearing protection was poor or non-existent in one of four employers. The wearing of ear protection was often not supervised (taking hearing protection off in high noise levels can damage the hearing in just a few minutes, rendering the wearing of hearing protection the rest of the time useless for the prevention of hearing loss). Noise control at source and enclosure was very limited. Audiometry, or hearing tests, were carried out in one in four workplaces.

Given the results of this survey, the results of the 1996 HSE survey[90] were no great surprise. This survey found the average cost of the noise at work regulations to be £36.60, or about the cost of a good pair of ear muffs. The total annual costs to industry were estimated to be around £50 million in 1990 in the first year of operation of the 1989 noise regulations, and £37 million a year since. The benefits were estimated, in a very rough and dubious way, to be around one-quarter (25 per cent) of the costs. Therefore, overall, they estimated the costs to employers to be around £27.9 million per year. But what price do you put on not going deaf? This second HSE report estimated there were some 80,000 establishments that had noise levels of at least 85 decibels (see page 194).

NOISE PREVENTION

The HSE provides plenty of guidance on noise, and the free HSE booklet[91] is as good an introduction as can be found. In summary, the noise regulations require an employer to:

O   decide whether there is a noise problem (if you have to raise your voice to be heard, you have a noise problem) also, if your employees are irritated with the noise levels or type of noise, such as high whines or low hums, you have a noise problem.

O   get the noise levels professionally assessed (or have members of your staff professionally trained)

○ tell the employees of the noise levels, the hazards, what to do about them and mark out and label noisy areas and/or machinery
○ reduce the noise levels, 'as far as is reasonably practicable'
○ if it is not possible to reduce noise below the safe level (80 decibels), then provide an 'ear protection programme' (ear muffs or plugs, training, cleaning, etc.)
○ check that the above programmes are working on a regular basis.

NOISE MEASUREMENT

There are three key problems with the measurement and control of noise at work: (1) the decibel scale for measuring noise levels; (2) the so-called 'safe' levels of noise exposure allowed by law; and (3) the poor protection offered by ear defenders (ear plugs or muffs).

Noise levels are measured in a logarithmic scale called 'decibels' or dB for short. This means that a doubling of the sound pressure on the ear, as measured by the dB scale, would only be recorded by a 3-dB increase. The measurements are further complicated by an adjustment to the noise scale at different frequencies, because hearing is more sensitive to damage at different frequencies (crudely, the higher the frequency, the more the damage). So the dB scale is adjusted to the human ear with a so-called 'A' weighting to give the abbreviation most often seen: dBA. This is best illustrated by the following figures shown in Table 5.4 for the time allowed to certain dBA levels before the hearing is damaged.

TABLE 5.4   Noise level versus allowed exposure time

Noise level (dBA)	Time allowed (hours or minutes) (unprotected ear)
90	8 hours
93	4 hours
96	2 hours
99	1 hour
102	30 minutes
105	15 minutes

The second problem relates to what is a 'safe' level of exposure to noise levels. The 1989 Noise at Work Regulations define three basic 'action levels':

1. Where the noise level is at least 85 dBA and not above 90dBA, a noise assessment must be made by a competent person. This must be reviewed when there are significant work changes and at least once every two years.

The employees may ask for ear protectors and then the employer must provide them. There is no obligation on the employee to wear ear protectors, nor on the employer to enforce such wearing. Manufacturers, suppliers, designers and importers of plant and equipment with noise levels at above 85 dBA must supply purchasers with 'adequate' information on the noise generated by the equipment.

2. Where the noise level is above 90 dBA, the employer is required to reduce noise level, 'so far as is reasonably practicable', by means other than ear protectors (e.g. machine modification or acoustic enclosure). If this is not possible, suitable ear protection must be provided and the employees must wear it. Employers must provide training, instruction and supervision on the wearing of ear protectors. The areas where noise levels are above 90 dBA must be designated as 'ear protection zones'. 'As far as is reasonably possible', employers must ensure that people entering such zones have suitable hearing protection.

3. There is a 'peak' action level where the employee is exposed to very loud intermittent noise of 140 dB, where the requirements of (2) also apply.

HOW SAFE IS 85 dBA OR 90 dBA?

Is your hearing protected after a lifetime at work in these levels? Even the HSE admits that if the unprotected ear is exposed to 90 dBA for a lifetime (say 40 years and 8 hours a day), then up to half the workforce would have significant hearing loss. About one in three of those exposed to 85–90 dBA will suffer from significant hearing damage after a working lifetime, if their ears are unprotected.

It is generally agreed that noise levels below 75 dBA, in the working environment, are not harmful. Evidence of damage to hearing, after a lifetime of working, has been found in the range 80–90 dBA. Therefore, something below 75 dBA would appear to be a safe level to hearing to be aimed for, and the current levels are *not* safe, in that they do not protect the hearing fully.

ASSESSMENTS

Only 14 per cent of non-unionised organisations had undertaken a noise assessment, whereas 45 per cent of establishments with unions had measured noise levels.[90]

A key requirement of the 1989 Noise at Work Regulations is a 'noise assessment'. How can you deal with a problem if you do not know the extent of it and where it is? The 1996 HSE survey[90] found that about half the workplaces surveyed had carried out such an assessment, at a first average cost of around £20 per noise-exposed person assessed. Subsequent assessments were much cheaper, dropping to an average of £6.50 per person assessed.

CASE STUDY 21: ELECTRICAL ENGINEERING COMPANY

The use of sound-level meters for monitoring noise was adequate under the old production line system. Since the organization moved to a cellular manufacturing system (i.e. all processes are combined together), noise has become more dispersed throughout the site. This new manufacturing system means that people are walking around between quieter and noisy areas more often. Thus, the organization has resorted to personal dosimetry in order to measure the individual's exposure to noise.[90]

But assessments alone do not reduce noise levels. I have been in many organizations where there are piles of noise assessments, carried out over many years, on shelves (or, more recently, in the computer), but they have led to no reduction in noise levels. Assessments must be used to: purchase quieter equipment, reduce the noise at source by modification and/or enclosure, provide soundproof booths for operatives and, as a last resort, assess the type and level of noise reduction required ('attenuation') or any personal hearing protection (ear muffs or plugs) required. They must also be repeated on a regular basis, the HSE suggests every two years, where there is no substantial change in the process. This is because machinery tends to get noisy as it ages, especially if it is not serviced well. Also, parts fall off and/or get removed by service engineers, and these parts may be vital to the noise control on the equipment.

CONTROL

The main emphasis on noise at work should be the control of the noise[92] in the first place. The main ways of controlling noise are as follows:

○ Replace the noisy equipment with new, less noisy equipment (the best and cheapest solution by far, in the long run).
○ Adapt and modify it, so it emits less noise.
○ Move it or make other structural changes.
○ Enclose it in a specially designed noise enclosure.

The HSE survey of almost 2000 workplaces[90] found that less than half of those organizations with a noise problem had bothered to take any precautions to reduce the noise levels. There was also little evidence of the impact of the Supply of Machinery (Safety) Regulations 1992, which are supposed to control noise at source (by far the cheapest method).

CASE STUDY 22: A CHEMICAL COMPANY

Over the course of 15 years, at a company making synthetic fibres, the average noise levels had fallen from 102 dBA to 82 dBA. This was mainly due to a proactive noise policy, which laid an emphasis on the purchase of quieter equipment. In some cases there was an extra expense of 2–3 per cent of the overall price when extra insulation panels, etc. were involved. As the factory manager said, 'You don't buy plant and machinery on noise alone. It is also whether it does the job better or quicker. You have to show a direct payback. However health and safety is now part of the investment equation.'[90]

CASE STUDY 23: A PLASTICS MOULDING FACTORY

Compressed air guns were used to clean powder deposits off the plastic moulds. The noise levels produced were 105 dBA. By replacing the air guns' nozzles, at £40 each, with ones reducing the turbulence within the tube, noise levels were reduced to 95 dBA. The new tools were also stronger. The unprotected ear is damaged after just 15 minutes at 105 dBA, whilst it takes around two hours at 95 dBA.[93]

CASE STUDY 24: THE CAR INDUSTRY

In one company, the noise produced during the machining of alternator end-casting was 104 dBA. By reducing the amount of vibration with £40 worth of dampers, the noise levels were reduced to 88 dBA. In addition, the quality of the cut improved and the machining time was reduced. The unprotected ear is damaged after just 15 minutes at 105 dBA, whilst it takes around eight hours at 88 dBA.[93]

HSE CHECKLIST

It is this area that the HSE has produced, for many years now, one of its most useful publications ever: *Sound Solutions – Techniques to Reduce Noise at Work*.[92] By means of 60 detailed – including cost – noise control case studies, the HSE has covered almost every conceivable way of reducing noise and shown the great value in doing so. It is essential reading for any manager or trade union safety representative with a noise problem. The book also includes a very useful checklist for managers with a noise problem, the main elements of which are as follows.

Observe, listen to and touch (where safe) the noise source

O   What is the problem?
O   Where is it?
O   Is vibration the problem?
O   What is the main source of the noise?
O   Is the dominant source of the noise being treated first?
O   How many employees will benefit from noise control measures?

○ What is the cost per protected person?

Consider the source of the noise

○ Is it reasonable to replace the source with one causing less noise?
○ Could the machine be removed from all or some employees' hearing?
○ Could the working area be modified to reduce the noise exposure to workers?
○ Could worn or faulty parts be replaced?
○ Is it possible to modify noisy parts of the source?

Consider how the source radiates noise

○ Are there vibrating panels?
○ Are there vibrations in the building?
○ Can continuous impact noise be dampened?
○ Are machine guards causing noise?
○ Can noisy exhaust and/or air inlets be modified and/or silenced?

Consider the path of the noise

○ Can the worker be positioned away from the noise source (doubling the distance could reduce the effect of noise by 6 dB).
○ Can the noise be enclosed?
○ Can the employees be enclosed in a noise-free haven?
○ Can barriers or screens be erected between employees and the noise source?
○ Is the building and/or room where the noise source is located making the problem worse by having no scount-proofing and/or absorbent panels on the walls, floor or ceiling?

Finally, measure the new noise levels after the control method(s) have been implemented. Continually monitor these levels.

There is another, very useful, checklist for avoiding pitfalls – of which there are many – when introducing noise control measures included in the HSE book[92] that I have not summarized here. I remember a long struggle to get a good extraction system in an engineering company to remove oil fumes from the lathes and milling machines. When I next visited the workshop it seemed as misty as ever, despite the obvious existence of a gleaming extraction system – installed at a cost of around £10,000. 'It's not on', the manager told me, adding that, 'The men complain of the noise levels when I turn it on!' It is not uncommon to replace one hazard, in this case oil fumes, with another, noise. In this case £100 worth of vibration dampers on the ducting did the trick and we got rid of most of the oil fumes and the noise problem caused by the ducting vibrating.

PERSONAL PROTECTIVE EQUIPMENT (PPE)

As noted above, the provision of hearing protection was the main response of employers to the 1989 Noise at Work Regulations. The HSE survey[90] showed that two out of three organizations with noisy areas provided hearing protection. Nine out of ten employers provided ear muffs, as opposed to ear plugs. The average cost for a pair of ear muffs was £10 and for ear plugs 40p.

Hearing protection should be provided by employers as follows:

○ If the noise levels are between 85 and 90 dBA, protection must be provided when asked for by employees – the wearing of them is voluntary.
○ At or above 90 dBA, the employer must provide suitable hearing protectors and ensure that they are worn.

Employees must wear the hearing protection provided. The hearing protection must be clean and comfortable and be suitable for the job. An assessment of the noise levels is required to ensure that the hearing defenders provide adequate protection, or 'attenuation', for the noise levels that the employees are exposed to. Ear plugs are only suitable for low levels of noise, as they do not give adequate protection and are usually supplied new each day (at about 10p per pair). More expensive, comfortable and protective plugs moulded to the shape of the ear can cost £25 per pair.

FIGURE 5.10   Ear defenders must be worn all the time to be effective, and can be much less effective when combined with head protection.

CASE STUDY 25: AN AIRLINE

Employees affected by high levels of noise are provided with ear muffs. The ear muffs used were recommended by consultants who carried out the noise assessment. These cost £8 to £10 a pair and the company buys four to five dozen a year. All the remaining staff are given ear plugs and these cost 60p a pair.[90]

It is vital to note that whatever type of ear protection is worn, *it must be worn all the time in high-noise areas*. As Table 5.4 clearly shows, if you remove your hearing protection for just 15 minutes at 105 dBA the damage to hearing is done. In other words, you may as well not wear the hearing protection at all. Many employees do not realize this and are therefore putting their hearing at risk by taking their defenders off for 5–10 minutes every hour or so to give themselves a 'break' (most ear defenders are not very comfortable if worn all day, as to be effective they have to press into the ears/head) and possibly talk to colleagues, etc.

HEARING TESTS OR 'AUDIOMETRY'

Although there is no legal requirement for hearing tests, or 'audiometric testing', to be carried out under the noise regulations, an HSE survey[89] of 400 workplaces found that one in four (25 per cent) did in fact carry out audiometric testing on their employees. A larger, more recent HSE survey[90] of some 1889 workplaces found the same figure, of one in four (25 per cent), of employees carrying out audiometric testing when the noise levels were above 85 dBA. As would be expected, the larger the workplace, the more likely audiometry was to be offered: in workplaces with more than 300 people, two out of three (67.6 per cent) carried out such testing. This most probably reflects the availability of an occupational health nurse or similar. A small-scale, HSE-funded, study into the audiometric provision in 12 companies noted:

> In all cases the main reason for carrying out pre-employment audiometry was to ... protect the employer against future claims for compensation for noise-induced hearing loss ... No case was reported by any of the employers in which noise control action was carried out as a direct result of the results of audiometry.[94]

Whilst it is no substitute for noise control at source and/or hearing protection, if done professionally audiometry can be a very useful tool in a hearing protection programme. It alerts employees to early hearing loss and makes them more aware of the need to protect their valuable hearing, and it is an important check that any hearing protection, if used, is actually effective (or worn) in that it protects the hearing. The cost per employee was around £8 and the tests took around ten minutes (longer in some organizations). Large companies had in-house testing facilities, and others used the NHS. Employers gave the main reason for carrying out audiometry as defending themselves against future common law claims. One employer in the HSE survey noted that audiometry was, 'about the only way to see whether the measures we have taken are working.'

CASE STUDY 26: PAINT COMPANY

Audiometry has been carried out since 1993. All existing employees have been tested and it is compulsory for new employees. It was suggested by the insurance company. Also, the closure of a nearby, noisy brick company meant that some new employees at the company already had damaged hearing. Compulsory testing is carried out every three years. Six employees have been found to have had hearing problems and been referred to their own GP or the company medical adviser. People with hearing problems are tested every year and moved to a less noisy area if appropriate. In the case of one employee, with a severe hearing problem, an £800 disability grant from the job centre enabled a pager to be purchased for the fire alarm.[93]

The HSE recommends[91] that the following audiometric records are kept, in addition to giving each employee a copy of their audiogram, explaining its significance, and a copy of the following information:

○ personal identity, including name and works/pay or national insurance number
○ job details, including when work in noisy areas started and ended
○ details of any known previous jobs involving exposure to high noise levels
○ details of noise exposure
○ the dates on which hearing checks were carried out
○ the forms of ear protection in use

ENVIRONMENTAL NOISE

For ten years, residents of a tower block in east London had complained about the noise levels in their flats, but nothing was done. Then, in 1995, a noisy party, three floors up on the 13th floor, caused 35-year-old British Telecom engineer, and father of two, Peter Thurston to crack. Dressed in combat gear and with a fake machine gun, he firebombed the party. He then cut the electricity which plunged the flat into darkness. Panic spread among the 40 guests and one, 26-year-old mother of one, Donna O'Dwyer, fell 13 floors to her death. (See Noise-raged man 'bombed flat', *Guardian*, 13 September 1995.) In September 1995 Peter Thurston was found guilty and sentenced to serve at least 22 years in prison. Prosecutor John Bevan said, 'It is unusual because the Crown says that this defendant's primary motive was not to kill … it was to stop the music.' (See 22 years for killer who firebombed his noisy neighbour, *Daily Mirror*, 28 September 1995.)

This is an extreme case, of course. But noise complaints to local councils did rise massively from 3314 in 1982–83 to 111,152 in 1992–93, and by 10 per cent on the previous year to almost 145,000 in 1994–95. A 1994 Building Research Establishment study found that the home life of one in three people was blighted by noise from traffic or neighbours.[95] Some studies have shown evidence of stress among children living near airports and high blood pressure in children in kindergartens near busy roads. I had a very reasonable, mature, student who was driven crazy by music when trying to study. He broke in one night and smashed up the sound system. He was charged with criminal damage and only just escaped a prison sentence. He was lucky, but the stress of the trial still caused him to miss one year of his course. Some councils now run mediation centres to try and bring the two sides together, and these seem to be quite successful.

The law on environmental noise has, from 1 April 1997, been tightened up under the Housing Act 1996. Local council EHOs, often with the aid of the police, now have the power to fine people who create excessive noise at night – in most cases set at more than 35 dBA – and to confiscate noisy equipment. However, this has led to rising threats of violence to EHOs; a man was jailed for four months after he knocked over and repeatedly kicked an EHO who had been called to his home.[96]

In addition, The Noise Act 1996 was passed in July 1997 and, where adopted, enforced from 19 September 1997.. It only applies to domestic premises (including gardens, outhouses and court yards) and sets 'permitted noise levels' between 11 p.m. and 7 a.m. The permitted noise level is 35 dBA, or 10 dBA above the underlying noise level, in cases where the underlying noise level exceeds 25 dBA. A free booklet[97] describes the new law.

Although strong on personal noise control (above), the former Conservative government backed off from controlling traffic noise. Aircraft and traffic noise is a great, and growing, problem. In the Netherlands, it is illegal to build houses in areas where the 24-hour average noise level exceeds 50 dBA. A 1990 survey found that seven out of 100 British homes had noise levels above 68 dBA.[95] Quiet road surfaces are available, but expensive, and the previous Conservative British government shied away from requiring them. In Austria, Belgium, The Netherlands and Sweden, trials with porous asphalt (required by law in The Netherlands for any road with more than 35,000 vehicles a day) have shown a halving, or 5 dBA reduction, of sound levels, and 'whisper concrete' can reduce the noise by up to one-quarter or by 10 dBA.

A 1995 survey, by the Council for the Protection of Rural England, has shown that the number of quiet and tranquil areas (i.e. 3 km from a large town, 2 km for major roads and 1 km from main railway lines) in Britain has shrunk by one-fifth (21 per cent).[95] The problem of environmental noise is now on everyone's agenda.

CONCLUSION

On paper the 1989 Noise at Work Regulations are pretty good. There is much good HSE advice available and the emphasis is on controlling noise at source. However, the noise level effectively allowed – 90 dBA for an eight-hour day – is too high and will allow people's hearing to be damaged.

Unfortunately, as we have seen, the regulations have been ineffective in controlling noise at the workplace. To be effective, and to provide a 'level playing field', the noise regulations have to be enforced. They are not. In 1996–97 (HSE, 1997), two prohibition notices, 82 improvement notices and no prosecutions were undertaken under the Noise at Work Regulations 1989.

The 1996 HSE-sponsored survey of nearly 2000 workplaces[90] found that 'pressure from HSE or local government inspectors was generally felt to be relatively unimportant' (p. 93). They quoted one apparently fairly typical employer's view, from a paper products manufacturer, who said:

> HSE inspectors are always rather vague and rarely specific about noise reductions. They might say the noise level is too high, but they don't say what level it should be and what could be done to reduce it. (page 93)

VIBRATION

> Stephen Bard started using road drills and breakers in the mid-1980s. In 1992, the 32-year-old driller was 'medically retired'. Unlikely to find work again, Stephen's fingers can be painful, numb and clumsy especially in cold weather. The nerves and blood vessels in his hands are permanently damaged by the vibration from the tools he used at work. ((1994) Bad vibrations, *Hazards*, **48**, 8–9)

The hazards of the type of vibration that Stephen suffers from – so-called 'hand–arm' vibration have been known since the turn of the century. 'Vibration white finger', VWF, or 'dead man's hand' was described in Italy in 1911 and in the USA in 1918.[98] The medical and scientific literature on the health hazards of hand–arm vibration grew as more and more jobs produced vibration – pneumatic tools (replacing chisels and mallets), air hammers and drills, chipping hammers, chain saws and pneumatic screwdrivers, with a flurry of medical papers around the time of the Second World War because of the pressures of mass production. By the time I wrote my 1975 booklet[99] enough was known to have prevented Stephen Bard (above) developing his VWF. Yet, in 1994 Drs Jack Collin and Roy Palmer of St Thomas' Hospital, London, just went out into the London streets and quizzed 53 roadside workers who used pneumatic tools. They found that one in five complained of stiff hand joints and at least three were diagnosed as suffering from VWF.[100] Only four of the 53 were aware of the preventative measures that could be taken to reduce VWF. It is not surprising that Professor Bill Taylor, the doyen of VWF research in the UK,[101] concluded, after a lifetime's research into the disease and its prevention: 'The pioneers of occupational medicine of the 16th, 17th and 18th century would not be impressed by our lack of progress in the hand–arm vibration syndrome in the 20th century.'[98]

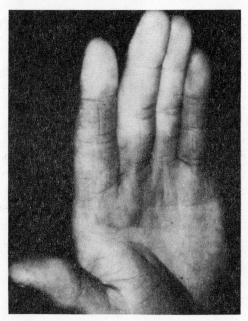

FIGURE 5.11   Vibration White Finger (or 'dead hand') can be very painful and disabling

The health hazards of vibration are generally divided into two areas:

1.   Hand–arm vibration.
2.   Whole body vibration.

The hazards arise from very different processes or machinery, with different vibration characteristics, and lead to different diseases. However, it is possible to be subject to both types of vibration in some occupations and therefore to suffer from both types of diseases. For convenience, they will be discussed separately. The hazards of hand–arm vibration have been known longer and they have been investigated more fully. That is not to say that they are the most important.

HAND–ARM VIBRATION

The HSE (1997) estimates:

○   In 1995, 30,000 people self-reported suffering from hand–arm vibration syndrome. This was double the 1990 figure.
○   There were 3016 DSS-assessed cases of vibration white finger in 1995–96 (compared with 5403 in 1990–91 and 1425 in 1993–94). To qualify for DSS assessment you have to have more than 14 per cent disability.
○   232 RIDDOR (see page 123) cases of hand–arm vibration syndrome (HAVS) were reported in 1996–97 one of the most common diseases reported.

O   Other diseases, such as carpal tunnel syndrome (CTS), may be caused by vibration. In 1995–96, 265 new cases of CTS were assessed.

The new name for VWF is hand–arm vibration syndrome (HAVS), because, as a 1995 report from the government's independent Industrial Injury Advisory Council (IIAC) noted, 'exposure to vibration causes neurological disturbances as well as blanching of the fingers'.[102]

The incidence of this disease is known to be high in many occupations, such as road drilling, chain sawing, grinding.[98] Other information comes from two compensation sources: the government's industrial injury and disease scheme, and common law claims where victims sue their employer (or, more commonly, the employer's insurance company).

COMPENSATION

Since 1954 the trade unions have been campaigning for the government to compensate those injured by hand–arm vibration at work. Under such pressure, the IIAC has held several investigations: between 1954 and 1984 it produced four reports on the subject, but no compensation was recommended. A breakthrough occurred in 1985, when the IIAC recommended some limited compensation[102] and the government accepted its recommendations. From that date the number of cases prescribed rose rapidly to peak at 5403 in 1990–91, and then fell back to 1747 in 1994–95 (but up from 1425 in 1993–94). However, a disability must be assessed at 14 per cent or more before compensation is payable, and in 1994–95 only one in ten (11 per cent) HAVS claims were so assessed. In 1995 the DSS estimated that there were only 1830 people receiving payment for HAVS, including cases assessed in earlier years. It is also possible for some HAVS sufferers, who have developed 'carpal tunnel syndrome' (a form of RSI), to claim a DSS pension.

The progress, until recently, on common law claims has been slow and the awards small. In 1979 Mr Justice Eastham awarded a Mr Mustoe £2000 for general damages and labour market handicap and set the date of knowledge about VWF, for a company with medical and nursing staff, at March 1969. In 1982 Mr Justice Kilner-Brown set general bands of awards from £500 to £3,000, depending upon the severity of the VWF, and said that industry as a whole would have little excuse for ignorance after 1975. A breakthrough in HAVS common law claims occurred in 1997 with the full outcome of a judgement against British Coal. In 1995 Judge Stephenson ruled that British Coal should have known of the hazards of VWF since 1 January 1975 (the normal date is 1 January 1976), and in October 1997 he gave the final awards to seven of nine coal miners (two were rejected) who were backed by their union, the NUM. The total awards to the seven were £124,735, with the seven individual amounts ranging from £5000 to £41,085.

There are at least another 500 coal miners' claims waiting and the final bill could be £150–500 million to the government (as British Coal is due to be wound up). The insurance industry says there are around 8–9000 claims for HAVS per year. The Amalgamated Engineering and Electrical Union (AEEU) is reported to have won £636,000 for its members in HAVS compensation alone. The general union, GMB, claims to have settled 12,384 'no-fault' vibration compensation claims in the past eight years. The coal miners' decision might open the floodgates for many other HAVS cases, such as the construction industry.

THE MAIN SYMPTOMS OF HAVS

○ Tingling and/or numbness in the fingers (if felt after 5–10 minutes of continuous use regard the machine/task as a vibration risk).
○ Loss of sensation and manual dexterity.
○ Finger blanching (white finger).
○ Aching fingers and limbs (depending on type of job).

There is no effective treatment for HAVS: prevention is the only cure. A recent medical follow-up of 102 HAVS sufferers found that one in five (22 per cent) said that their attacks of blanching and numbness had decreased, whilst almost one in three (32 per cent) said that they had increased.[103] People were more at risk if they continued to work with high-vibration hand tools, smoked, suffered from other circulatory diseases and were younger when first diagnosed with HAVS.

A comparison is often made between noise and vibration, as they often occur together and the same basic equipment, with some key modifications, can be used to measure both. However, there is one key different between the two hazards: there is no personal protection available to prevent vibration exposure. In fact anti-vibration seats, and some so-called anti-vibration gloves, can actually increase the vibration that the hands and arms receive.

VIBRATION MEASUREMENT

> It is safest to regard regular prolonged use of any high-vibration tool or machine as suspect, especially if it causes tingling or numbness in the user's fingers after about 5 to 10 minutes continuous operation.[104]

Whilst it is true the same equipment that is used to measure noise, with the use of a vibration sensor (an 'accelerometer') instead of a microphone, can be used to measure vibration, the actual measurements are more difficult and more subject to error, and the 'safe' standards are much less sure for vibration than for noise.[105]

The measurements must be carried out by specialists with knowledge of vibration measurements, evaluation and control. Because the vibration has to be measured in three planes, the measurements are more difficult. A common problem is the attachment of the accelerometer to the vibrating equipment; if it is not firmly screwed or clipped on, the measurements will be inadequate. Accelerometer cables are fragile and a common source of problems. Errors of up to 20 per cent or more are not uncommon. Also, laboratory vibration levels found in equipment rarely mimic those in real life. The measurements found are then compared with various national and international guidelines. In the UK, the common standard used is BS 6842:1987. The allowance for time versus vibration exposure are:

Vibration level found (m/s²)	2	2.8	4	5.6	8	11.2
Exposure time allowed per day (hours)	16	8	4	2	1	0.5

However, these action levels are not completely safe levels. For example, *the eight-hour exposure to 2.8 m/s² may allow up to one in ten people so exposed, after ten years of exposure, to develop white finger.* The US government suggests that exposure to vibration be reduced as far as is possible, both by reducing the acceleration of the vibration and by cutting down exposure times.

VIBRATION PREVENTION

There are no specific laws to control and prevent vibration, although at some time in the future the EU Physical Agents Directive will come into force and it does cover the hazards of vibration. At the moment, the only specific UK law concerned with vibration is The Supply of Machinery (Safety) Regulations 1992. These regulations require suppliers to provide installation and assembly instructions to minimize vibration. Further, suppliers must provide information on the vibration levels if hand-held or hand-guided machinery is likely to subject workers to vibration exceeding 2.5 m/s². The HSE guidance says: 'Where (vibration) hazardous jobs are identified they should be taken into account in the general risk assessment required by the *Management of Health and Safety at Work Regulations 1992.*'[106] A 1993 AEEU survey of 263 companies, employing 87,000 workers, found that one-third had *not* carried out risk assessments of vib-ration levels and only a quarter of them provided any form of protection from vibration. All of the companies surveyed used tools or machines known to cause vibration-related diseases. (See (1993) Bad vibrations, London: AEEU.)

Twenty years ago I surveyed some of the anti-vibration advances available,[99] there were plenty then and there are many more now. Even then there were cases, such as the Forestry Commission, who clearly, through extensive research, identified the chain saw with the least vibration. However, they did not then recommend that saw, but used a cheaper one. According to the HSE, there are about 35,000 road breakers in use in the UK today. Most of them exceed the safe standards, according to an HSE review.[107] Measuring the vibration from a wide range of road breakers, the levels went from 5.6m/s^2 on a Lifton LH20 Hydraulic which would allow two hours of continuous use to a JCB 292-08200 Hydraulic with a vibration of 54/5 m/s^2, way above any official recommendations. The average vibration was in the area of 17 m/s^2, which would only allow about 30 minutes of use a day to reduce the risk of HAVS. The HSE report makes a series of control measure recommendations: modified, suspended and cushioned handles (the new Ingersoll-Rand hammer has a vibration level of only 7 m/s^2) to the use of a road breaker on a suspended arm from a JCB (see Figure 5.12). The HSE report also points out that new working methods such as 'cut and break' when digging up road surfaces can reduce vibration exposure. In June 1997 the HSE published[106] an excellent set of useful, and practical, case studies on handarm vibration prevention. In some cases the prevention cost only a few pounds.

FIGURE 5.12   Remote controlled pneumatic hammers offer the best method of vibration control on road breakers; they are more efficient, too

CASE STUDY 27: FASTEST CHAIN SAW SHOWS LEAST VIBRATION

A study of 186 common hand-held tools in the construction industry showed that many of them subjected the user to harmful vibrations. A detailed study of the vibration levels of five different models of 'sabre saw', when cutting a steel tube of diameter 48mm and with a 4-mm wall thickness, found that the safest – from a vibration point of view – was also the fastest. Thus the Milwaukee 6522-4 had a vibration of 5.6–6.8 m/s^2 and took 155 seconds.[108]

CASE STUDY 28: PEDESTAL GRINDING

A process involved holding aluminium components against an abrasive band to remove flash. The operator carried out this task for 4 hours and 10 minutes each day. A vibration assessment showed the levels to be 44.4m/s^2, giving a 10 per cent risk of finger blanching in only 8.5 months. This level of vibration is over ten times the HSE guidance of 32 m/s^2 for daily exposure. In fact the HSE action level is exceeded in only two minutes of continuous deflashing. Engineering modifications were introduced to reduce the vibration at a cost of around £20 for half a day's work for one person fitting the modification. The vibration level fell to only 1.5 m/s^2 and only half the HSE action level.[106]

WHOLE BODY VIBRATION

As noted above, far less is known about the health hazards (and the 'safe' standards) for whole body vibration. Nevertheless, in January 1997 the HSE published a ground-breaking leaflet that – at long last – recognized the harmful effects that whole body vibration can have on the backs of certain groups of drivers.[109] As Christopher Bowden of the HSE said, when launching the booklet:

> There is evidence of a link between back problems in drivers and 'whole-body vibration', which is the vibration or jolting from a vehicle, transmitted through drivers' seat into their spines. This is particularly prevalent in tractors, dumper trucks, life trucks and quarry vehicles, which are driven over rough ground or poorly paved surfaces. When this sort of exposure goes on for several hours day after day, it can cause drivers to suffer back injury and back pain. Sufferers may have to take long spells off work and in some cases have to give up work altogether. The costs to employers in lost production time, re-training and general disruption can be substantial, especially to small firms and owner drivers.[110]

In fact, a wide range of other health problems have been associated with exposure to whole body vibration, as well as backache. Some of these are stomach problems, problems with balance (associated with inner ear problems) such as motion sickness, piles, tiredness, menstrual problems and increased miscarriage rates.[111] Vibration exposure in the 4-hertz range is said to result in changes in electrical activity in the brain. Although many of these observations have been dismissed because the research was carried out in eastern Europe, further research is needed to prove or disprove these observations, and anecdotal evidence[99] from drivers and other exposed to whole body vibration supports the former eastern European researchers.

A 1986 review of over 180 publications on whole body vibration concluded that there was a definite health risk to: the spine, peripheral nervous system and digestive system and possibly the peripheral veins.[112] Others have reported backache, numbness of the arm and leg, headache, stiff shoulder and stomach pains and noted that many drivers and operators of construction equipment are exposed to both whole body and hand–arm vibration.

According to the HSE,[109] young people are especially at risk from whole body vibration ('because the strength of the muscles is still developing and the bones have not yet fully matured'), as are those operating the following machinery:

○   construction and quarrying vehicles and machinery
○   tractors and other agricultural and forestry machinery
○   industrial trucks, such as lift trucks and straddle carriers
○   road haulage vehicles, rail vehicles, buses etc.
○   hammer mills and mobile crushers

The HSE advises that employers should consider anyone to be at risk who drives or works on the above equipment for most of the day. Manufacturers should warn users if the whole body vibration is a hazard when they supply new machinery. The HSE advises that it may be necessary for employers to use a consultant to measure the levels of vibration and recommend what can be done to reduce such levels. The HSE recommends the following measures to reduce whole body vibration.

○   Purchase low-vibration vehicles and equipment.
○   Ask manufacturers to advise you how to use and maintain equipment to keep vibrations to a minimum.
○   Ensure that vehicles and machinery are adequately maintained, particularly suspension components.
○   Check that the driver's seat is in good repair, and gives good support.
○   Check whether a suspension seat is fitted suitable to the vibration characteristics of the machine and, if not, whether a suitable seat can be fitted. You may need to talk to the machine's manufacturer about this.
○   If a suspension seat is fitted, ensure that it is correctly adjusted to the operator's weight according to the manufacturer's instructions (some seats adjust automatically to the driver weight).
○   Ensure that where equipment in vehicle cabs can be adjusted, it is set to suit the size and reach of drivers expected to use it.
○   Check that drivers have the right tyres and that they are inflated to the correct pressure for the ground surface.

○ Identify the vehicles or machines with the highest levels of vibration and arrange for a rota of operators or drivers to reduce the time spent on them by individuals.
○ Plan work site routes with the smoothest terrain.
○ If possible, improve the ground surface over which vehicles have to be driven regularly, for example by repairing pot holes, clearing debris or levelling out.
○ Train all employees in the hazards of vibration, good posture, how to adjust suspension seats, the correct tyre pressure, keeping low speeds over uneven terrain, varying work patterns to reduce exposure, to report increased vibration over new/serviced vehicles and to report backache or other problems that they feel may be associated with exposure to vibration to medical authorities (e.g. works doctor, GP), management union and enforcement agencies.

Several recent scientific papers support some of the above recommendations. Some suspension seats, in construction equipment lorries, fork-life trucks and tractors, can actually increase the amount of vibration that the driver receives.[113] Many were found not to protect the driver over a whole working day. In France alone, some 200,000 fork-life trucks are used by around 700,000 drivers. A study of five common makes, using different tyres, seats, tracks, drivers and whilst empty and loaded, concluded that:[114]

○ the roughness of the terrain is a very important factor, as a rough track can increase vibration levels by up to 70 per cent
○ a suspended seat is useful (especially with a cut-off frequency lower that 4 hertz)
○ if the previous point is fulfilled, then inflated tyres are best (otherwise, and with 'low cost', or normal seats, cushion tyres may be better)
○ in any case the driving speed should be adjusted to the track, load, truck, etc.

SMOKING, ALCOHOL AND DRUGS AT WORK

These issues were until very recently, private issues for the individual and, except in some instances (e.g. drinking and driving), nothing to do with the workplace. However, with the knowledge of the hazards of passive smoking and more public awareness about the harmful effects of drinking and drug-taking, these issues are now becoming more important at the workplace. These are sensitive issues, ranging from personal habits that, if they do not interfere with the ability to work, are none of the business of the employer, to personal habits that are clearly workplace issues (e.g. passive smoking) and on which the employer even may have a legal duty to act (e.g. drinking and driving). On all three issues – smoking, alcohol and drug abuse at work – the HSE has produced some very readable, useful and free literature.[115]

FIGURE 5.13   The workplace ashtray - to be confined to history?

The issue of workplace smoking hazards is more clear-cut, the guidance better and there are even some newer health and safety regulations that mention smoking, so it is the easiest place to start.

WORKPLACE SMOKING

For years Veronica Bland had to put-up with being exposed to other people's cigarette smoke at her work with Stockport Metropolitan Borough Council. Eventually it caused her to develop chronic bronchitis. In January 1993 she received £15,000 compensation from the council for the damage caused to her health by passive smoking.[116]

The ventilation system in Beryl Roe's office was shut down and this increased her exposure to cigarette smoke. Since 1983 she suffered from eye, nose, throat irritation and bronchial hypersensitivity due to the cigarette smoke. In 1987, aged 51, she retired from Stockport Council on ill-health grounds. She has been unable to work since and her symptoms return if she goes into a smoky atmosphere. With the help of her union, UNISON, in July 1995 she received £25,000 compensation.[116]

Most people now accept that smoking causes lung cancer, other chest diseases and an increase in heart disease. There has been a steady decrease in smoking, with only around one in three people smoking as compared with one in two ten or so years ago. However, there are still worrying trends in smoking increases among women and young people. Since an authoritative UK government report of 1988, it has been known that passive smoking – inhaling someone else's smoke – can cause a small increase in lung cancer. Passive smoking also has an immediate ('acute') irritant effect in the eyes, throat and respiratory tract, and can aggravate asthma. Recent research has suggested a possible connection with heart disease, and a possible association between heavy exposure to tobacco smoke of women during pregnancy and smaller babies.

For these reasons both the government and the HSE advise that:

○   non-smoking should be regarded as the norm in enclosed workplaces
○   smokers should be segregated from non-smokers

The law

Section 2 of the 1974 Health and Safety at Work Act requires all employers to ensure, so far as is reasonably practicable, the health, safety and welfare of all employees. Clearly, with current knowledge, workplace smoking hazards would be considered under this section. More specifically, The Workplace (Health, Safety and Welfare) Regulations 1992, section 25, requires that employers provide 'rest facilities' that protect non-smokers from smokers. The HSE has noted that cigarette smoke contributes to a 'sick-building syndrome' (see page 113) and, as noted in the two cases above, there is the possibility of a common law claim, by suing the employer for negligence. Clearly, the law is changing in favour of the non-smoking workplace and the non-smoker.

No-smoking policies

For both employers and employees, the restriction of smoking at the workplace is not always easy and it must be carried out with the full consultation of all employees both smokers and non-smokers. Smokers who were taken on to work in a workplace that allowed smoking have employment rights. And the rights of natural justice – and the fact that many smokers want to give up but are addicted – means that if management tries to crudely victimize smokers, even non-smokers will support smokers against such victimization. With regard to a total ban on smoking in the workplace, the HSE guidance[115] says: 'In some situations a complete ban on smoking may be justified for safety reasons, for example if there is a risk of fire or explosion' (p. 8). In all other cases, the HSE recommends that all employers should have a specific policy on smoking in the workplace. The policy should be written down and generally available. The policy should 'give priority to the needs of non-smokers who do not wish to breathe tobacco smoke' (p. 8). Plenty of guidance is now available on: the benefits of such a policy (both to management and staff); how to draw up a no-smoking policy; how to implement it (a key point being the time it takes to introduce); and how to monitor the effectiveness of such a policy.[117]

The key points of a no-smoking policy are as follows.[116]

○ Consult the employees (including trade union safety representatives or delegates of employee safety):
  - survey staff about smoking at work
  - ask managers and unions to comment on the draft policy
  - publicize the intention to go smoke-free

○ Write a policy:
  - explain the health risks of passive smoking
  - give guidance on who will implement the policy, and how

○ Make it happen – convene site working groups to:
  - identify limited separate designated smoking areas
  - put up signs
  - work to a smoke-free deadline
  - organize local publicity

○ Keep a check on progress:
  - nominate two monitors per site
  - create a checklist for monitoring
  - institute regular monitoring procedures
  - deal with problems as they arise

ALCOHOL AND DRUG ABUSE

> A television executive's known previous drinking habits were considered important, and valid, in the refusal to offer him a job.
>
> Industrial tribunal case during 1996.

So it is now possible to not even get a job, let alone lose it, through known drinking habits. There is also a small, but slow, increase in the number of employers carrying out pre-employment (e.g. urine testing) testing for drug abuse, especially for staff in safety sensitive jobs, locations or industries (e.g. oil and transport). A recent Institute of Personnel and Development (IPD) survey of more than 1500 personnel professionals found that one in ten employers carried out pre-employment drug testing, but that only half were randomly testing employees.[118] The IPD survey also discovered that, of employers surveyed:

○ nine out of ten (90 per cent) had a smoking policy
○ three out of five (63 per cent) had a policy on alcohol
○ one out of two (54 per cent) had a policy on drugs
○ one in three (35 per cent) had cases of alcohol abuse reported
○ one in seven (15 per cent) had received reports of employees using illegal drugs in the past year
○ one in five (18 per cent) personnel professionals said that employees who test positive for illegal drugs should be dismissed, regardless of the nature of their job

○ seven out of ten (72 per cent) personnel professionals said that employees who tested positive for drugs, and were carrying out safety-critical work, should be dismissed.

The IPD survey also claimed that:

> Research from the United States also suggests that employees who use drugs are a third less productive than their colleagues, 3.6 times more likely to injure themselves or somebody else in a workplace accident, and 2.5 times more likely to be absent from work for eight days or more. (page 2)

In the UK, a lot more is known about the effects of alcohol abuse at work than drug abuse, as drug users often hide their habit from their employer. As Oonagh Ryden, an IPD policy adviser involved in the IPD survey says, 'A coke addict is not going to do a line in full view of colleagues, although a heavy drinker may go to the pub with their manager because alcohol is legal and therefore more socially acceptable.'
According to the HSE,[115] alcohol abuse at the workplace:

○ causes 3–5 per cent of all absences from work each year; about 8–14 million lost working days each year
○ costs industry about £2 million a year
○ is a fairly minor problem for nine out of ten personnel directors, and a 'major problem' for almost one in five (17 per cent).

The Health and Safety at Work Act, section 2, will cover general work hazards from both alcohol and drug abuse. More specifically, The Transport and Works Act 1992 makes it a criminal offence for certain workers to be unfit through drink and/or drugs while working on railways, tramways and other guided transport systems. Employers operating these transport systems would also be guilty of an offence unless they had shown 'all due diligence' in trying to prevent such an offence being committed. Many employers, especially in the driving and other industries, state in the contract of employment that being found unfit to drive or work through drink and/or drugs is a sackable offence.
    The government and the HSE suggest that it is best not to drink at all in the following situations:

○ before or during driving
○ before using machinery, electrical equipment or ladders
○ before working or in the workplace when appropriate functioning would be adversely affected by alcohol

They suggest that a model alcohol policy would:

○ have aims (best for all staff)
○ have a senior manager responsible for implementing the policy
○ have understandable rules to ensure that their employees' alcohol consumption does not have a detrimental affect upon their work

○   make clear whether the rules apply in all situations or whether there are exceptions
○   have a statement saying that all employees with an alcohol problem will be treated in strict confidence
○   have a description of the support available to employees who have problems because of their drinking
○   have a commitment to provide employees with general information about the effects of drinking alcohol on health and safety
○   have the circumstances in which disciplinary action will be taken

The HSE guidance[115] on a policy on drug abuse at work is similar to the above, but different in a number of key respects, and the main points are that the policy should:

○   clearly define drug abuse
○   explain the health hazards of drug abuse
○   encourage employees with drug problems to seek help
○   provide the necessary help and advice
○   stress the confidential nature of any discussions on this issue
○   make clear that absence for treatment and rehabilitation will be regarded as normal sickness
○   recognize that relapses may occur
○   enable employees to return to the same job, after treatment, if possible or otherwise offer alternative employment
○   explain that if help is refused and/or impaired performance continues, disciplinary action is likely
○   explain that dismissal action may be taken in cases of gross misconduct
○   state that trafficking will be reported immediately to the police; there is no alternative to this procedure
○   provide for the policy to be monitored and reviewed regularly in consultation with workplace representatives.

A recent review of company alcohol and drug policies notes that they are still relatively rare, but growing fairly fast as a result of the 1992 Transport and Works Act.[119] It gives detailed examples of 12 such policies in a wide range of companies and organizations. The important issue of infringement of freedom is discussed more fully in a recent article, where it is noted that a recreational joint, E or other soft drug can be found in the urine days, and sometimes weeks, later.[120] In most jobs, it should be no business of an employer what an employee does or does not do, at the weekend or after work.

I have recently been involved in advising trade union safety representatives at a large food company, where the management became concerned about drug use by the mainly young workforce. Several perfectly good employees – who did their jobs well and were no risk to either themselves or others – whose urine showed drug use weeks before were sacked. This does not make sense, it made the rest of the workforce both scared and angry, apart from being unfair. What is the point of the drug testing programme? To follow the HSE guidance[115] *before* any drug testing programme is introduced seems vital:

> The agreement of the workforce to the *principle* of screening should be obtained, and in each case the *written consent of the individual* must be obtained. Medical confidentiality must be assured: managers should only be told whether an employee is considered fit or unfit for work. (page 12; original emphasis)

PERSONAL PROTECTIVE EQUIPMENT (PPE)

> The employer shall ... give collective protective measures priority over individual protective measures.
> Article 6.2.(h) of the EU Framework Directive on the introduction of measures to encourage improvements in the safety and health of workers at work, 391 (1989)

Several mentions have been made before of the use of PPE in connection with hearing protection and chemical/biological hazards and dust protection. But the use of PPE goes much wider than that. It includes safety helmets (now compulsory on building sites), safety boots, safety glasses, respirators, hearing protectors, anti-vibration gloves, general protective gloves, breathing equipment, back belts (of unproven value, see page 190) and general overalls and so on. Often PPE is the employer's first cheap and nasty choice of protection. Yet in the hierarchy of the Control of Substances Hazardous to Health (COSHH) Regulations, and that of all decent safety professionals, such as safety officers, safety engineers, doctors, nurses and occupational hygienists, PPE is the *last* – and often least effective – means of health and safety protection.

Recognizing the problems, the HSE, as one of the 'six-pack' regulations, brought in the Personal Protective Equipment Regulations 1992.[121] In a recent, very useful and important review of PPE, R. M. Howie notes that 'competent hygienists have recognized for many years that PPE performance in the workplace is difficult to guarantee and is probably lower than indicated by standard tests.'[122]

CASE STUDY 29: TOP OF THE RANGE ASBESTOS MASKS DO NOT PROTECT

In 1996 some workers removing asbestos on a Scottish power station noticed asbestos inside their face masks. Their masks were 'top of the range'. They complained to management and an independent analysis confirmed their fears. Apparently, this 'top of the range' mask did not provide protection when using a chipping hammer and grit blasting on asbestos lagging above head height (a very common situation). This situation was publicized by Clydeside Action on Asbestos and by the TGWU in Scotland.

After some pressure from the TGWU, and others, the HSE-sponsored 'Howie Report' on the failure of asbestos masks to protect was finally published in 1996. The report showed quite clearly that face masks with a supposed protection factor (i.e. the ratio of the dust outside to inside the mask) of 2000 often only had a protection factor of 40! This report led the HSE to concentrate much more on safer working methods for asbestos removal and not to rely just on personal protection. But what of the health of all the asbestos removers who thought that their 'top of the range' masks would protect them in any amount of asbestos dust?

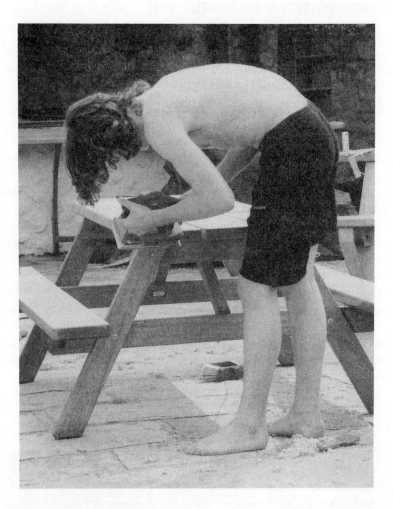

FIGURE 5.14   Eye/face, hair, head, hand, feet and sun protection are missing for this young worker.

CHECKLIST ON PPE SAFETY

Howie has outlined a key checklist,[122] reproduced below, for anyone using PPE, most of whose requirements are contained in the 1992 PPE regulations. In his article he expands on most of the items listed below:

○ Assess risks and identify where control is required.
○ Implement all reasonably practicable control measures.
○ Identify who needs protection.
○ Inform wearers of the consequences of exposure.
○ Select adequate PPE to control residual exposure.
○ Match PPE to wearer.
○ Ensure that the PPE does not crease risks.
○ Ensure that different PPE's are mutually compatible (e.g. ear muffs and safety helmet).
○ Involve wearers in the PPE selection process.
○ Provide PPE free of charge.
○ Train wearers in the correct use of their PPE.
○ Minimize wear periods.
○ Supervise wearers to ensure the correct use of PPE.
○ Maintain the PPE in efficient and hygienic conditions.
○ Inspect PPE to ensure that it is correctly maintained.
○ Provide suitable storage facilities for the PPE.
○ Record usage, maintenance and inspection data.
○ Monitor programme to ensure effectiveness.

If the above is fully carried out by management, then the cheap and nasty option does not look so attractive. Of course, PPE is very often the cheapest: protective glasses, ear muffs or face mask, bought quickly off the shelf at the lowest price, and given to the worker, with no training or instructions in their use and limitation (and, of course, no real assessment of the hazard and risk) and no cleaning, maintenance or regular replacement.

In 1996–97 (HSE 1997), 68 improvement and prohibition notices were issued under The Personal Protective Equipment Regulations 1992. There were six successful prosecutions, with an average fine of £1350. The safety representative regulations (page 76) make it a legal requirement for the employer to consult the manufacturers, if in doubt, about the effectiveness of their PPE for the workplace tasks that they are using them for. Howie recommends that 'If suppliers are unable to provide the required information, they should be reported to the relevant enforcing authority, i.e. in the UK, the local trading standards office' (in the local council). Of course, the PPE should *not* be worn in such cases.

Face masks or ear muffs that fit a large male will not be suitable for a small female, for example. Wearing face masks, especially with impermeable clothing, in hot conditions will place a considerable strain on the heart of the wearer, and their fitness and health must be monitored. Rest regimes are required. Does the wearing of PPE restrict vision or impair hearing in a way that could cause another hazard (e.g. an accident)? There are many important questions to ask when wearing PPE. The HSE has produced much free and priced[121] advice and guidance on the selection and maintenance of PPE for a wide range of occupations and hazardous tasks.

CASE STUDY 30: A UNIQUE PPE SURVEY

In 1986 I conducted what remains, unfortunately, one of the only large-scale surveys of PPE from the user's viewpoint. I received 607 responses (mainly from trade union safety representatives) from 245 workplaces that employed over 43,000 employees. The survey revealed that less than half the respondents were trained in PPE use and less than half the safety representatives were consulted in the choice of PPE.

There were problems with many types of PPE, and much of the PPE was designed for men not women. Studies in American coal mines, where women have worked since 1974, have shown that PPE for men that fits women badly is the cause of accidents and ill-health among women (as well as considerable discomfort). The positive aspect of the survey was that when the manufacturers were confronted with the problems the wearers complained of, many were only too ready to listen or had suitable PPE available. As the director of one large PPE supplier told me, 'Frankly, most of the points raised in your survey could be overcome if companies did not purchase on price alone.'[123]

NOTES

1. C. Cooper and S. Cartwright (1996) *Mental Health and Stress in the Workplace*, London: HMSO; An excellent summary of the causes of implications of and what to do about workplace stress. Most of the symptoms, illness and cost data for stress that I have quoted come from this authoritative, but little known, report.
2. Managing Stress (1995) *The Industrial Society*, Managing Best Practice, Number 18 – a good review of stress problems and solutions with some useful case studies.
3. A. Spurgeon, J. M. Harrington, and C. L. Cooper (1997) Health and safety problems associated with long working hours: a review of the current position, *Occupational and Environmental Medicine*, **54**, 367–75.
4. R. B. Briner (1996) Absence from work, *British Medical Journal*, **313**, 874–7.
5. Stansfield *et al.* (1995) Sickness absence for psychiatric illness: the Whitehall II study, *Social Science and Medicine*, **40**, 189–97.
6. Jill Earnshaw and C. Cooper (1996) *Stress and Employer Liability*, London: Institute of Personnel and Development. An excellent guide to stress compensation and prevention.
7. Judgement of the European Court, Case c-84/94, paragraph 15, 12 November 1996.
8. Anne Spurgeon (1997) Health and performance: effects of shiftwork and long working hours, *TUC Seminar on Working Time*, 7 February.

9. Martin Moore-Eden (1993) *The 24-Hour Society*, London: Piatkus Books.
10. *Working Time – LRD's guide to the European directive* (1996), London: The Labour Research Department.
11. Time to act (1997) *Hazards*, **57**, 1–2.
12. A. J. P. Dalton (1997) Under pressure, *T&G Health and Safety Record 3*, 7.
13. Eleanor Carty (1996) £175,000 for workload stress, *The Guardian*, 27 April.
14. £66,000 Stress payment to residential social worker, UNISON press release HS/25/96, July 1996.
15. Rory O'Neill (1996) *Stress at Work – Trade Union Action at the Workplace*, London: TUC. A good overview, with a very useful reading list.
16. A. J. P. Dalton (1988) *Stress at Work*, London: The Labour Research Department.
17. Health and Safety Executive (1990) *Managing Occupational Stress – A Guide for Managers and Teachers in the Schools Sector*, HSE.
18. Tom Cox (1993) *Stress Research and Stress Management*, HSE Contract Research report no. 61/1993.
19. Health and Safety Executive (1995) *Stress at Work – A Guide for Employers*, HSE, HS(G)116. Very general, but the right approach.
20. Andrea Adams (1994) *Bullying at Work*, London: Virago.
21. UNISON (1996) *Bullying at Work – Guide for Branches, Stewards and Safety Representatives* London: UNISON. An excellent guide, with full discussion of the issues, further reading, draft survey for members and draft policy.
22. Labour Research Department (1997) *Stress, Bullying and Violence – A Trade Union Action Guide*, London: The Labour Research Department.
23. Health and Safety Executive (1996) *Violence at Work*, HSE, IND(G)69L (Rev).
24. Department of Transport (DoT) (1995) *Protecting Bus Crews*. The Standing panel on assaults against bus staff, DoT, Room S15/09, 2 Marsham Street, London SW1P 3EB.
25. Health and Safety Executive (1995) *Preventing Violence to Retail Staff*, HSE, HS(G)133. The HSE has produced much more guidance on preventing violence at work, especially in banks, education and the health service.
26. Ian Burrell (1997) This woman is allergic to modern life, *The Independent*, 7 March, p. 6.
27. (a) A. A. Ashford and C. S. Miller (1991) *Chemical Exposure: Low Levels and High Stakes*, London: Van Nostrand Reinhold; (b) W. J. Rea (1995) *Chemical Sensitivity*, London: Lewis/Times Mirror International Publishers Ltd, (four volumes); (c) M. R. Cullen (ed.) (1987) *Workers With Multiple Chemical Sensitivities*, Philadelphia: Hanley and Belfus.
28. A. A. Ashford and C. S. Miller (1996) Low-level chemical sensitivity: current perspectives, *International Archives of Environmental Health*, **68**, 367–76.
29. *Hazards*, **42**, 2 (1993); **47**, 7 (1994).
30. S. M. Barlow and F. M. Sullivan (1982) *Reproductive Hazards of Industrial Chemicals*, London: Academic Press.
31. A. C. Fletcher (1985) *Reproductive Hazards of Work*, London: Manufacturing, Science and Finance Union.
32. National Institute for Occupational Safety and Health (1996) *The Effects of Workplace on Male Reproductive Health*, Washington: NIOSH.
33. Theo Colborn, John Peterson Myers and Dianne Dunanoski (1996) *Our Stolen Future: How Man-made Chemicals are Threatening Our Fertility, Intelligence and Survival*, London: Little, Brown and Company.

34. Rory O'Neill (1995) *Asthma at Work: Causes, Effects and What to Do About Them*, Sheffield Occupational Health Project, 37 Exchange Street, Sheffield, S2 5TR.

35. Health and Safety Executive (1994) *Preventing Asthma at Work – How to Control Respiratory Sensitizers*, HSE, L25.

36. COSHH – the HSE's 1991/92 evaluation survey, *Occupational Health Review*, July/August, i–vi.

37. Employers ignore COSHH regulations (1996) *The Safety and Health Practitioner*, February, 4.

38. Health and Safety Executive (1997) *Industries Perception and Use of Occupational Exposure Limits*, HSE Contract Research Report 144/1997, London: HSE Books.

39. (a) Health and Safety Executive (1996) *COSHH – the New Brief Guide for Employers*, HSE, IND(G) 136L (revised); (b) Health and Safety Commission (1997) *General COSHH ACOP*, HSC, L5; (c) Health and Safety Executive (1993) *A Step by Step Guide to COSHH Assessment*, HSE, HS(G)97; (d) Health and Safety Executive (1994) *Steps to Successful Substitution of Hazardous Substances*, HSE, HS(G)110; (e) Health and Safety Executive (1992) *COSHH and Peripatetic Workers*, HSE, HS(G)77.

40. Department of Health (1989) *The Control of Substances Hazardous to Health – Guidance for the Initial Assessment in Hospitals*, London: HMSO. The HSE has produced many free small COSHH guides of specific industrial sectors (print, agriculture, etc.).

41. (a) Health and Safety Commission (1996) *Safety Data Sheets for Substances and Preparations Dangerous for Supply*, 2nd edn. HSC, L62; (b) Health and Safety Executive (1985) *Substances for Use at Work: Provision of Information*, HSE, HMSO, HS(G)27.

42. (a) I. Ashton and F. S. Gill (1992) *Monitoring for Health Hazards at Work*, London: Blackwell Scientific Publications; (b) J. L. Perkins (1997) *Modern Industrial Hygiene*, London: Van Nostrand Reinhold.

43. Post-traumatic stress award made to carpenter too afraid to use solvents (1997), *Health and Safety Information Bulletin*, January.

44. Health and Safety Executive (1990) *The Maintenance, Examination and Testing of Local Exhaust Ventilation*, HSE, HS(G)37, HMSO.

45. A. J. P. Dalton (1986) *A Guide to Protective Clothing*, London: The Labour Research Department.

46. Health and Safety Executive (1996) *A Short Guide to the Personal Protective Equipment at Work Regulations 1992*, HSE, IND(G)174(L).

47. Richard Preston (1994) *The Hot Zone*, London: Doubleday.

48. (a) J. Lederberg, R. E. Shope and S. C. Oaks (eds) (1992) *Emerging Infections – Microbiological Threats to Health in the United States*, Washington: National Academy Press. (b) Bernard Dixon (1994) *Power Unseen – How Microbes Rule the World*, Oxford: W. H. Freeman. (c) Arno Karlen (1995) *Plague's Progress – A Social History of Man and Disease*, London: Victor Gollancz. (d) M. R. Berenbaum (1995) *Bugs in the System: Insects and Their Impact on Human Affairs*, Wokingham: Addison-Wesley Publishing Co.

49. Control of Substances Hazardous to Health Regulations 1994 (1997) *Approved Codes of Practice*, L5, HSE Books.

50. Robert Emery *et al.* (1992) Release of bacterial aerosols during compacting infectious waste, *American Industrial Hygiene Association Journal*, **53**, 339–45.

51. J. M. Goodley *et al.* (1994) Environmental sampling for aspergilli during building construction on a hospital site, *Journal of Hospital Infection*, **26**, 27–35.
52. Anna-Liisa Pasanen *et al.* (1993) Microbial growth of respirator filters from improper storage, *Scandinavian Journal of Work and Environmental Health*, **19**, 421–5.
53. Health and Safety Executive (1996) *Contained Use of Genetically Modified Organisms*, HSE, IND(G)86(L) (revised).
54. Susan Gordon *et al.* (1992) Reduction of airborne allergenic proteins from laboratory rats, *British Journal of Industrial Medicine*, **49**, 416–22.
55. MRSA – what nursing and residential homes need to know (1996) Free from The Department of Health, PO Box 410, Wetherby LS23 7LN.
56. W. A. Muraskin (1995) The role of organised labor in combating the Hepatitis B and AIDS epidemic, *International Journal of Health Services*, **25**, 129–52.
57. HIV on the rise in inner-city Britain (1996) *New Scientist*, 23 November. 5.
58. Jeremy Lawrence (1997) Nurses' dirty hands put patients at risk *The Independent*, 1 May.
59. Health and Safety Executive (1996) AIDS and the workplace – a guide for employers, HSE.
60. HIV/AIDS and the workplace – the trade unionists' guide (1995) London: The Labour Research Department.
61. George Browning (1997) Returning to surgical work with HIV, *Occupational Health Review*, March/April, 33–6.
62. (a) P. F. Holt (1987) *Inhaled Dust and Disease*, Chichester: John Wiley and Sons. (b) J. E. Cotes and J. Steel (1987) *Work-Related Lung Disorders*, Oxford: Blackwell Scientific Publications. (c) R. Parkes (1994) *Occupational Lung Disorders*, 3rd edn. Oxford: Butterworth-Heinemann. (d) W. Morgan and C. Seaton (1995) *Occupational Lung Diseases*, 3rd edn. London: Harcourt Brace.
63. *The Use of the Dust Lamp* (1997) London: HSE Books.
64. (a) A. J. P. Dalton (1979) *Asbestos Killer Dust – A Worker/Community Guide to the Hazards of Asbestos and its Substitutes*, London: British Society for Social Responsibility in Science. (b) A. J. P. Dalton (1995) Asbestos hazards: past, present and future, *Occupational Health Review*, **57**, 34–6. The best book on this subject is: B. I. Castleman (1996) *Asbestos: Medical and Legal Aspects*, 4th edn. Aspen: Aspen Law and Business.
65. A 'regulated fibre', for health and HSE purposes, has a length three times its diameter and is greater than five micrometres long with a diameter of less than three micrometres.
66. Health and Safety Executive (1996) *Review of Fibre Toxicology*, EH65/30. London: HSE Books.
67. P. F. Infante, L. D. Schuman, J. Dement and J. Huff (1994). Fibrous glass and cancer, *American Journal of Industrial Medicine*, **26**, 559–84.
68. Health and Safety Executive (1990) *Man-Made Mineral Fibres*. EH46 (revised), London: HSE.
69. Man-Made Mineral Fibres (1996) *HELA Document LAC 37/3*, 30 April. Available, by quoting the government's Code of Practice on the Freedom of Information, from the environmental health department of your local council.
70. M. Holmstrom, G. Rosen and B. Wilhelmsson (1991) Symptoms, airway physiology and histology of workers exposed to medium-density fibre board, *Scandinavian Journal of Work and Environmental Health*, **17**, 409–13.

71. Akosua Buckman (1997) Employer liable for failure to warn of rest breaks, *Occupational Health Review*, May/June, 33–5.

72. Annelle Yassi (1997) Repetitive strain injuries, *The Lancet*, **349**, 943–7.

73. Health and Safety Executive (1996) *Upper Limb Disorders – Assessing the Risks*, IND(G)171(L), HSE. An excellent guide with a very useful ergonomic risk assessment checklist.

74. Health and Safety Executive (1994) *A Pain in Your Workplace: Ergonomic Problems and Solutions*, HSE, HS(G)121. An excellent set of practical case studies; (b) Health and Safety Executive (1990) *Work-related Upper Limb Disorders: A Guide to Prevention*, HSE, HS(G)60. Useful but a bit limited (e.g. no mention of DSEs) and dated now.

75. Barrie Clement (1993) Judges' RSI ruling scorned, *The Independent*, November 1993.

76. Julia Gallagher (1996) *Designing RSI Out of the Workplace*, TUC. A report of a joint conference with the Ergonomics Society. A short, but useful and positive guide with some good contact addresses.

77. Evaluation of the Display Screen Equipment Regulations 1992, *HSE Contract Research Report 130/1997*.

78. Kirton Gill (1995) *An Office Worker's Guide to Work Related Upper Limb Disorders*, London: The City Centre. A very useful, quick guide on identification, prevention and sources for treatment.

79. Carmel McHenry (1995) WRULDs – policies and practice, *Occupational Health Review*, 19–25.

80. Repetitive Strain Injury Association, Chapel House, 152 High Street, Yiewsley, West Drayton, Middlesex, UB7 7BE (01895 431134); there are local RSI groups up and down the country.

81. M. I. V. Jayson (1996) Back pain, *British Medical Journal*, **313**, 355–8.

82. J. W. Frank (1996) Disability resulting from occupational low back pain, *Spine*, **21**, 2908–17.

83. Health and Safety Executive (1993) Getting to grips with manual handling – a short guide for employers, HSE, IND(G)143L.

84. US Centre for Disease and Control (1994) Workplace use of back belts, NIOSH.

85. Health and Safety Executive (1994) Manual handling – solutions you can handle, HSE(G)115. (b) Health and Safety Executive (1996) A pain in your workplace? – ergonomic problems and solutions, HSE, HSE(G)21.

86. Investigator criticised by judge (1996) *The Scotsman*, 6 November.

87. P. A. B. Raffle, P. H. Adams, P. J. Baxter and W. R. Lee (eds) (1994) *Hunter's Diseases of Occupations*, 8th edn, pp. 271–94. London: Edward Arnold.

88. A. P. Smith and D. E. Broadbent (1991) Non-auditory effects of noise at work: a review of the literature, *HSE Contract Research Report 30/1991*.

89. Health and Safety Executive (1994) Assessment of compliance with the Noise at Work Regulations 1989, *HSE Research Paper 36*.

90. Health and Safety Executive (1996) The costs and benefits of the Noise at Work Regulations 1989, *HSE Contract Research Report No 116/1996*.

91. Health and Safety Executive *The Noise at Work Regulations – A Brief Guide to the Requirements for Controlling Noise at Work*, HSE, IND(G)75(L)(Rev).

92. Health and Safety Executive (1995) *Sound Solutions – Techniques to Reduce Noise at Work*, HSE, HS(G)138.

93. Health and Safety Executive (1996) *Employer's Guide to Good Health is Good Business*, phase 1, London: HSE.
94. Robert Taylor (1988) A small scale survey into the use of audiometry in practice, *HSE Contract Research Report 3/1988*, para. 4.4.
95. Michael Bond (1996) Plagued by noise, *New Scientist*, 16 November, 14–15.
96. Peter Gruner (1997) Rising violence threatens noise pollution officers, *The Evening Standard*, 8 May.
97. *Bothered by Noise? There's No Need to Suffer* (1997) Department of the Environment, Transport and the Regions, Publications Despatch Centre, Blackhorse Road, London SE99 6TT.
98. Bill Taylor (1989) Bad Vibrations, *New Scientist*, 14 January, p. 47.
99. A. J. P. Dalton (1975) *Vibration – a Workers' Guide to the Health Hazards of Vibration*, London: British Society for Social Responsibility in Science.
100. Grant Prior (1994) Crippling disease is spreading, *Construction News*, 28 April.
101. Obituary, *The Guardian* 3 June 1994.
102. *Hand Arm Vibration Syndrome*, IIAC, DSS, Cm. 2844, 1995.
103. Rolf Petersen *et al.* (1995) Prognosis of vibration induced white finger: a follow up study, *Occupational and Environmental Medicine*, 52, 110–15.
104. Health and Safety Executive (1994) *Hand Arm Vibration* HSE, HS(G)88.
105. *Hand–Arm Vibration Management Manual* (1996) Industrial Noise and Vibration Centre (01753 5304114).
106. *Vibration Solutions – Practical Ways to Reduce the Risk of Hand–Arm Vibration Injury* (1997) HS(G)170.
107. P. Hanley (1994) Vibration Hazards from Road Breakers, HSE *Specialist Report Number 44*.
108. Bert Jacobsson (1992) Vibrating hand-held machines in the construction industry, *Safety Science*, **15**, 367–73.
109. Health and Safety Executive (1997) In the driving seat, HSE, IND(G)242L.
110. Health and Safety Executive (1997) New leaflet warns of damage to drivers' backs from vibration and jolting, Press Release E00:97, 23 January.
111. Patrick Donati (1993) *Health Practitioner*, August, 17–19.
112. Quoted in: K. Miyashita (1992) Symptoms of construction workers exposed to whole body vibration and local vibration, *International Archives of Occupational and Environmental Health*, **64**, 347–51.
113. (a) Patrick Donati (1993) Vibration in industrial vehicle and earth-moving machines. *The Safety and Health Practitioner*, May, 20. (b) Alex Burdorf and Paul Swuste (1993) The effect of seat suspension on exposure to whole-body vibration of professional drivers, *Annals of Occupational Hygiene*, **37**, 45–55.
114. J. Malchaire, A. Pietta and I. Mullier (1996) Vibration exposure on fork-lift trucks, *Annals of Occupational Hygiene*, **40**, 79–91.
115. (a) Health and Safety Executive (1993) *Passive Smoking at Work*, HSE, IND(G)63(L) (revised). (b) Health and Safety Executive (1996) *Don't Mix It! – a Guide for Employers on Alcohol at Work*, HSE, IND(G)40L (revised). (c) Health and Safety Executive (1994) *Drug Abuse at Work – a Guide for Employers*, HSE, IND(G)01L (revised).
116. *Ashes to Ashes – Dealing with Workplace Smoking* (1995) London: UNISON.
117. (a) Action on Smoking and Health (ASH), 109 Gloucester Place, London WIH 3PH. (b) Health Education Authority, Hamilton House, Marbledon Place, London WC1H 1TX.

118. Institute of Personnel and Development (1996) Sorted out for E's, booze and work? Press release, 24 October 1996.
119. Alcohol and Drug Policies (1994) Incomes Data Services Study, 553, May.
120. Just say no to drugs testing (1996) *Hazards*, **55**, 8-9.
121. Health and Safety Executive (1992) Guidance on the Personal Protective Equipment at Work Regulations 1992 London: HSE. The HSE has also produced a very useful free guide to these regulations and much other free, and priced, guidance on PPE (e.g. an annual guide to HSE-approved respirators).
122. R. M. Howie (1995) Personal protective equipment. In J. M. Harrington and K. Gardiner (1995) *Occupational Hygiene*, 2nd edn. Oxford: Blackwell Science.
123. A. J. P. Dalton (1986) *A Guide to Protective Clothing*, London: The Labour Research Department.

6

SOME KEY WORKPLACE ENVIRONMENTAL ISSUES

Corporate attitudes to the environment have changed significantly.
Frances Cairncross, Green Inc. 1995.

In her recent and useful overview of companies and the environment,[1] former environmental editor on *The Economist* magazine, Frances Cairncross, gives the following reasons why an increasing number of companies and organizations are turning green:

- ○ *Management morale* – managers, especially those of the post-Stockholm generation often want to have an environmental record they can be proud of; some feel it improves the quality of management too.
- ○ *Staff* – in many companies, the pressure to adopt sound environmental policies came initially from the workforce.
- ○ *Consumer tastes* – shoppers suddenly became more interested in the environmental pedigree of the products they bought.
- ○ *Desire for good publicity* – companies began to see the value in a reputation for good environmental citizenship.
- ○ *Fear of incurring the costs of environmental damage* – these have risen dramatically as regulations have tightened and also become increasingly unpredictable.
- ○ *Savings* – companies found that reductions in their use of raw materials and energy, and the amount of toxic waste they produced, could yield savings, partly because of the rising costs of waste disposal.

In March 1997, the second *UK Business and The Environment Trends Survey*[2] was released. Three hundred interviews with top executives responsible for the environment in the UK's top companies formed the basis of the survey. In addition, 50 key 'opinion formers' (e.g. senior representatives of environmental campaigns, business groups and government) on the environment were also interviewed. The results were compared with a similar survey in 1996. The top five corporate issues were health and safety, air pollution, water pollution, waste disposal and energy conservation.

The main results of the survey were as follows:

○ Two-thirds (67 per cent) of the companies attached more importance to environmental issues than they did in 1996, although concern was growing a bit less than in 1996.

○ One in three companies acknowledged that their commercial activities have a major or significant impact on the environment.

○ The number of companies looking to go beyond legal requirements on the environment had risen from one in four (25 per cent) in 1996 to one in three (37 per cent) in 1997.

○ The business case for investing in the environment seemed far from proven, with costs of implementation still seen as a major barrier in over half (58 per cent) of companies surveyed.

○ Two-thirds (66 per cent) of those questioned thought that existing environmental regulations are not too stringent and the policing of regulations should be more rigorous.

○ Half (54 per cent) of the companies questioned thought that the government should put more emphasis on using taxes and charges, rather than regulations, to improve the environment.

The survey suggested that the companies would back the introduction of several policy measures that would encourage industry to improve its environmental performance. These include:

○ investments allowances for clean technology
○ changes to advertising regulations to outlaw misleading 'green' product claims
○ an EU code on environmental liability
○ compulsory environmental liability insurance
○ compulsory environmental reporting
○ full public access to information about actual levels of pollutants produced by individual companies

Finally, in May 1997, the environmental consultants KPMG published their fifth annual survey[3] of the *Financial Times* (FT) top 100 UK companies. In general, the survey showed that environmental reporting was now established practice: with 79 of the top 100 FT companies producing one. Thirty produced separate environmental reports, of which 14 had quantifiable targets. However, the number of reports with 'external verification' fell from 13 in 1996 to 10 in 1997.

As with health and safety workplace auditing and inspection (page 113), it is worthwhile taking a brief look at some wider environmental issues – or some very useful and imaginative 'environmental tools' – before plunging inside the company and organization to carry out an environmental audit. The approaches are more widely developed in the USA, where 'industrial ecology', or 'cradle to grave' analysis, life cycle analysis (LCA) and cleaner technology are much researched, discussed and applied. In the UK we are in our infancy in this respect, as my experience with ICI, quoted below, clearly demonstrates.

INDUSTRIAL ECOLOGY

In a 1989 pathbreaking article,[4] Robert Frosch and Nicholas Gallopoulos laid down the basic principles of 'industrial ecology'; these were modelled on biological ecosystems. In the essence, the idea is that the by-product(s) of one polluting industry could serve as the raw material(s) for another industry, and so on in a cycle that, ideally, would end with the final company feeding its waste into the first company as 'raw material'. This, is course, is practically impossible for complex manufacturing. But there are examples of limited on-site, and even better in-company, recycling already in existence. Since that time there have been several experiments with 'industrial eco-parks', such as Kalundbork Park, in Denmark (page 230) and, perhaps the more generally applicable – since it takes an existing industrial park – Burnside Industrial Park, Nova Scotia, Canada, which has over 1200 businesses.[5] This exciting approach to pollution prevention has been the subject of a recent review.[6]

LIFE CYCLE ASSESSMENT (LCA)

In essence, the LCA procedure tries to look at a product or process from the 'cradle to the grave'.[7] The key areas to be looked at are:

- natural resources
- raw material acquisitions
- material manufacture
- product manufacture
- product use
- product disposal

Although simple to write down, the process of carrying out a LCA is rarely simple and many assumptions have to be made during LCAs (through lack of good data) that can often invalidate the LCA. Thus, it is often possible for two detailed and independent LCAs – on, say, the use of disposable plastic versus washable china cups or disposable nappies versus washable nappies – to come to diametrically opposite conclusions. Sometimes the LCA conclusions are simply related to the sponsoring organization! B&Q called their 1993 environmental report *How Green is My Hammer?*[8] When they looked into doing an LCA on a 'simple' product like a hammer (see p. 232), they found the following environmental impacts:

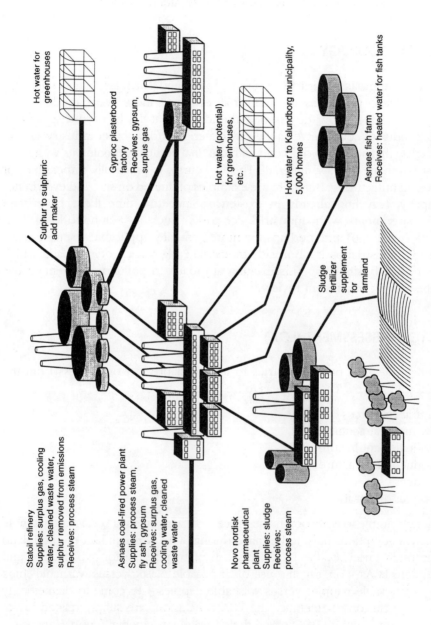

Hot water for
greenhouses

Sulphur to sulphuric
acid maker

Gyproc plasterboard
factory
Receives: gypsum,
surplus gas

Hot water (potential)
for greenhouses,
etc.

Hot water to Kalundborg municipality,
5,000 homes

Asnaes fish farm
Receives: heated water for fish tanks

Statoil refinery
Supplies: surplus gas, cooling
water, cleaned waste water,
sulphur removed from emissions
Receives: process steam

Asnaes coal-fired power plant
Supplies: process steam,
fly ash, gypsum
Receives: surplus gas,
cooling water, cleaned
waste water

Novo nordisk
pharmaceutical
plant
Supplies: sludge
Receives:
process steam

Sludge
fertilizer
supplement
for
farmland

FIGURE 6.1   Symbiotic relationships in Kalundborg, Denmark: one model of an industrial ecosystem

○ *Ash/pine shaft* – visual damage, wildlife loss, soil acidity, river pollution, energy use, dust and solvent emissions.
○ *Forged steel head* – landscape degradation, dust, noise, wildlife disturbance, energy use, air emissions, acid gases, greenhouse effect, heavy metal pollution of water, site contamination, waste lubricants and swarf for recycling.

How do you balance up the sometimes competing pollutants? As early as 1990, McDonald's fast food chain converted from polystyrene to paper-based containers for its foods. On the basis of an LCA it claimed that there would be a reduction in packaging, energy consumption, air emissions and water pollution as a result. Since that time many other LCAs have bee completed, but fewer published, for commercial confidentiality reasons. But it is already clear that LCA has a great future and, indeed, is already being used, in a primitive way, to give consumer products 'eco-labels'.

ECO-LABELS AND LCA

A 1996 study of the green claims on a variety of consumer products concluded that 'Many of the claims made on products are unverifiable, and/or vague, woolly, specious or misleading. Most are accompanied by a bewildering range of logos and symbols.'[9] Although there are more standardized eco-labelling schemes in other countries (e.g. German 'Blue Angel' and Nordic 'Swan'), it has only been in the last four years that the UK has had a small eco-labelling scheme.[10] Using criteria developed in both the UK and other EU countries, a 'life cycle' matrix is applied to the products submitted for an eco-label.

The following factors are considered at five stages of production:

○ pre-production
○ production
○ distribution
○ utilization
○ disposal

The environmental factors considered are: waste relevance, soil pollution and degradation, water contamination, noise, consumption of energy, consumption of natural resources and effects on ecosystems.

Progess in the UK has been very slow, and, by January 1997, only one washing machine, three types of toilet paper, three types of kitchen towels and four types of paints had received an approved UK eco-label. Within the EU, eco-labels have been awarded for 26 products in four groups: washing machines, toilet rolls, kitchen towels and paints. The scheme, slowly, appears to be gaining momentum. However, the EU appears to want the scheme to be self-financing by 2002,[11] and

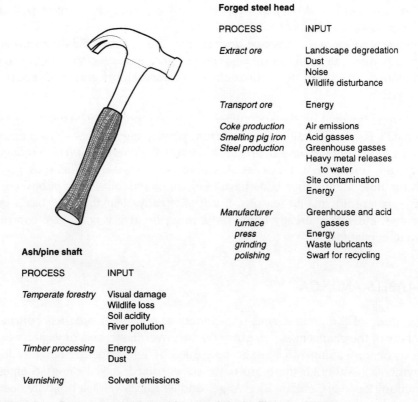

Forged steel head

PROCESS	INPUT
Extract ore	Landscape degredation
	Dust
	Noise
	Wildlife disturbance
Transport ore	Energy
Coke production	Air emissions
Smelting pig iron	Acid gasses
Steel production	Greenhouse gasses
	Heavy metal releases to water
	Site contamination
	Energy
Manufacturer	Greenhouse and acid
furnace	gasses
press	Energy
grinding	Waste lubricants
polishing	Swarf for recycling

Ash/pine shaft

PROCESS	INPUT
Temperate forestry	Visual damage
	Wildlife loss
	Soil acidity
	River pollution
Timber processing	Energy
	Dust
Varnishing	Solvent emissions

FIGURE 6.2   Environmental impacts associated with a hammer

this may spell the death of this innovative scheme, which would be a great pity. It urgently needs more EU, and national (e.g. UK), funding and support, not less.

CASE STUDY 31: US GOVERNMENT USES LCA FOR CLEANING AGENTS

There has been some criticism that the UK government has not greened itself, despite having green ministers in all departments. In the US, where the Federal government purchases more than $200 billion worth of goods and services each year, in October 1993 President Clinton signed the Federal Acquisition, Recycling and Waste Prevention Order 12873, which required environmental factors to be taken into account in government purchasing. The first products to which this law was applied were biodegradable cleaners and greasers. Using a seven-item LCA (skin irritation, food chain exposure, air pollution potential, fragrance, dye, packaging and minimizes exposure) – which unusually in an LCA, recognized the health and safety needs of the user – a table of products was drawn up and published (Table 6.1). This is a major initiative in a very important area and an excellent model for other countries and companies.[12]

TABLE 6.1 Biodegradable cleaners and degreasers – US Life Cycle Assessment (LCA)

Product Attribute Matrix

Product	Skin Irritation	Food chain exposure (Bio concentration factor)	Air pollution potential (% VOC)	Contains fragrance	Contains dye	Reduced/ recyclable packaging	Product minimizes exposure to concentrate?
Alfa Kleen AK-020	Not reported	Not reported	N/A	No	No	Yes/Yes	–
Allied Clean Free	ST	Not reported	N/A	Yes	Yes	Yes/Yes	–
ASP Alpine Cleaner	Not reported	Not reported	N/A	No	No	Yes/Yes	–
Caljen Fast Clean	ST	12000	3.5	No	No	Yes/Yes	–
Charlie	M	Exempt	Not reported	No	No	No/NA	NA
Chemco Enviro-Chem 095A	M	Not reported	8	No	Yes	Yes/Yes	–
Chemco Kleenzol 148	SL	Not reported	10	No	Yes	Yes/Yes	–
Cooke Tuff Job	M	12000	4.2	No	Yes	Yes/Yes	–
Cooke Easy Job	SL	Exempt	0.5	No	No	Yes/Yes	–
Earth Clean Systems Degrease	N-SL	Exempt	NA	No	No	Yes/NA	–
Electro ECD-101	SL	Exempt	NA	No	No	No/Yes	NA

TABLE 6.1 Biodegradable cleaners and degreasers *(cont.)*

Product Attribute Matrix

Product	Skin irritation	Food chain exposure (Bio concentration factor)	Air pollution potential (% VOC)	Contains fragrance	Contains dye	Reduced/ recyclable packaging	Product minimizes exposure to concentrate?
ERL E-Z Does It	M	Not reported	NA	Yes	Yes	No/NA	NA
ERL Grease Cutter	M	Not reported	34.7	No	No	No/NA	NA
Gaylord Formula G-510	Exempt	8165	NA	No	No	Yes/Yes	–
L&B (Arrowak) Klean E-Z	Not reported	Exempt	12.7	Yes	Yes	Yes/Yes	–
L&B (Arrowak) Klean E-Z Concentrate	Not reported	Exempt	12.7	Yes	Yes	Yes/Yes	–
PCI Hurrisafe 9010	N-SL	Exempt	2	No	No	No/NA	NA
PCI Hurrisafe 9030	SL	Exempt	8	No	No	Yes/NA	–
PCI Hurrisafe 9040	SL	Exempt	15	No	No	Yes/NA	–
Rochester Biogenic 377C	SL	Exempt	1	No	No	Yes/NA	+
Sunshine Simple Green	N-SL	Exempt	0.8	Yes	Yes	Yes/Yes	0, Larger units, (-) smaller units
SOQ Ecomate	SL	Exempt	NA	No	No	Yes/Yes	–

TABLE 6.1 Biodegradable cleaners and degreasers *(cont.)*

Product Attribute Matrix

Product	Skin Irritation	Food chain exposure (Bio concentration factor)	Air pollution potential (% VOC)	Contains fragrance	Contains dye	Reduced/ recyclable packaging	Product minimizes exposure to concentrate?
Webaco Scuzz-RTU	ST	Exempt	3.3	No	No	No/NA	NA
Webaco Scuzz	ST	Exempt	3.3	No	No	Yes/NA	–
West Penetone Citrikleen Aerosol	M	Exempt	31	No	No	No/NA	NA
West Penetone Citrikleen	M	Exempt	6	No	No	Yes/NA	–
West Penetone Citrikleen HD	M	Exempt	10.5	No	No	Yes/NA	–
West Penetone Penair HD-1	M	Exempt	10	No	No	No/NA	NA

CLEANER TECHNOLOGY

One of the major criticisms of the government's integrated pollution control (IPC) approach has been that it has promoted expensive 'end-of-pipe' technology and not 'cleaner technology'. ICI is the UK's largest chemical company, and one of the world's largest. As would be expected, it is UK leader in environmental reporting and auditing methods in the chemical industry.[13] However, sitting on a top-level government committee, the HSE's Advisory Committee on Dangerous Substances (ACDS), late in 1996, I was surprised by the primitive nature of a paper presented to us by one of ICI's top scientists entitled 'Inherent SHE (Safety, Health and Environmental) – 20 years of evolution.' It was clear that ICI was slowly stumbling towards, with some good specific examples, what American and Japanese companies had been practising for years: the value of taking a 'life cycle' and 'clean technology' approach to pollution control in the chemical industry, in particular. With a starting slide illustrating Darwin and Lenin, he made the point that ICI had taken the 'evolutionary' and not the 'revolutionary' approach. Indeed, he admitted that there had been five 'Wilderness Years' at ICI during 1986–91, when little had been done to develop SHE techniques. Perhaps the 'revolutionary' approach – as taken by the Americans and Japanese – would have been more fruitful, profitable and improved the environment. Ironically, during 1997, ICI became infamous for its many public pollution leaks and ended up being 'taken to task' by the Environment Agency. If this is the UK's best, what of its worst?

But for some, 'cleaner technology' has arrived now. The term 'clean production'[14] was coined by a 1989 working group of the United Nations Environment Programme's Industry and Environment Office (UNEP/IEO) to describe a:

> Conceptual and procedural approach to production that demands that all phases of the life-cycle of a product or of a process should be addressed with the objective of prevention or minimisation of short- and long-term risks to human health and the environment. (p. 1)

Thus 'cleaner technology', a more accurate term than 'clean technology', involves the raw materials, the process or chemical reaction (is it the cleanest possible?), the product, distribution and final disposal. However, unlike LCA (page 229), it tends to concentrate on the more *specific* production process itself. Thus, the use of 'cleaner technology' is often one of the tools used in an LCA, and the approach of most cleaner technology reports is case study, in that specific processes are examined to see if they can be carried out in a cleaner manner, rather than use the expensive solution of end-of-pipe technology. Although it is early days for cleaner technology, as it is for LCA, there is gradually emerging in the literature of cleaner technology a set of principles and theory which it will be possible to apply to any new product or process at the earliest design stage.

As mentioned above, the United Nations Environment Programme started the interest in cleaner technology in 1989, and they have continued to maintain interest by means of a set of worldwide case studies on clean production.[14] In the UK, early reports on cleaner technology were produced, in 1991, by the Department of Trade and Industry[15] and in 1992 by the Advisory Council on Science and Technology (ACST).[16] These reports have led to the setting up of a clean technology unit[17] which issues a regular bulletin, sets of detailed case studies and an annual directory of clean technology research (mainly in universities).

Two years ago the Environmental Industries Commission (EIC) was launched[18] to represent the interests of the UK's emerging environmental technology sector. Although it is dominated by end-of-pipe pollution control companies, as would be expected, some of the newer cleaner technology companies are well represented and the EIC has done a lot to promote the commercial and environmental benefits of a healthy UK environmental industry sector, including the growth area of cleaner technologies. The practice, and some of the theory, of cleaner technology has been reviewed in two recent books.[19] In 1994, the Manufacturing, Science and Finance (MSF) trade union produced its own excellent guide to the subject,[20] written by David Gee, a former director of Friends of the Earth and former head of health and safety at the GMB trade union. All of these books and reviews give many examples of the environmental and economic value of using the cleaner technology approach. To give just one example, quoted in the MSF book, 'Coca-Cola, identified savings of £1.6m a year from which the unions negotiated and "eco-bonus" for employees of £1,000 a year as their direct share in the savings'.

GREENING COMPANIES AND ORGANIZATIONS

It must be admitted that only a few UK companies are really taking environmental issues seriously, although many more pay lip service in their annual reports to shareholders than ever before. In increasing order of importance, the way to 'green' companies and organizations can be classified as follows:

○ *Ad hoc* methods (e.g. recycle paper, switch off unused lights, use energy-efficient light bulbs, monitor water use).
○ Produce an environmental report.
○ Establish an environmental 'stakeholder' group.
○ Adopt Agenda 21.
○ Obtain either ISO 14001 (formerly BS 7750) or Eco-Audit and Management System (EMAS) Registration, examples of environmental management systems (EMS).

Of course, if a company is subject to control under the 1990 Environmental Pollution Act (1990 EA, see page 63) then there are two other key sources of environmental information publicly available on that company:

1. If the process is more polluting, a so-called Part A process of 1990 EA, then the local office of the Environment Agency (EA) will hold a large file on the pollution levels in air, land and water.
2. If the process is less polluting, a so-called Part B process of 1990 EA, then the local authority environmental health department will hold a thinner file, just on the air pollution from that process.

There may be a small charge for photocopying, but the information contained in these files (especially 1, which can be very revealing, but also very technical) are essential starting points for the greening of any company to which they apply.

AD HOC METHODS

> By the installation of a series of simples measures – such as the installation of low-flush toilets and low flow taps – the plant's water consumption was cut by 46% during 1995.
>
> Nortel Telecommunications, Monkston, Northern Ireland.

Many employers, often prompted by concerned employees, start from sometimes very effective *ad hoc* green initiatives. Why not recycle all the copying paper? Can the other sides of reports be used as scrap pads? Do we really need to produce all the copies of these reports? Can reports and minutes be made shorter to save both paper and time? After all, this is supposed to be the age of the 'paperless office'. We have fire wardens, so why not have 'energy wardens' to ensure that unused lighting and heating is switched off? But studies show that many of these initiatives fall off after some initial enthusiasm without a real management (and employee) commitment to workplace environmental improvement.

Transport is an issue that some employers are looking into. About 80 per cent of the 50,000 people working at Heathrow Airport commute by car, with 12 per cent using the bus, coach and underground and only 8 per cent motor cycling, cycling or walking. The British Airlines Authority (BAA) has 4000 employees at Heathrow Airport and some staff have free parking places. In November 1996 BAA offered £200 to anyone willing to give up their car park passes; only 40 employees took up the offer. It also gave bicycles to 100 car-using volunteers from its own staff and other local employers. They cycled to work for six months and reported to BAA on what extra facilities – cycle lanes, showers, sheds – would persuade them to travel to work by bike permanently. There is also an official BAA company car-sharing scheme: 800 employees, 12 per cent of the total, now use it compared with 8 per cent five years ago. Other organizations, like Derriford Hospital, near Plymouth, and Boots in Nottingham, are trying out similar schemes: raising the costs of car parking; co-operating with local bus services to provide efficient and regular provision; giving 20 per cent off bus passes; offering interest-free loans on cycles, etc.

Of course, *ad hoc* initiatives, like the announcement in August 1997 that the Post Office, with some 30,000 vans and lorries on the roads, was going to use rapeseed oil instead of diesel to power its 6000 or so vehicles in London and other large cities, must be seen as real advances. Trials had shown that pollution was cut by one-quarter (25 per cent). But, alone such initiatives are not enough and can often be seen as simply 'green publicity' (which they often are).

ENVIRONMENTAL REPORTS

For some years now, several companies have led the way on voluntary environmental reporting and even making the 'greenness' a selling point. The Body Shop immediately springs to mind in this respect.[21] Of course, more fundamental questions could be asked about most of the 'green' products that The Body Shop sells, their real value to society and so on. In many ways much more radical, and relevant to more people's lives and UK society as a whole, has been the imaginative campaign[8] of the massive B&Q do-it-yourself company. It began an amazing 'life cycle' or 'cradle to the grave' approach of looking at all of its 40,000 product range and the environmental standards of its suppliers. This project leads the way for an imaginative and radical way of looking at the environmental impact of one company's commercial activities.

There are now at least several hundred companies in the UK who produce some form of 'green' environmental report, to very varying standards. There are several companies and consultancies who review and audit these green reports, and a recent detailed review looks at these and the wider developments in international environmental reporting, including 12 very interesting case studies.[22] The government's Advisory Committee on Business and the Environment (ACBE) has recently produced guidelines on what financial information, relative to environmental performance and liability, should be produced in company annual reports.[23]

Perhaps one of the most amazing industries to suddenly start turning green is the construction industry. Clearly educated in environmental issues by the Newbury protesters, and their very effective demonstrations, Tarmac – the giant 20,000-employee and £3 billion pound construction group – produced a very impressive, and, even more rare, independently monitored 'green report'.[24] Around the same time, the Building Research Establishment (BRE) looked at the environmental impact of many common building materials.[25] Finally, the European Construction Institute has produced a useful checklist approach to SHE standards in construction.[26]

TABLE 6.2   Blue Circle Cement environmental statement 1997, with some input from 'stakeholders'. But is it still cement-wash?

1   To assign environmental responsibility throughout the Group

Group Chief Executive **appoints a main board Director who**:

O   is responsible for co-ordinating implementation of this Policy
O   ensures that sufficient personnel and financial resources are made available
O   monitors progress against environmental targets as Chairman of the Environment committee

Operating Division **assign responsibility to a senior executive for**:

O   divisional environmental performance
O   certifying compliance with this Policy as part of the annual audit of management practices
O   preparing specific Environmental Policies applying the commitments in this Policy to their own operations
O   cascading responsibility for implementing the specific Policies to site management

2   **To implement environmental management systems at all manufacturing sites**

O   introduce an environmental management system compatible with international standard ISO 14001 at major manufacturing sites by the year 2000
O   carry out regular environmental audits to monitor progress

3   **To set objectives and targets to manage and reduce its environmental impacts**

O   address impacts through specific Environmental Policies
O   identify key environmental performance indicators
O   set objectives and detailed targets within site environmental management systems

4   **To train its employees to achieve high standards of environmental performance**

O   provide employees with environmental awareness training and encourage their commitment to continuous improvement of environmental performance
O   give specific training to those with responsibilities in particular areas

5   **To integrate environmental considerations into business decision-making at all levels**

O   follow procedures to ensure that environmental issues are given high priority and considered alongside commercial, safety and other factors in all business decisions

6   **To adopt the principle of product stewardship**

O   research and develop new products and processes with a reduced life-cycle impact on the environment
O   consider the use of by-products arising in other industries
O   seek suppliers and contractors with high standards of environmental performance
O   encourage customers to ensure the environmentally responsible use and eventual disposal of Blue Circle's products

7   **To communicate openly and consult with stakeholders on environmental issues**

O   communicate openly on issues of concern
O   conduct regular two-way consultation with a core group of stakeholders
O   make this Policy and specific Environmental Policies publicly available
O   report progress against stated objectives and performance indicators in independently verified environmental reports by the year 2000

8   **To review this Environment Policy annually and update and re-issue it as required**

K Orrell-Jones Group Chief Executive

Although shareholders at Shell's May 1997 Annual General Meeting voted down, by a margin of about eight to one, a resolution trying to force Shell to establish an independent audit of its environmental and human rights policies, the writing is on the wall. Even the outgoing chair, John Hennings, said he accepted the principle of independent verification. The main point of contention, it seems, is time. Shell executives point out that it took 500 years to agree accountancy rules for external financial auditing. But, with the environment, we may not have 500 years.

ENVIRONMENTAL 'STAKEHOLDER' GROUPS

In the past few years one of the new buzzwords has been the 'stakeholder' society, not least several senior members of Prime Minister Tony Blair's Labour government and the Trade Union Congress (TUC). Stakeholders appear to be any group with a legitimate say in the way a company or organization operates: consumers, employees, enforcement agencies, environmental groups, shareholders etc. Table 6.2 gives an example of the environmental stakeholder group that I belong to for Blue Circle Industries, in this case there are 63 'stakeholders'. With regard to the environment, this appears to mean a group of worthy and independent people who oversee and comment upon the environmental policy of an organization. There is not yet any general agreement as to what powers, if any, they have, or even if they ever meet (as in my case).

It is very early days with this concept and it may yet turn out to be another worthy, but ineffective, public relations exercise for some companies and organizations. In principle, such groups and their reports and policies should be more effective than just uncritical in-house environmental reports produced by companies and organizations. We shall have to wait and see (see also page 47).

AGENDA 21

At the 1992 Earth Summit, in Rio, the various states of the United Nations adopted an extensive work programme called Agenda 21. With 150 programmes and 2509 activities, it is a very wide programme, and yet its 41 chapters have been criticized for some notable exceptions, such as energy, tourism and transport. In the UK, at national level, the government set up the Advisory Panel on Sustainable Development (APSD). 'Sustainable development' has been defined as development which 'meets the need of the present generation without compromising the needs of future generations' (*The Bruntland Report*, 1987).

The most useful Agenda 21 activity is that taking place at the local level via local councils[27] throughout the world.[28] In fact, two-thirds of the actions set out in the report of the Earth Summit involve local government.

The new agenda[29] before local councils is:

○ help 'save the planet' by becoming more sustainable
○ think global and act local
○ balance economic, social and environmental considerations in policies and service delivery to this aim
○ rally public service support
○ advocate best practice and develop partnerships with business and the wider community

In June 1997 the Audit Commission published an important review of local council progress on Agenda 21 in the week before the second Earth Summit.[29] The report concluded that 'Some local authorities have made good progress. But much remains to be done ...' In the UK it is said that over 90 per cent of local authorities are committed to some form of local Agenda 21 process. However, only 40 per cent of UK local authorities produced a 'local sustainable development strategy' by the 1996 deadline set by the Rio treaty. And, as the Audit Commission report acidly notes, 'Strategies alone are not enough; they must be translated into effective action.'

The Audit Commission is a very good, if sometimes depressing, read. It is the first authoritative, and critical, look at local council Agenda 21 in action. Some of the case studies quoted are very revealing and useful (and not always successful).

An interesting case study concerns the attempts of Coventry City Council – with the aid of a European Social Fund grant – to turn some of their less than successful 'adversarial approach to enforcement' to advice and education, by their environmental health officers (EHOs):

○ providing advice to companies on recycling and waste minimization
○ accumulating and disseminating good practice
○ developing good practice case studies
○ providing a reference library
○ servicing a business panel
○ developing links with major companies

It was noted that, 'Flagrant breaches of the regulations were challenged robustly but, where breaches resulted from ignorance, a better approach was to educate businesses of the need to improve their environmental practice' (page 29).

The Audit Commission study ended with a series of 34 key recommendations for the greening of local government.

Immediate objectives

Waste management

○ Promote home composting.
○ Limit the further introduction of large wheeled bins.
○ Create more 'bring' sites (one per thousand households).

○ Organize the home collection of newspapers.

Water conservation

○ Reduce water in toilet cisterns.
○ Check for leaks by analysing monthly meter readings.
○ Check meter sizes.
○ Intall and use pool covers.

Energy conservation

○ Check consumption in schools and other council buildings against bench-marks.
○ Install lagging, insulation and thermostatic radiators where not in place.
○ Survey council housing stock.
○ Prioritize investments according to payback period.

Car commuting

○ Limit car-parking in new office buildings.
○ Use the Department of Environment, Transport and the Regions, 'Transport Policy and Programmes' (TPP) system to promote alternatives to car travel.
○ Raise long-stay car-parking charges.
○ Undertake an environmental assessment of planning policies and adopt statutory plans that minimize traffic volumes.

Overall management

○ Establish a corporate approach to local authority Agenda 21, cutting across traditional service department and committee lines.
○ Establish an appropriate process specifically to co-ordinate policy, pro-grammes and undertake performance review.

Environment co-ordinators

Provide senior support for environmental co-ordinators to afford the necessary status and influences.

Staff

Involve and enthuse staff lower down the organizational hierarchy about environmental issues.

Monitoring

Monitor the impact of environmental initiatives, using EMAS.

Partnerships

Establish effective partnerships with the business and the wider community.

Further initiatives

Waste management

O   Process garden waste at 'bring' sites.
O   Create a 'bring' site for every 500 households.
O   Compare the incineration costs with forecast landfill costs.
O   Advise business on waste reduction.
O   Introduce 'kerbside' recycling.

Energy conservation

O   Use central government funding (PFI) to finance zonal controls and the replacement of electric space heating.
O   Evaluate local lighting controls.
O   Eveluate the use of central government funding (PFI) to replace out-of-date district heating schemes.

Car commuting

O   Introduce 'park and ride' schemes.
O   Promote alternatives to car travel for the 'school run'.
O   Create more cycle paths.
O   Ensure that cycle paths are present in the new housing developments.

Local Agenda 21 activities concern not only the local council they should involve the local business community, trade unions, community groups, tenants' and residents' associations, women's groups, disability groups and so on. A recent book reviews the success, or otherwise, of Agenda 21 worldwide.[30]

ENVIRONMENTAL MANAGEMENT SYSTEMS (EMS)

Once a company or organization has become aware of its environmental responsibilities, the most common environmental control policies implemented, according to a recent review,[2] are:

O   awareness of obligations on waste packaging (93 per cent)
O   operate a company-wide environmental policy (89 per cent)
O   recycle materials used in processes (88 per cent)
O   operate waste minimization programmes (85 per cent)
O   undertake environmental audits (76 per cent)
O   implement energy-saving programmes (76 per cent)
O   implement EMSs (67 per cent); although last in this list, with two out of three companies implementing an EMS, it is in fact the overall management tool that deals with all seven issues and any other environmental impact of the company or organization.

EMAS, BS 7750 and ISO 14001

There are currently two formal specifications for EMSs available in the UK: EMAS and ISO 14001 (formerly BS 7750). BS 7750 was withdrawn during 1997, in favour of ISO 14001. In brief summary, these are as follows:

O BS 7750 and ISO 14001 are voluntary standards, developed by the British Standards (BS) Institute or the International Standards Organization (ISO). Both of these standards are very similar and were designed to overlap with both EMAS and the BS 8800 *Guide to Occupational Health and Safety Management Systems* and the HSE management systems approach (see page 32). The intention is obviously that they will be integrated at some stage in the future to produce a SHE standard.

O The EU Eco-Management and Audit Scheme (EMAS) is also a voluntary EMS scheme introduced in the UK in April 1995, as a direct result of an EEC Regulation of 1993 (1836/83) allowing for voluntary participation in the scheme by companies in the industrial sector. In the UK EMAS has been extended to local authorities. Although closely related to BS 7750 and ISO 14001, while the former consists of five essential steps, EMAS has two major extra requirements to make seven key steps.

The two extra requirements of EMAS over ISO 14001 are as follows:

O The issuing of an annual public statement, outlining in clear and concise language how exactly the company or local council have met its stated objectives.

O Before publication, the EMS and the annual public statement must be validated by an independent accredited verifier, who is independent of the site's auditor.

In April 1997 the EU officially recognized ISO 14001 and a bridging document (CEN CT 12969) was produced for users of ISO 14001 who wish to transfer to EMAS. The main differences are as follows:

O EMAS requires companies to move towards levels of performance compatible with Economically Viable Application of Best Available Technology (EVA-BAT), whilst ISO-accredited companies only have to demonstrate that they have 'measures in place to achieve this objective'.

O An 'environmental review' is required under EMAS, but is only recommended under ISO 14001.

O The language of the two documents is different, especially Annex 1B(3) of EMAS.

O EMAS requires an audit and ISO 14001 does not.

O There is no specification of 'audit cycle' in ISO 14001, whilst EMAS specifies an audit cycle of at least once every three years.

O EMAS requires communication to 'public authorities and the public and contractors', but ISO 14001 does not.

○ The definitions of site, company, industrial activity and organization are different for EMAS and ISO 14001.

○ EMAS states that companies must comply, whilst ISO 14001 requires only a commitment to compliance.

○ EMAS requires registration and the preparation and publication of an environmental statement. ISO 14001 does not require the compilation of registers.

There are now many books about these various EMS schemes, the background, the pros and cons, the methods and the benefits,[31] but what follows is summarized from the excellent materials produced by the UK EMAS Competent Body.[32] These publications are authoritative, detailed but readable, include videos (for both private and local government sectors) and case studies and have the added advantage that they are free.

The real value of the EMAS scheme, over the BSI/ISO standards, is the independent validation. The shareholders of a company can insist on an independent audit of the company accounts, and so it should be for (safety, health and) environmental auditing. The disadvantage of the EMAS scheme is its limitations – to industrial sites and local authorities – and, more importantly, the small number of companies and local councils who have achieved EMAS accreditation in the two years of its existence: about 30 in the UK to April 1997. Even within the EU, the registration to EMAS is very low. Germany dominates with 516 of 713 EU EMAS registered sites. Austria and Sweden hold 56 and 45 registrations respectively. For this reason, both Denmark and Holland have plans to extend the principles of the voluntary EMAS scheme, in the manner of 'green accounting', and make it compulsory in certain industrial sectors.[33] In Denmark this will cover 2000–3000 companies, and in Holland some 300 companies will be affected. The take-up of ISO 14001 was said to be fairly slow during 1996, with around 584 certificates issued by the middle of 1997: 289 of these are said to be in the UK (including BS 7750).[33]

The essentials of EMAS

There are seven key steps to gaining EMAS accreditation:

1. *A company environmental policy*, which should commit the company to compliance with existing legislation and to reasonable continuous improvement of environmental performance.
2. *An environmental review*, which should identify all the environmental impacts of the site to be registered.
3. *An environmental programme*, which is designed to put the company's environmental policy into practice.
4. *An environmental management system* (EMS), which organizes and documents the above programme.

5. *An environmental audit cycle*, which checks the programme's progress at regular intervals.
6. *An environmental statement*, an annual public statement that outlines in clear and concise language exactly how the company has met its stated objectives.
7. *External validation* – before publication both the EMS (4, above) and the statement (6, above) must be validated by an accredited verifier, who is independent of the site's auditor.

EMAS has produced several case studies – Loudwater, printers; Woodcote Industries Ltd, an engineering and drop forging company; Layezee Beds, a leading UK bed manufacturer; Design to Distribution, an electronics company; and Hereford City Council – which show clearly the environmental and commercial value of EMAS accreditation.[32] In addition, manufacturing companies with less than 250 employees are eligible for financial assistance from the Small Company Environment and Energy Management Assistance Scheme (SCEEMAS) along the following lines:

○ Stage 1 of EMAS, environmental review – up to 40 per cent grant.
○ Stage 2, management systems – up to 40 per cent grant.
○ Stage 3, environmental statement – up to 50 per cent grant (plus 10 per cent from stages 1 and 2).

There are slight differences between the private industry EMAS scheme and EMAS for local government (e.g. individual operational unit registration is allowed but in doing so requires more obligations of the local authority as a whole). EMAS in local authority is also tied in much more with Local Agenda 21, which requires a much broader look at local environmental issues by local councils worldwide. There is no reason why EMAS should not be extended to all types of workplace and, indeed, article 14 of the original 1993 EU EMAS Regulation allows for this on an experimental basis and includes the public sector. The NHS, with around one million employees, is the biggest employer in Europe. Hospitals are large polluters[34] in that they consume large amounts of energy and produce large amounts of waste (some of it toxic) and, with the increasing use of disposable items (e.g. gowns, forceps, scissors, syringes, drainage bottles, ventilation tubes, oxygen masks, face masks), that waste is growing. The University Hospital in the Black Forest town of Freiburg in Germany is one of Germany's largest. In 1995 it had 1724 beds, 5368 employees and 53,255 hospital admissions. Although environmentally aware since the 1980s, it has now taken the first steps to carry out an environmental audit and to seek EMAS accreditation.[35]

PRODUCT STEWARDSHIP

We have seen above that the more innovative green companies (e.g. B&Q) and organizations are cascading their greenness down to their supplier and

FIGURE 6.3   Cover of the Rover Group's publication

subcontractor companies and organizations, and this can obviously be done with ISO 14001 and EMAS. In 1994 the Rover Group published the results of their pilot 'product stewardship' scheme with six volunteer car company supplier companies:[36]

- ○ BSK Aluminium Ltd
- ○ PPG Industries (UK) Ltd
- ○ Brisco Engineering Ltd
- ○ Callow and Maddox
- ○ Avenell Engineering
- ○ Pulleys

Birmingham City Council, the City of Coventry and Oxfordshire City and County Council are collaborative partners. The main conclusion, evaluated with the help of the University of Central England, was that:

> For some companies the savings were relatively low, and would not justify the exercise on purely short term economic grounds. For the majority, however, the savings were both environmentally and economically significant, with a rapid payback on the resources required. (p. 5)

The Rover report contains some useful information and checklists, including two in-depth case studies of a service company and manufacturing company and the quick checklist on the 'key points' on implementation, reproduced below.

TABLE 6.3 A quick checklist for examination of potential environmental effects

---

☐ **Resource Consumption and Eco-System damage**

Minerals/raw materials
Energy usage
Fuels usage
Disturbance/loss of habitats
Stock exploitation

	YES	NO
– Are the materials used from renewable sources?	☐	☐
– Is the material(s) re-usable?	☐	☐
– Could any of the materials you use be replaced with lower grade or waste materials?	☐	☐
– Are energy bills/usage monitored by individual operation?	☐	☐
– Is the product designed to maximise useful life and thus minimize resources?	☐	☐

☐ **Land**

Hazardous wastes
Radioactive wastes
Non-hazardous wastes
Site contamination
Soil erosion

	YES	NO
– Can you identify ways of reducing the quantity of waste generated?	☐	☐
– Can any hazardous materials be contained and made harmless?	☐	☐

– Are wastes stored on site securely and in a manner
   which minimizes environmental risks?   □   □
– Do you segregate your waste to facilitate recycling?   □   □
– Do you have appropriate contingency plans in the event
   of spillage, fire etc?   □   □

□ **Air**

Potential climate change eg. CO_2/CH_4/N_2O - Fossel fuel combustion.
Stratospheric ozone layer eg. CFCs/Halons/other compound.
Acid emissions and deposition eg. SO_2/NO_x/NH_3.
Tropospheric ozone eg. Volatile Organic Compounds. (VOCs) NO_x.
Hazardous gases/fumes.
Dust.
Smoke.
Radioactive substances.
Radiation eg. Radioactive sources electromagnetic sources.

	YES	NO
– Do you minimize the use of environmentally damaging materials?	□	□
– Is there a formal system to review plant operations in order to prevent or contain fugitive or accidental emissions and discharges?	□	□
– Do you review your processes as a result of complaints from the local community?	□	□

□ **Water**

Oxygen demand eg. General organic load.
Hydrocarbon spills.
Eutrophication eg. Phosphorus - nitrogen compounds.
Hazardous organisms eg. Pathogens
Acidification.
Thermal discharges.
Radioactivity.
Foaming, colour, litter.
Taste.
Water usage.

	YES	NO
– Do you recycle or re-use energy, water and materials where practicable?	□	□
– Have all discharge release pounds which require control been identified?	□	□

– Are there contingency pans for external pollution control
in the even of a control system breakdown?   ☐   ☐

☐ **Nuisance**

Visual eg. litter, buildings.
Dust.
Odour.
Noise/Vibration.

	YES	NO
– Have there been any complaints of noise from neighbours?	☐	☐
– Is there a policy to take noise output into account when purchasing new equipment?	☐	☐

Reproduced with permission from the Rover Group.

CONCLUSION

As we have seen above, it is very early days for companies issuing 'green annual reports', voluntary EMS schemes, ISO 14001 and EMAS itself. During 1997 an article in the *Financial Times* pointed out that:

> The fact that Severn Trent, one of the worst polluters in the water industry, also ranked in the higher echelons of the (environmental) league table illustrates how environmental management tools do not necessarily guarantee good performance.

In February 1997 the Rover Group became the first BS 7750 certified company to be prosecuted for an environmental offence (and fined £4000), followed by Akzo in March 1997 (also fined £4000), so the possession of an EMS certification clearly does not remove the need for fair and effective environmental enforcement. In America and worldwide, there is a hope in some industrial sectors (e.g. chemical) that the achieving of these voluntary EMS standards will allow for less enforcement and inspections by the environmental regulators. Environmental groups, and others, see this approach as a form of 'de-regulation'. In the UK it appears that the Environment Agency takes the view that ISO 14001 and EMAS should, in the words of the director of the EA, Dr David Slater, 'bring its own reward' (in terms of waste reduction, saving money and reducing its liabilities); he added that 'I don't think a lightening of the regulatory load automatically follows'.[37]

Some, like Professor Richard Welford, director of the Centre for Corporate Environmental Management at Huddersfield University, consider (Welford, 1997) that much of what business has done on the environment so far – environmental management systems, green auditing and so on – is just 'another corporate lie' and that 'It is simply ridiculous that we allow businesses to continue to destroy our planet.'

At an EU-funded trade union conference I helped organize in 1996,[38] there was considerable enthusiasm for EMAS both from UK trade unionists and throughout Europe.[39] Indeed, as a direct result of this conference, the TGWU, with 900,000 members the UK's second largest union, now has a policy of:

○ campaigning for a statutory EMAS scheme (i.e. 150,000 EMAS-accredited companies and not 30)
○ negotiating for EMAS at a plant level
○ educating all our estimated 10,000 safety representatives in environmental issues.

NOTES

1. Frances Cairncross (1995) *Green Inc. – a Guide to Business and the Environment*, London: Earthscan.
2. Entec Environmental Consultants/The Green Alliance, (1997) *The 1997 UK Business and the Environment Trends Survey*, Moffat Associates Partnership, 72 Boston Place, London NW1 6EX.
3. KPMG (1997) *The KPMG Survey of Environmental Consulting*, KPMG, PO Box 695, 8 Salisbury Square, London EC4Y 8BB.
4. (a) R. A. Frosch and N. E. Gallopoulos (1989) Strategies for manufacturing, *Scientific American*, September, 94–102. (b) National Academy of Engineering (1994) *The Greening of Industrial Ecosystems*, Washington: National Academy Press. (c) T. E. Graedel and B. R. Allenby (1995) *Industrial Ecology*, New Jersey: Prentice Hall Inc.
5. R. P. Cote *et al.* (1994) *Designing and Operating Industrial Parks as Ecosystems*. School for Resource and Environmental Studies, Dalhousie University.
6. D. T. Allen and K. S. Rosselot (1997) *Pollution Prevention for Chemical Processes*, Chichester: John Wiley and Sons, Inc.
7. (a) Sustainability Ltd (1993) *The LCA Sourcebook – a European Business Guide to Life-cycle Assessment*, London: SustainAbility Ltd. (b) M. A. Curran (1996) *Environmental Life-cycle Assessment*, London: McGraw Hill.
8. B&Q plc (1993) *How Green is My Hammer?* B&Q plc, 1 Portswood House, Hampshire Corporate Park, Chandlers Ford, Eastleigh, Hants SO53 3YX.
9. National Consumer Council (1996) *Green Claims – a Consumer Investigation into Marketing Claims about the Environment*, London: The National Consumer Council.
10. UK Ecolabelling Board, 7th Floor, Eastbury House, 30–34 Albert Embankment, London, SE1 7TL.
11. *Self-financing plan casts new pall over EC eco-labelling scheme* (1997) ENDS Report 267, 27–29 April.
12. *Environmentally Preferable Purchasing Program*, US EPA, 401 M Street, S.W. (7409), Washington, DC 20460, USA.
13. *ICI establishes its environmental burden* (1997) Environmental Bulletin 66, 5.
14. *Cleaner Production Worldwide* (1993) United Nations Environment Programme, Industry and Environment, Programme Activity Centre, 39–43 quai Andre Citroen, 75739 Paris Cedex 15, France.

15. Department of Trade and Industry (1991) *Cleaner Technology in the UK*, London: HMSO.
16. Advisory Council on Science and Technology (1992) *Cleaner Technology*, London: HMSO.
17. Cleaner Technology Unit, Polaris House, North Star Avenue, Swindon, Wilts SN2 1ET.
18. *The EIC Guide to the UK Environmental Industry* (1997) The Environmental Industries Commission, 6 Donaldson Road, London NW1 6NB.
19. (a) Tim Jackson (ed.) (1993) *Cleaner Production Strategies*, London: Lewis Publishers. (b) Ian Christie, Heather Rolte and Robin Legard (1995) *Cleaner Production in Industry*, London: Policy Studies Institute.
20. David Gee (1994) *Cleaner Production: from Industrial Dinosaur to Eco-efficiency*, London: Manufacturing, Science and Finance Union.
21. *The Green Book* (1996) The Body Shop International plc, West Sussex BN17 6LS.
22. *The Benchmark Survey – the second international progress report on company environmental reporting* (1996) SustainAbility/United Nations Environment Programme, Sustainability, 49–53.
23. *Environmental Reporting in the Financial Sector* (1997) Advisory Committee on Business and the Environment, C11/18, 2 Marsham Street, London SW1P 3EB.
24. *Tarmac in the environment – first report of the independent advisory panel* (1995) Tarmac plc, Hilton Hall, Essington, Wolverhampton WV11 2BQ.
25. *Environmental Standard – homes for a greener world* (1995) Building Research Establishment, Gaston, Watford WD2 7RJ.
26. European Construction Institute (1992) *Total Project Management of Construction Safety, Health and Environment* (SHE), London: Thomas Telford Services Ltd.
27. *First Steps – local agenda 21 in practice* (1994) London: HMSO. A report of various practical initiatives and case studies on LA 21 throughout the world.
28. *Earth Summit II Briefing* (1997) UNED-UK, c/o United National Association, 3 Whitehall Court, London SW1A 2EL.
29. *It's A Small World – Local Government's Role as a Steward of the Environment* (1997) London: Audit Commission Publications.
30. Felix Dodds (ed.) (1997) *The Way Forward – Beyond Agenda 21*, London: Earthscan.
31. (a) D. Hunt and C. Johnson (1995) *Environmental Management Systems – Principles and Practice*. London: McGraw-Hill Book Company. (b) Richard Welford (1996) *Corporate Environmental Management – Systems and Strategies*, London: Earthscan Publications Ltd. (c) P. A. Marcus and J. T. Willig (1997) *Moving Ahead with ISO 14000 – Improving Environmental Management and Advancing Sustainable Development*, Chichester: John Wiley and Sons, Inc.
32. The EMAS Competent Body, Department of the Environment, C11/09, 2 Marsham Street, London SW1P 3EB. Details of EMAS for local authorities may be obtained from EMAS Help-Desk, Local Government Management Board, Layden House, 76–86 Turnmill Street, London EC1M 5QU.
33. ISO14001-certified businesses pass the 200 mark (1997) *ENDS Report* 267, April, 6–7.
34. M. Dettenkofer *et al.* (1997) Environmental auditing in hospitals: approach and implementation in a university hospital, *Journal of Hospital Infection*, **36**, 17–22.
35. F. D. Daschner and M. Dettenkofer (1997) Protection of the patient and the environment – new aspects and challenges in hospital infection control, *Journal of Hospital Infection*, **36**, 7–15.

36. *BS7750/EMAS Environmental Management Standard – a practical introduction for small companies* (1994) Corporate Communications, Rover Group, International Headquarters, Warwick Technology Park, Warwick CV34 6RG.
37. Agency resists light touch for sites with ISO 14001, EMAS (1997) *Ends Report* 266, 3.
38. (1996) *Trade Unionists and Eco-Auditing*. London: TGWU.
39. The European Trade Union College (ETUCO) has recently published a number of publications on trade unions and the environment: a source book on resources; eco-auditing and EMAS and case studies on trade unions and environmental bargaining. ETUCO, Boulevard Emile Jacqmain 155, B-1210 Brussels, Belgium.

APPENDIX: WHERE TO GET HELP AND/OR FURTHER INFORMATION

INTRODUCTION

At this moment in time it is still convenient to divide the sources of information and help into two areas: (1) health and safety, and (2) the environment. This is because the agencies who regulate the hazards at both EU and UK level and other non-governmental groups (NGOs) (e.g. hazards centres, trade unions, environment groups) still see these two areas as separate. As this book has argued, this distinction will become less and less clear as safety, health and environmental (SHE) issues merge into one subject for discussion, investigation, action and enforcement. However, we have not yet reached that time.

I have made no distinction between the types of person or organization seeking the help or information. Agencies like the Health and Safety Executive (HSE) and Environmental Agency (EA) should make no distinction, and nor should professional bodies. However, some organizations like trade associations and trade unions clearly exist to serve specific groups and will be more useful (and friendly!) to those groups. Others, such as the larger environmental organizations and the hazards centres, may appear more friendly to the individual, community group or trade unionist, but they will often serve the business community with very useful information, training and consultancy if asked (this will have to be paid for, of course). In general, I have found that people concerned with SHE issues are keen to help, wherever you come from, if you really want to do something to reduce SHE hazards at the workplace.

Where I have covered an issue, then the notes at the end of the section should provide the basic guide to reading materials and sources of help and information, including, sometimes, self-help groups. In addition, the annotated reading list (page 261) may provide some useful information on hazards and issues not dealt with in the main body of the book.

HEALTH AND SAFETY

ENFORCEMENT AGENCIES

As I have indicated throughout this book, the Health and Safety Executive (HSE) and local council environmental health officers (EHOs), in addition to enforcing the law on health and safety at the workplace, provide a large amount of excellent, and often free, materials and guidance. Indeed, some of us think they provide *too* much help and guidance and not enough enforcement. Clearly, they should be the first port of call on this subject. Do not worry about whether your workplace is covered by the HSE or an EHO; when you contact one or the other, they will soon pass you on if they do not cover your workplace!

HSE advice by phone: HSE Infoline -- 0541 545500.
HSE advice: HSE Information Centre, Broad Lane, Sheffield S3 7HQ.
Tel: 0114 289 2345. Fax: 0114 289 2333.
HSE free and priced leaflets: HSE Books, PO Box 1999, Sudbury, Suffolk
CO10 6FS. Tel: 01787 881165. Fax: 01787 313995.

You can also visit the library and information centre of one of 22 local HSE offices that are situated throughout the UK. Their address and phone number can be obtained from your phone book or above. You are also entitled to see and copy the enforcement guidance issued to HSE enforcement officers, improvement and prohibition notices issued and details of prosecutions taken, all under the government's Code of Practice on the Freedom of Information.

Your local council environmental health department (which might go under another name, such as 'health and consumer services') will provide a similar, if less detailed, service as the HSE to the public, employers, trade unionists and community groups, etc.

OTHER ADVICE AGENCIES

Many of the larger companies who are members of trade associations have health and safety officers and the smaller ones have access to consultants in the specialist area who often run health and safety course. The Confederation of British Industry (CBI), Centrepoint, London, WC1 may be able to help with local business contacts and publish widely on SHE issues.

Most trade unions have a specialist health and safety office and produce publications on health and safety. In addition, most unions and the Trades Union Congress (Health and Safety Department, TUC, Congress House, Great Russell Street, London WC1B 3LS (0171 636 4030; Fax 0171 636 0632)) run health and safety courses for trade unionists. The Labour Research Department (LRD) is an independent, trade-union funded organization that provides very useful advice and publications on safety, health and environmental issues for trade unionists (LRD, 78 Blackfriars Road, London SE1 8HF (tel. 0171-928 3649)).

There are three major UK professional organizations concerned with health and safety issues and all provide advice services (to members), library facilities/searches and publish a regular magazine and run health and safety courses:

1. The British Safety Council (BSC), National Safety Centre, Chancellor's Road, London W6 9RS. Tel: 0181 741 1231/2371. Fax: 0181 741 4555.
2. The Royal Society for the Prevention of Accidents (RoSPA), Edgbaston Road, 353 Bristol Road, Birmingham B5 7ST. Tel: 0121 248 2000. Fax: 0121 248 2001.
3. Institution of Occupational Safety and Health (IOSH), The Grange, Highfield Drive, Wigston, Leicester LE18 1NN. Tel: 0116 257 1399. Fax: 0116 257 1451.

The HSE information service publishes, every few years, a useful free directory of 'organizations concerned with health and safety information' (including some abroad), the latest one being in January 1997; this is available from HSE publications (above).

The Health and Safety Manager's Year Book 1997, AP Information Service, Roman House, 296 Golders Green Road, London NW11 9PZ (Tel: 0181 455 4550; Fax: 0181 455 6381) is a very useful guide to a wide range of health and safety organizations including consultants.

A source of very useful health and safety information are the various 'hazards centres', 'occupational health projects' and 'victims support groups' (e.g. asbestos, RSI, stress, death at work) that operate up and down the country. As many of these are voluntary and/or run on a shoe string, they come and go, and names and addresses change. The best source for the latest list is: *Hazards* magazine, PO Box 199, Sheffield S1 1FQ (issue 58, April/June 1997, has a list of over 30 such organizations).

Finally, a very good guide to international 'workers' occupational health contacts' is available from *Hazards* magazine (above).

PUBLICATIONS

Books

ILO Encyclopedia of Health and Safety, International Labour Office, ILO, Vincent House, Vincent Square, London SW1P 2NB. Tel: 0171 828 6401. Fax: 0171 233 5925. The guide to health and safety; a new edition was published in 1998 in both paper and electronic versions. The ILO also publishes many other health and safety guides (e.g. on stress in various occupations) and codes of practice.

Croner's Health and Safety, Croner Publications Ltd, Croner House, London Road, Kingston-upon-Thames, Surrey KT2 6SR. Tel: 0181 547 3333. Fax: 0181 541 4275. Authoritative health and safety and environmental information in a useful, looseleaf, updated format.

Tolley's Health and Safety at Work Handbook 1997, Tolley Publishing, Tolley House, 2 Addiscombe Road, Croydon, Surrey CR9 5AF. Tel: 0181 686 9141. The standard, if dry, health and safety text.

Redgrave, Fife and Machin Health and Safety, John Hendy and Michael Ford, 2nd edition, 1993 plus cumulative supplement 1996. The old 'Factory Inspector's Bible', comprehensive with a good introduction, but very legalistic.

Hazards at Work – TUC Guide to Health and Safety, 1997, TUC, Congress House, Great Russell Street, London WC1B 3LS. Tel: 0171 636 4030. A useful, up-to-date and looseleaf guide for trade union safety representatives.

Journals

Health, Safety and Environmental Information Bulletin, monthly, IRS, 18–20 Highbury Place, London N5 1QP. Tel: 0171 354 5858. A very authoritative, readable and comprehensive journal that covers environmental issues well too.

Hazards magazine, four times a year, *Hazards*, PO Box 199, Sheffield S1 1FQ. Tel: 0114 276 5695. The guide for trade union safety representatives, full of very useful information, campaigns and contacts. Also covers environmental issues.

The Worker's Health International Newsletter (WHIN), four times a year, is an excellent, and unique, guide to what is happening worldwide on the SHE front, from a trade union and community perspective available from the *Hazards* address (above).

Health and Safety at Work, Tolley Publishing, Tolley House, 2 Addiscombe Road, Croydon, Surrey CR9 5AF. Tel: 0181-686 9141. A useful and informative publication.

The three major professional health and safety organizations mentioned above also publish regular, monthly, health and safety journals that complement these four publications.

THE ENVIRONMENT

ENFORCEMENT AGENCIES

There are two main enforcement agencies for environmental laws, depending on whether the polluting process is 'major' or 'minor'; a part A or part B process respectively under the 1990 Environment Protection Act. (See page 63.)

Major polluting processes are enforced by The Environment Agency (Rio House, Waterside Drive, Astec West, Almonsley, Bristol BS12 4UD), who have area offices up and down the country. At these offices the file on the pollutants (in air, land and water) from a Part A process is recorded and is open to the public and can be copied. The EA has a general enquiry line (0645 333111) and an emergency pollution hotline (0800 807060).

For minor polluting processes, and for all other general pollution incidents, the first port of call is the environmental health department (or similar) of your local council. There will be a similar, if smaller (air pollution only), file for EA part B processes and it is also open to the public for inspection and copying.

OTHER ADVICE AGENCIES

The two main environmental pressure groups are Friends of the Earth (FoE) and Greenpeace, although many other large organizations, (e.g. The Royal Society for the Protection of Birds, The Ramblers Association) and small (e.g. The London Cycling Campaign, Toxic Waste Campaign Network), plus many local environmental groups and campaigns exist and are very active on environmental issues; they can usually be located via FoE magazine or local groups.

Friends of the Earth, 56–58 Alma Street, London N4 3HQ. Tel: 0171 263 7424. Fax: 0171 263 7424.

Greenpeace, Canonbury Villas, London N1 2PN. Tel: 0171 865 8100. Fax: 0171 865 8200.

BOOKS AND PUBLICATIONS

The range, and rapidly growing number of environmental books are very large and any good bookshop will have many of them. I have indicated those useful for greening the workplace fully in the relevant section in the book and added a few more in the recommended reading (page 261).

The key journal in this area is the *ENDS Report*, monthly, (Environmental Data Services, Finsbury Business Centre, 40 Bowling Green Lane, London EC1R 0NE; Tel: 0171 278 4745). This is the authoritative journal in this area; it is packed with useful information and is practical case study-orientated. It is essential reading. It is supplemented by the IRS *Environment Bulletin*, mentioned above, *Hazards* magazine (above) for trade unionists and FoE and Greenpeace publications for environmental activists.

THE INTERNET

Clearly, more and more SHE information will become available on the net. Many organizations (e.g. HSE, EA, Friends of the Earth, Greenpeace) already have web sites and many more (e.g. the TUC) plan to have a network of such sites in the near future. The problem at the moment is too much information, a lot of it unreliable, so you have to be very wary of the sources of the information. For example, when I surfed for information on asbestos, one of the most easy to find, up-to-date and user-friendly web sites, which was packed full of 'useful' information, was run by the Canadian asbestos industry, although it was not too clear what the source of the information was if you were not already knowledgeable. Most of the journals mentioned have regular updates and features on the net, one recent one being in *Hazards* 57, Jan./March 1997.

RECOMMENDED READING

There are many key books mentioned in the relevant sections of the text and, in general, they are not repeated here. However, in the absence of any comprehensive UK SHE book, I have also found the following publications of use and/or interest over the years. Some of them are historical. But in dealing with SHE workplace hazards as in any other area a knowledge of history can sometimes prevent the same mistakes being made again. A number of the historical texts read very well, even today.

Adams, John (1995) *Risk*, London: University College Press. A stimulating essay on risk management's many pitfalls, but the author offers no solutions to the risk management dilemma.

Aldridge, W. N. (1996) Mechanisms and concepts in toxicology, London: Taylor and Francis. An important overview of the subject by one of the UK's leading toxicologists.

Allen, Robert (1992) *Waste Not, Want Not*, London: Earthscan. One of the early books on toxic waste.

Asante-Duah, D. K. (1996) *Managing Contaminated Sites*, Chichester: John Wiley and Sons Ltd. A practical guide to what can be done and how to do it.

Ashford, N. A. (1976) *Crisis in the Workplace*, London: MIT Press. An excellent overview of the American health and safety scene, as it was then.

Ashford, N. A. and Miller, C. S. (1991) *Chemical Exposures – Low Levels and High Stakes*, London: Van Nostrand Reinhold. One of the first popular, yet detailed, books to establish MCS as a real disease.

Ashton, Indira and Gill, F. S. (1992) *Monitoring for Health Hazards at Work*, Oxford: Blackwell Scientific Publications. The basic guide on occupational hygiene measurements.

Atherley, G. R. (1978) *Occupational Health and Safety Concepts*, London: Applied Science Publishers Ltd. A biologically based look at workplace health and safety, with some interesting ideas.

Baldwin, Robert (1995) *Rules and Government*, Oxford: Clarendon Press. Looks at the use of rules and regulations and uses the HSE as a case study.

Barlow, S. M. and Sullivan, F. M. (1982) *Reproductive Hazards of Industrial Chemicals*, London: Academic Press. One of the first compilations of the reproductive effects of a wide range of chemicals.

Bate, Roger (ed.) *What Risk? Science, Politics and Public Health*, Oxford, Butterworth-Heinemann. A rightwing look at many common hazards that, as you might expect, underestimates the risks.

Bayer, Ronald (ed.) (1988) *The Health and Safety of Workers*, Oxford: Oxford University Press. An excellent collection of essays that show clearly the political nature of occupational health.

Bearg, D. W. (1993) *Indoor Air Quality and Heating, Ventilating and Air Conditioning Systems (HVAC)*, London: Lewis Publishers. A very useful book that describes the sources, poor HVAC, of many sick building syndrome problems.

Bentham, Peggy (1996) *VDU Terminal Sickness*, London: Jon Carpenter. Lots of information gathered in a dense and uncritical manner. If VDUs were really this bad, all VDU users would be very sick and I would not have been able to write this book!

Bertell, Rosie (1985) *No Immediate Danger – Prognosis for a Radioactive Earth*, London: The Women's Press. A thoughtful, and worrying, book about the possible hazards of low-level radiation.

Beaumont, Peter (1993) *Pesticides, Policies and People*, London: The Pesticides Trust. Written by the director of the Pesticides Trust, all you will ever want to know about the subject.

Beaumont, P. B., Coyle, R., Leopold, P. and Schuller, S. (1990) *The Determinants of Effective Joint Health and Safety Committees*, Glasgow: Glasgow University. A useful and unique survey.

Beck, Ulrich (1986) *Risk Society*, London: Sage Publications. One of the original theorists of risk assessment; hard going.

Beckerman, William (1995) *Small is Stupid*, London: Duckworth. A small-minded, and cynical, attack on the greens.

Berman, Dan (1978) *Death on the Job – Occupational Health and Safety Struggles in the United States*, London: Monthly Review Press. A great book, by a great activist, and the first of this type.

Billatos, S. B. and Basaly, N. A. (1997) *Green Technology and Design for the Environment*, London: Taylor and Francis. A book full of stimulating chapters on specific projects in 'green engineering'.

British Medical Association (1992) *Pesticides, Chemicals and Health*, London: Edward Arnold. An important, and useful, review of this controversial area.

British Retail Consortium (1997) *Retail Crime Costs*, London: British Retail Consortium.

Brock, W. H. (1977) *Justus von Liebig The Chemical Gatekeeper*, Cambridge:

Cambridge University Press. The first environmental chemist? A great book for chemists.

Brodeur, Paul (1973) *Expendable Americans*, New York: The Viking Press. The first American book that really blew the lid off the asbestos horror.

Brown, L. R. (ed.) (1996) *Vital Signs 1996–1997*, London: Earthscan Publications Ltd.

Brown, M. H. (1979) *Laying Waste the Poisoning of America by Toxic Chemicals*, New York: Random House. The horrifying story of Love Canal and more.

Bruntland, G. H. (1987) *Our Common Future – Commission on Environment and Development*, Oxford: Oxford University Press. One of the key environment books of the past 20 years and the one to invent and define 'sustainable development'.

Burge, H. A. (1995) *Bioaerosols*, Florida: CRC Press. A useful review, from an American source, in an area of growing concern.

Burgess, John (1995) *Recognition of Health Hazards in Industry*, Chichester: Wiley. A very useful compilation of the hazards, and methods of control, in many common industrial processes.

Business Council for Sustainable Development (1992) *Changing Course*, London: MIT Press. One of the first books to see a role for the greening of industry.

Cahill, L. B. (1996) *Environmental Audits*, Maryland: government Institutes. One of the first of its kind and still very useful, although the book is American.

Cairney, Tom (1995) *The Re-use of Contaminated Land*, Chichester: Wiley. A useful discussion of risk assessment, problems and practice.

Carson, Rachel (1962) *Silent Spring*, London: Penguin Books. The book that alerted us to the environmental and occupational hazards of pesticides, still in print and deserving to remain so; a classic.

Carson, W. G. (1982) *The Other Price of Britain's Oil*, Oxford: Martin Robertson. A detailed study that shows clearly the lack of health and safety in North Sea oil production.

Cartwright, Sue and Cooper, Cary (1994) *No Hassle! Taking the Stress Out of Work*, London: Random House. A useful, practical guide by two of the UK's leading workplace stress experts.

Castleman, Barry (1996) *Asbestos – Medical and Legal Aspects*, Aspen: Aspen Law and Business. The book on asbestos diseases, and the cover-up, by America's principal campaigner/expert on the subject; a classic.

Caufield, Catherine (1989) *Multiple Exposures – Chronicles of the Radiation Age*, London: Secker and Warburg. A detailed, and very readable, look at the history of radiation hazards and how the so-called safe standards are set.

Charney, W. and Schirmer, J. (1993) *Essentials of Modern Hospital Safety*, 2 volumes, London: Lewis Publishers. Excellent reviews of specific topics in hospital safety; both hazards and management systems.

Cherniack, Martin (1986) *The Hawk's Nest Incident*, London: Yale University Press.

One of America's worst industrial disasters, where hundreds died of silicosis building a tunnel, is fully exposed in this in-depth, very readable, story.

Chivian, Eric *et al.* (eds) (1993) *Critical Condition – Human Health and the Environment*, London: MIT Press. A very thought-provoking series of essays.

Clarke, Lee (1989) *Acceptable Risk Making Decisions in a Toxic Environment*, London: University of California Press. A useful discussion, with case studies, of some of the key issues.

Colborn, Theo, Dumanoski, Dianne and Myers, John Peterson (1996) *Our Stolen Future*, London: Little, Brown and Co. The new 'Silent Spring', it deals with the reproductive effects of chemicals.

Cole, L. A. (1993) *Elements of Risk – the Politics of Radon*, Oxford: Oxford University Press. A very detailed, fascinating look at this cancerous gas.

Commoner, Barry (1963) *Science and Survival*, New York: Ballantine Books. One of the key books that stimulated interest in the 1970s on environmental issues

Confederation of British Industry (CBI) (1990) *Developing a Safety Culture*, London: Confederation of British Industry. Some useful tips from a CBI survey..

Cook, Judith (1989) *An Accident Waiting to Happen*, London: Unwin. Reviews some of the major 'accidents' of the 1970s and concludes that a society that puts profit before all else creates such risks.

Cook, Judith and Kaufman, Chris (1982) *Portrait of a Poison – the 2,4,5,-T Story*, London: Pluto Press. How the farmworkers' union fought a weedkiller that was used in the Vietnam war (agent orange) and won, eventually. Reminiscent of the problems with organophosphates in the 1990s.

Cox, R. A. F. (ed.) (1995) *Fitness for Work*, Oxford: Oxford University Press. A fair look at a whole range of work-related and other disorders that need to be considered at the workplace.

Craig, Marianne (1991) *Office Workers' Survival Handbook*, London: The Women's Press. A very useful and radical look at office hazards and what you can do about them.

Cullen, M. R. (ed.) (1987) *Workers with Multiple Chemical Sensitivities*, Philadelphia: Hanley Belfus Inc. One of the first books to consider MCS seriously.

Cutter, S. L. (1993) *Living with Risk*, London: Edward Arnold. An interesting look at some of the problems of risk assessment.

Dalton, A. J. P. (1979) *Asbestos Killer Dust*, London: British Society for Social Responsibility in Science.

Dalton, A. J. P. (1981) The attitude of the trade unions. In: Chissick, S. S. and Derricott, R. (eds) *Occupational Health and Safety Management*, Chichester: Wiley.

Dalton, A. J. P. (1982) *Health and Safety at Work for Managers and Supervisors*, London: Cassell.

Dalton, A. J. P. (1991) *Health and Safety – an Agenda for Change*, London: Workers' Education Association.

Dalton, A. J. P. (1995) *A Manager's Guide to Safety Representatives*, London: Technical Communications (Publishing) Ltd.

Dawson, Sandra, Willman, Paul, Bamford, Martin and Clinton, Alan (1988) *Safety at Work – the Limits of Self-regulation*, Cambridge: Cambridge University press. An important survey of health and safety at that time and a book that killed off the idea of 'self regulation', for a while at least.

Day, Martyn (1998) *Environmental Action – A Citizen's Guide*, London: Pluto Press. A very good guide to the possibilities, and limits, of legal action in community environmental action, written by a leading solicitor in this area.

Dembe, A. E. (1996) *Occupation and Disease*, London: Yale University Press. By means of three excellent and in-depth case studies – RSI, backache and noise – questions the role of the doctor in awarding (or not) compensation; a classic.

Department of Energy (1988) *The Public Inquiry into the Piper Alpha Disaster* (the Cullen Report), London: HMSO.

Department of Trade and Industry (1993) *Regulation in the Balance – a guide to risk assessment*, London: DTI.

Department of Transport (1988) *Report of Formal Investigation into the Loss of the Herald of Free Enterprise* (the Sheen Report), London: HMSO.

Department of Transport (1988) *Investigation into the King's Cross Underground Fire* (the Fennel Report), London: HMSO.

Department of Transport (1989) *Investigation into the Clapham Junction Railway Accident* (the Hidden Report), London: HMSO.

Dinham, Barbara (1993) *The Pesticide Hazard*, London: Zed Books. The horrifying truth about the global hazards of pesticides.

Dodds, Felix (ed.) (1977) *The Way Forward – Beyond Agenda 21*, London: Earthscan. A collection of interesting essays on how we can go forward from the Earth Summit in Rio 1992.

Douglas, Mary (1992) *Risk and Blame*, London: Routledge. A broader view of the risk debate.

Doyal, Lesley (1979) *The Political Economy of Health*, London: Pluto Press. One of the first books to show the wider political nature of public and occupational health.

Doyal, Lesley (1983) *Cancer in Britain: the Politics of Prevention*, London: Pluto Press. A critical look at preventable cancer in Britain, with much emphasis on the workplace.

Doyal, Lesley (1995) *What Makes Women Sick*, London: Macmillan. Thought-provoking and wide-ranging, including workplace hazards.

Duffus, J. H. and Worth H. G. J. (1996) *Fundamental Toxicology for Chemists*, Cambridge: The Royal Society of Chemistry. A fairly standard look at toxicology.

Dul, J. and Weerdneester B. (1993) *Ergonomics for Beginners*, London: Taylor and Francis. A good introduction to a very large subject.

Earnshaw, Jill and Cooper, Cary (1996) *Stress and Employer Liability*, London: Institute of Personnel and Development. An excellent guide to stress hazards, symptoms, the law and prevention.

Egginton, Joyce (1980) *Bitter Harvest*, London: Secker and Warburg. A w ll-researched, and told, story of how the poisoning of US cattle by poly-brominated biphernyl (PBB) fire retardants was covered up and eventually exposed.

Elkington, John (1985) *The Poisoned Womb – Human Reproduction in a Polluted World*, London: Penguin Books. One of the first books to identify this growing problem.

Elkington, John (1987) *The Green Capitalists*, London: Victor Gollancz. One of the first UK books to look at the greening of the workplace for profit.

Elling, Ray (1986) *The Struggle for Worker's Health*, New York: Baywood Publishers Inc. A really great book about American health and safety struggles; a classic.

Elliot, David (1997) *Energy, Society and Environment*, London: Routledge. A very good introduction to a wide and important subject.

Elvin, Ann (1995) *Invisible Crime – the True Life Story of a Mother's Fight Against the Cover-up of Workplace Manslaughter*, from Ann Elvin, 24 Gravesend Road, Rochester, Kent ME2 3PJ. An amazing book, by an amazing woman.

Emsley, John (1994) *The Consumers Good Chemical Guide*, Oxford: W. H. Freeman. Chemicals are good for you, according to this apologist for the chemical industry.

Engles, Frederick (1974) *The Conditions of the Working Class in England*, London: Panther. First published in 1892, this still readable classic tells of horrible working conditions.

Epstein, Sam (1979) *The Politics of Cancer*, New York: Anchor Books. The book that revealed the preventable nature of much cancer, including much at the workplace; a classic.

Fagin, Dan and Lavelle, Marianne (1996) *Toxic Deception – How the Chemical Industry Manipulates Science, Bends the Law and Endangers your Health*, Secancus, NJ: Carol Publishing Group.

Flynn, Laurie (1992) *Studded with Diamonds and Paved with Gold*, London: Bloomsbury Publishing. A horrifying, but true, story of the South African mines and their hazards by a great investigative journalist.

Francis, John (1993) *The Politics of Regulation*, Oxford: Blackwell. Uses regulating environmental health risks as a case study.

Frankel, Maurice (1978) *The Social Audit Pollution Handbook – How to Assess Environmental and Workplace Pollution*, London: Macmillan Press. A book that was way ahead of its time, as was social (read: environmental and more) auditing.

Franklin, Jane (ed.) (1998) *The Politics of Risk Society*, Cambridge: Polity Press. A leftwing look at 'risk' in a more general sense. Useful.

Frazier, L. M. and Hage, M. L. (1998) *Reproductive Hazards of the Workplace*, London: Chapman and Hall. An up-to-date, encyclopedic review of this important topic.

Gersuny, Carl (1981) *Work Hazards and Industrial Conflict*, London: University of Rhode Island. Gives a useful account of some of the issues of conflict on occupational health in America.

Gillespie, Richard (1991) *Manufacturing Knowledge – a History of the Hawthorne Experiments*, Cambridge: Cambridge University Press. The infamous 'Hawthorne effect' is something everybody who investigates real workplaces must be aware of.

Goldsmith, F. and Kerr, L. R. (1982) *Occupational Safety and Health – the Prevention and Control of Workplace Hazards*, New York: Human Sciences Press Inc. An important book on the politics of occupational health in America.

Gould, K. A., Schnaitberg, A. and Weinberg, A. S. *Local Environmental Struggles*, Cambridge: Cambridge University Press. Case studies on people participation in environmental issues in America.

Graham, J. D. and Hartwell, J. K. (1997) *The Greening of Industry – the Risk Management Approach*, London: Harvard University Press. By means of detailed case studies, argues for risk assessment.

Graham, J. D. and Wiener, J. B. (eds) (1995) *Risk versus Risk – Tradeoffs in Protecting Health and the Environment*, London: Harvard University Press. Uses case studies to argue for risk analysis.

Harr, Jonathan (1995) *A Civil Action*, London: Century. A real story of an American fight for compensation from toxic chemicals. Fact seems worse than fiction!

Harrington, J. M. (1994) Shift work and health, *Annals of the Academy of Medicine*, **23**, 699–705.

Harrington, J. M. and Gardner, K. (1995) *Occupational Hygiene*, Oxford: Blackwell. A good general overview of all the key topics; good on sampling but weak on control measures.

Harris, J. A., Birch, P. and Palmer, J. (1996) *Land Restoration and Reclamation*, London: Longman. An introductory overview of the principles and practice.

Harrison, Barbara (1996) *Not only the 'Dangerous Trades'*, London: Taylor and Francis. Highlighting the social and political significance of women's health and safety struggles in the nineteenth century.

Harrison, Kathryn and Hoberg, George (1994) *Risk, Science and Politics*, Montreal and Kingston: McGill–Queen's University Press. A very interesting, and instructive, set of case studies (pesticides, asbestos, urea–formaldehyde foam, radon), comparing American and Canadian approaches.

Hawken, Paul (1993) *The Ecology of Commerce*, London: Phoenix. A popular, and logical/profitable, argument for the greening of industry, from an industrialist.

Hay, Alastair (1982) *The Chemical Scythe – Lessons of 2,4,5,-T and Dioxin*, London: Plenum Press. Agent orange in Vietnam, Love Canal, Seveso and many other warnings are documented in detail here, many years ago.

Headapohl, D. M. (1993) *Women Workers*, Philadelphia: Hanley and Belfus. A useful collection of essays on the specific hazards facing women at work.

Health and Safety Commission (1975) Press releases, 9 April.

Health and Safety Commission and Executive (1977) *Headline Workplace Health and Safety Statistics 1996/97*, London: HSE Books.

Health and Safety Executive (1996) *Health and Safety Statistics 1995/96*, London: HSE Books.

Health and Safety Executive (1997) *Health and Safety Statistics 1996/97*, London: HSE Books.

Health and Safety Executive and Commission (1991) *Annual Report 1990/91*, London: HSE Books.

Health and Safety Executive and Commission (1993) *Annual Report 1992/93*, London: HSE Books.

Health and Safety Executive and Commission (1996) *Annual Report 1995/96*, London: HSE Books.

Hendy, John, Day, Martyn and Buchan, Andrew (1992) *Personal Injury Practice*, London: Legal Action Group. The guide to personal injury claims.

Hendy, John and Ford, Michael (1993) *Redgrave, Fife and Machin Health and Safety*, London: Butterworths. The classic legal 'factory inspector's Bible', with supplements. A great introduction and a classic.

Hendy, John and Ford, Michael (1995) *Munkman on Employer's Liability*, 12th edn, London: Butterworth. The key addition to their previous book.

Holt, P. F. (1987) *Inhaled Dust and Disease*, Chichester: John Wiley. Written by one of the most concerned respiratory toxicologists, still a good read, if a bit dated.

Hood, C. and Jones, D. K. C. (1996) *Accident and Design*, London: University College Press. Some of the key issues in risk management, including criminal law and corporate responsibility.

Houghton, John (1997) *Global Warming – the Complete Briefing*, 2nd edn, Cambridge: Cambridge University Press. If you really want to know about this subject, read this book.

House of Lords (1993) *Occupational Health and Hygiene Services*, Select Committee on Science and Technology 2nd report, 2 vols, London: HMSO. A very detailed enquiry that went nowhere.

Howes, Rupert, Skea, Jim and Whelan, Bob (1997) *Clean and Competitive? A Motivating Environmental Performance in Industry*, London: Earthscan. A useful reader that covers all the major workplace environmental issues in a general way.

Hunter, Donald (1955) *Diseases of Occupations*, London: The English Universities Press. The book on workplace health for some forty years (with many revisions); earlier editions have a fascinating view of workplace ill-health history.

Hunter, Donald (1994) *Hunter's Diseases of Occupations*, 8th edn, edited by Raffle, P. A. B., Adams, P. H., Baxter, P. J. and Lee, W. R., London: Edward Arnold. Still the best general UK occupational health textbook available.

Hurst, Peter, Hay, Alastair and Dudly, Nigel (1991) *The Pesticides Handbook*, London: Journeyman Press. An early, and useful, compilation of pesticide hazards.

Inequalities in Health (eds P. Townsend and N. Davidson) (1988) The Black Report, London: Pelican. A report on health inequality, including the workplace.

Hutter, B. M. (1988) *The Reasonable Arm of the Law?* Oxford: Clarendon Press. Looks at the enforcement role of environmental health officers.

Ives, J. H. (ed.) (1985) *The Export of Hazard*, London: Routledge and Kegan Paul. One of the first books to look at what transnationals were doing around the world with hazards.

Jeyaratnam, J. (ed.) (1992) *Occupational Health and Developing Countries*, Oxford: Oxford University Press. A useful look at the worldwide issues of workplace hazards.

Jones, Tara (1988) *Corporate Killing – Bhopals Will Happen*, London: Free Association Books. The true story of Bhopal and the horrible implications.

Karasek, Robert and Theorel, Tores (1990) *Healthy Work – Stress, Productivity and the Reconstruction of Working Life*, New York: Basic Books. One of the first, and leading, authorities on why work causes stress and the importance of job design and content.

Kazis, Richard and Grossman, R. L. (1982) *Fear at Work – Job Blackmail, Labor and the Environment*, New York: The Pilgrims Press. One of the first books to identify the attacks on workplace and environmental SHE issues by big business in the USA.

Khail, T. M. *et al.* (1993) *Ergonomics in Back Pain*, New York: Van Nostrand Reinhold. Looks at backache mainly from the point of view of prevention and changing the workplace.

Kinnersly, Patrick (1973) *The Hazards of Work: How to Fight Them*, London: Pluto Press. The great, and seminal, book for trade union safety representatives; a classic.

Kohn, Howard (1981) *Who Killed Karen Silkwood?* London: New English Library. Together with the film, it makes a powerful case for her being the first deliberate victim of the nuclear power industry.

Kroemer, K. H. E. and Grandjean, E. (1997) *Fitting the Task to the Human*, 5th edn, London: Taylor and Francis. A bit long in the tooth now, but still packed full of good information and advice.

Kumashior, M. and Megaw, E. D. (1991) *Towards Human Work*, London: Taylor and Francis. Towards a new, worker-centred, participatory ergonomics.

Lang, Tim and Clutterbuck, Charlie (1991) *P is for Pesticides*, London: Ebury Press. A good overview of the hazards of pesticides and some alternatives.

Lea, W. J. (1996) *Chemical Sensitivity*, 4 volumes, London: Lewis Publishers. The main books on the subject, by the expert on MCS.

Leslie, G. B. and Lunau, F. W. (1992) *Indoor Air Pollution*, Cambridge: Cambridge University Press. A useful overview of a complicated subject.

Margolis, Howard (1996) *Dealing with Risk*, London: University of Chicago Press. A short essay on risk assessment and why public involvement is import.

Marshall, V. C. (1987) *Major Chemical Hazards*, Chichester: John Wiley. Uses real-life chemical plant disasters to reveal poor plant design; a classic.

Marx, Karl (1867) *Capital*, vol. 1 (1974 edn), Moscow: Progress Publishers.

McCaffrey, David (1982) *OSHA and the Politics of Health Regulation*, London: Plenum Press. A useful overview of OSHA in America in the early days.

McKessock, Brenda (1995) *Mesothelioma – the Story of an Illness*, Argyll: Argyll Publishing. The moving story of the death of one asbestos victim and her daughter's search for justice.

Meadows, D. L., Meadows, D. H., Randers, J. and Behrens III, W. W. (1972) *The Limits to Growth*, London: Earth Island Ltd. Maybe the computer modelling got it wrong, but it made people start thinking about the finite nature of the Earth's resources; a classic.

Mitchell, Bruce (1997) *Resource and Environmental Management*, Harlow: Longman. An excellent introduction to the key environmental issues, with an emphasis on involving people in environmental planning and management.

Mol, A. P. J. (1995) *The Refinement of Production – Ecological Modernisation Theory and the Chemical Industry*, Oxford: Jon Carpenter. A thought-provoking look into a green future for the chemical industry, with three key case studies (paint, plastics and pesticides); may be a classic.

Murdie, Alan (1993) *Environmental Law and Citizen Action*, London: Earthscan. A useful guide to the subject.

National Research Council (1984) *In Situ Bioremediation – When Does it Work?* Oxford: National Academy Press. A very useful overview of what must be a safer way of clean-up than landfill and incineration.

Navarro, Vicente and Berman, Dan (1983) *Health and Work Under Capitalism*, New York: Baywood Publishers Inc. A very fine set of essays about capitalism and workplace ill-health.

Nelkin, D. and Brown, M. S. (1984) *Workers at Risk – Voices from the Workplace*, London: The University of Chicago Press. An interesting range of interviews with workers in a variety of dangerous trades.

Nichols, T. (1997) *The Sociology of Industrial Injury*. London: Mansell. A thought-provoking, and unique, look at UK industrial safety during the past 25 years.

Nichols, T. and Armstrong, P. (1973) *Safety or Profit*, Bristol: Falling Wall Press. The arguments against the Robens Report philosophy; a classic.

North, R. D. (1995) *Life on a Modern Plant*, Manchester: Manchester University Press. As you would expect from a book part-funded by ICI, not too friendly to many environmental issues. Basically, 'carry on as usual' is the message.

Oates, A. and Gregory, d. (eds) (1993) *Industrial Relations and the Environment*, Dublin: The European Foundation for the Improvement of Living and Working Conditions. A two-volume survey of trade unions and the environment in the EU which shows that they were doing very little at that time.

Ortolano, Leonard (1997) *Environmental Regulation and Impact*, Chichester: John Wiley and Sons. A very good overview of the American situation.

Parker, K. G. and Imbus, H. R. (1992) *Cumulative Trauma Disorders*, London: Lewis Publishers. Otherwise known as RSI in the UK. Useful for the fact that it takes a preventative, workplace-orientated, approach to the subject.

Pelmear, P. L. Taylor, W. and Wasserman, D. E. (1992) *Hand–Arm Vibration*, New York: Van Nostrand Reinhold. A very good guide to the symptoms, diagnosis and control.

Pepper, David (1993) *Eco-Socialism – from Deep Ecology to Social Justice*, London: Routledge: A thoughtful, and sometimes provocative, look at environmentalism from a left/green perspective.

Perkins, J. L. (1997) *Modern Industrial Hygiene*, Vol. 1, London: Van Nostrand Reinhold. Although American, a very useful overview with some good practical guidance.

Pope, A. M., Patterson, R. and Burge, H. (1993) *Indoor Allergens*, Washington: National Academy Press. A good overview of the biological and chemical hazards causing asthma indoors and how to control them.

Puchard, Ed (1989) *Piper Alpha – a Survivor's Story*, London: W. H. Allen. A moving, yet detailed story of why this disaster never should have happened.

Ramazzini, Bernadino (1713) *Diseases of Workers*. New York: Hafner Publishing Company (1964) reprint). The first, and the greatest, occupational medicine textbook, which is still very readable; a classic.

Rees, Joseph (1988) *Reforming the Workplace*, Philadelphia: University of Pennsylvania. A study of one experiment of self-regulation in the USA that seemed to work.

Report of the Formal Investigation into the Loss of the Herald of Free Enterprise (the Sheen Report) (1988), London: HMSO.

Ridley, John (1995) *Safety at Work*, 4th edn, Oxford: Butterworth-Heinemann. In many ways the standard textbook, but showing its age now, and with nothing on the environment.

Rimington, John (1995) *Valedictory Summary of Industrial Health and Safety since the 1974 Act*, London: The Electricity Association. A key review of the law from the Director General of the HSE during the crucial period and the claimed principle architect of the HSE philosophy of risk management.

Robinson, J. C. (1991) *Toil and Toxics – Workplace and Political Strategies for Occupational Health*, Oxford: University of California Press. A detailed, and readable, study of de-regulation and workplace ill-health in the USA.

Rodricks, J. V. (1992) *Calculated Risks*, Cambridge: Cambridge University Press. A useful introduction to toxicology, but one that is complacent about many hazards and that places too much faith in 'good' science alone solving toxicological problems.

Roelofs, Joan (1996) *Greening Cities – Building Just and Sustainable Communities*, New York: Bootstrap Press. Open your eyes to another world.

Rogers, Richard (1997) *Cities – for a Small Planet*, London: Faber & Faber. A radical and, to some extent, environmentally orientated architect's view of cities.

Rogers, R. and Salvage, J. (1988) *Nurses at Risk*, London: Heinemann. A very good, critical overview of the hazards of nursing.

Rom, W. N. (ed.) (1992) *Environmental and Occupational Medicine*, London: Little, Brown and Co. A brilliant American textbook and a model of how to write one; a classic.

Rosner, D. and Markowitz, G. (eds) (1989) *Dying for Work – Worker's Safety and Health and Twentieth-century America*, Bloomington: Indiana University Press. An amazing collection of detailed case studies that reveal the true extent of workplace ill-health in the USA, from the worker's perspective.

Rosner, D. and Markowitz, G. (1991) *Deadly Dust – Silicosis and the Politics of Occupational Disease in Twentieth-century America*, New Jersey: Princetown University Press. Reveals just how this deadly disease has been covered up in the USA for many years; a classic.

Rothman, Harry (1972) *Murderous Providence – a Study of Pollution in Industrial Societies*, London: Rupert Hart-Davies. A very neglected, and in its time forward-looking, book from the first wave of environmental texts.

Rowell (1996) *Green Backlash*, London: Routledge. Some of the reactions of industry and others to the success of the environmental movement.

The Royal Society (1992) *Risk Analysis, Perception and Management*, London: The Royal Society. The key guide to the subject, but it does not really consider people involvement in risk analysis.

Sagan, S. D. (1993) *The Limits of Safety*, New Jersey: Princeton University Press. A useful approach to accidents that looks at the organizational factors.

Sauter, S. L. (ed.) (1989) *Job Control and Worker Health*, Chichester: John Wiley. A useful collection of essays and key in reducing workplace stress.

Schumacher, E. F. (1973) *Small is Beautiful*, London: Blond and Briggs. A key UK book that made people think.

Schwab, Jim (1994) *Deeper Shades of Green,* San Francisco: Sierra Club Books. Shows that the American environmental movement has blue-collar, as well as white-collar, activists.

Seaton, Andrew (ed.) (1994) *Practical Occupational Medicine*, London: Edward Arnold. A good, brief introduction to the subject.

Selikoff, I. J. and Lee, D. H. K. (1978) *Asbestos and Disease*, London: Academic Press. A book by the world's top asbestos expert, who has saved many lives; a classic.

Seyle, Hans (1956) *The Stress of Life*, London: McGraw Hill. The first, and classic, book on stress; good on symptoms, poor on prevention.

Sharrant, Paul (ed.) (1995) *Environmental Management Systems*, Rugby: Institution of Chemical Engineers. Shows that the UK chemical industry can clean up, but no mention of life cycle analysis or any wider vision.

Snashall, David (ed.) (1977) *The ABC of Work Related Disorders*, London: BMJ

Publishing Groups. An excellent collection of authoritative reviews from the *BMJ* on key occupation health subjects.

Stacey, N. H. (ed.) (1993) *Occupational Toxicology*, London: Taylor and Francis. A useful introduction to the toxicity of many workplace materials.

Stellman, J. M. and Daum, S. M. (1973) *Work is Dangerous to Your Health*, New York: Vintage Books. The key US book that first discussed workplace hazards from a worker's point of view.

The Tavistock Institute (1997) *Review of Workplace-related Violence*, London: HSE Books.

Trades Union Congress (1991) *Greening the Workplace*, London: TUC. An excellent handbook for its time that was, unfortunately, not followed up with any real TUC workplace training or action until this day. A missed opportunity.

Trades Union Congress (1995) *The Future of Workplace Safety Reps*. London: TUC. An interim report of a TUC discussion group; not very imaginative.

Trades Union Congress (1997) *Hazards at Work – TUC Guide to Health and Safety*, London: TUC. A fairly comprehensive, useful guide, that is the basic guide for trade union safety reps on TUC training courses. Could be better designed, up-to-date more critical of government standards and say something about the environment. Some of these deficiencies may be corrected by future loose-leaf additions.

Tressell, Robert (1914) *The Ragged Trousered Philanthropists*, Herts: Granada Publishing. If you want to buy just one book, this is it.

Walters, D., Dalton, A. J. P. and Gee, David (1993) *Worker Representation on Health and Safety in Europe*, Brussels: Trade Union Technical Bureau. A useful survey of the situation for safety representatives throughout Europe.

Warr, Peter (1996) *Psychology at Work*, 4th edn, London: Penguin. Now showing its age (the first edition was in 1971), but useful for an insight into the isolated and conservative view that some occupational psychologists still take of work.

Watterson, Andrew (1991) *Pesticides and Your Food*, London: Green Print. From someone who has been exposing the misuse of pesticides for years.

Wehrmeyer, Walter (ed.) (1996) *Greening People – Human Resources and Environmental Management*, Sheffield: Greenleaf Publishing. A wide-ranging and stimulating series of essays on this subject.

Weindling, Paul (ed.) (1985) *The Social History of Occupational Health*, London: Croom Helm. A very interesting historical look at the subject with some useful essays on specific subjects.

Welford, Richard (1997) *Highjacking Environmentalism – Corporate Responses to Sustainable Development*, London: Earthscan. A good overview of why some of the fine words and corporate 'environmental management systems' are just so much 'greenwash'.

Wells, Celia (1993) *Corporations and Criminal Responsibility*, Oxford: Clarendon Press. Discusses some of the important issues in this area.

Wentz, Charles (1995) *Hazardous Waste Management*, London: McGraw Hill. An overview of the issues, methods and techniques.

Werksman, Jacob (1996) *Greening International Institutions*, London: Earthscan. It has got to happen, and this book explains why.

Williams. John (1960) *Accidents and Ill-Health at Work*, London: Staples Press. A much neglected work which was way ahead of its time and a forerunner of the great *Hazards of Work* by Pat Kinnersly.

Willums, Jan-Olaf and Goluke, Ulrich (1992) *From Ideas to Action – Business and Sustainable Development*, Oslo: ICC Publications. A useful compilation of company action and case studies on the environment.

Wilson, Des (1983) *The Lead Scandal*, London: Heinemann. Details of the UK campaign to get lead in petrol reduced.

Wilson, Graham (1985) *The Politics of Safety and Health*, Oxford: Oxford University Press. An early study of the American and British government approaches to controlling health and safety hazards at the workplace, which concludes that there is not much to choose between them.

Wolf, Susan and White, Anna (1997) *Principles of Environmental Law*, 2nd edn, London: Cavendish. A good basic guide.

Yocum, J. E. and McCarthy, S. M. (1991) *Measuring Indoor Air Quality*, Chichester: John Wiley. Gives some idea of the difficulty of measuring low-level indoor contaminants accurately.

Zenz, Carl (ed.) (1994) *Occupational Medicine*, Baltimore: Mosby. One of two key American medical texts and packed full of useful information.

INDEX

Numbers in italics refer to Figures; those in bold refer to Tables.